Children's
Health
Care

Issues in Children's and Families' Lives
AN ANNUAL BOOK SERIES

Senior Series Editor
Thomas P. Gullotta, *Child and Family Agency of Southeastern Connecticut*

Editors

Gerald R. Adams, *University of Guelph, Ontario, Canada*

Robert L. Hampton, *University of Maryland, College Park*

Bruce A. Ryan, *University of Guelph, Ontario, Canada*

Roger P. Weissberg, *University of Illinois at Chicago, Illinois*

Drawing upon the resources of the Child and Family Agency of Southeastern Connecticut, one of this nation's leading family service agencies, **Issues in Children's and Families' Lives** is designed to focus attention on the pressing social problems facing children and their families today. Each volume in this series will analyze, integrate, and critique the clinical and research literature on children and their families as it relates to a particular theme. Believing that integrated multidisciplinary approaches offer greater opportunities for program success, volume contributors will reflect the research and clinical knowledge base of the many different disciplines that are committed to enhancing the physical, social, and emotional health of children and their families. Intended for graduate and professional audiences, chapters will be written by scholars and practitioners who will encourage readers to apply their practice skills and intellect to reducing the suffering of children and their families in the society in which those families live and work.

*C*hildren's *H*ealth *C*are

Issues for the Year 2000 and Beyond

Editors
Thomas P. Gullotta
Robert L. Hampton
Gerald R. Adams
Bruce A. Ryan
Roger P. Weissberg

Vol. 12 *Issues in Children's and Families' Lives*

SAGE Publications
International Educational and Professional Publisher
Thousand Oaks   London   New Delhi

Copyright © 1999 by Sage Publications, Inc.

For information:

 SAGE Publications, Inc.
2455 Teller Road
Thousand Oaks, California 91320
E-mail: order@sagepub.com

SAGE Publications Ltd.
6 Bonhill Street
London EC2A 4PU
United Kingdom

SAGE Publications India Pvt. Ltd.
M-32 Market
Greater Kailash I
New Delhi 110 048 India

Printed in the United States of America

Library of Congress Cataloging-in-Publication Data

Main entry under title:

Children's health care: Issues for the year 2000 and beyond /
    edited by Thomas P. Gullotta . . . [et al.].
        p. cm.—(Issues in children's and families' lives; v. 12)
    Includes bibliographical references and index.
    ISBN 0-7619-1931-7 (acid-free paper)
    ISBN 0-7619-1932-5 (acid-free paper)
    1. Child health services—United States. 2. Child mental health services—United States. I. Gullotta, Thomas, 1948-. II. Series
    RJ102.C489 1999
    362.1'982'00973—dc21   98-58079

99 00 01 02 03 04 05 7 6 5 4 3 2 1

Acquiring Editor:	C. Deborah Laughton
Editorial Assistant:	Eileen Carr
Production Editor:	Astrid Virding
Production Assistant:	Nevair Kabakian
Typesetter/Designer:	Marion S. Warren

Contents

Introduction

Children's Health Care: Issues for the Year 2000 and Beyond

THOMAS P. GULLOTTA

As the United States approaches the millennium, one of the great issues facing this country is how it will provide health care services for young people. In particular, how will it address the mental health needs of its youth? Why focus on mental health issues? Simply because that is where the need is most urgent and societal consensus most lacking.

As an age group, young people are remarkably healthy. While some 2 million young people have chronic physical health conditions that impede activity (Gullotta & Noyes, 1995), this figure pales in light of the 1 in 5 young people who are estimated to be in need of mental health services in any given year (see Faenza & Steel, Chapter 3; Plant, Chapter 6; and Blau & Brumer, Chapter 8).

This volume is an effort to grapple with this pressing societal concern. Over the past 2 years, numerous reports have raised serious ethical debates within government and among service providers about the type and level of the care authorized by HMOs and other health insurance entities. At the same time, traditional service delivery systems and their methods of care have been challenged as being both costly and—worse still—ineffective. We are faced with claims that the past didn't work and the present offers no improvements as payer systems are accused of shifting their costs onto others in order to maximize their profits. This issue has great meaning for the Child and Family Agency, an organization founded as a charitable benevolent children's society. Our historic interest has been helping families find and develop the necessary skills to enable their children to grow into healthy and participating members of our society. Thus, this issue was identified by the editorial board for examination. Given the rapid changes occurring in this area, this volume must be treated as a work in progress. We have identified four broad areas for study and initiated that work.

In the first of four areas we give the reader a firm grounding in the development of children's health care. To accomplish this, John G. Day in Chapter 1 provides a thorough overview of the history of children's health care from colonial times to the present. In Chapter 2, Christie Provost Peters continues that historical perspective by focusing her attention on the federal government's involvement in health care services for low-income children and families. The third chapter, by Michael M. Faenza and Elizabeth Steel, discusses the concerns providers and advocates for children have for assuring young people have adequate and appropriate access to mental health care services.

In the next chapter the second concern of this volume is undertaken. In Chapter 4 we examine a frequently discussed model for service delivery—the School-Based Health and Social Services Center. Providing physical and mental health services from a school setting, these Centers offer an unique opportunity to improve access to care for children. Joy G. Dryfoos, one of the founders of this movement, discusses the development and the promise of this service delivery system within the full-service school model.

The third area examined in this volume concerns the effectiveness of outpatient mental health services. In Chapter 5, William D. Marelich and Mary Jane Rotheram-Borus review the literature and identify several research-proven forms of intervention for changing specific dysfunctional behaviors. Professional and payer barriers are examined, and provocative proposals emphasizing the use of manuals and paraprofessionals for delivering service are offered. This section concludes with Robert W. Plant's defense of psychotherapy and its use by professional clinicians.

The final area of concern for this volume offers a view of the current system of care and in two respects how it might be improved. In Chapter 7, Nancy J. Kennedy examines the cost effectiveness of primary prevention. Her review of the literature

confirms the opinion of John Day (Chapter 1) that primary prevention is a wise and cost-effective intervention in the lives of children.
In Chapter 8, Gary M. Blau and David A. Brumer offer a plan for
integrating service delivery systems for children and their families.
Their suggestions, which include model legislative action, would
improve a system in which too many young people are lost.

Readers should consider this volume a starting rather than an end
point. It will enable the mental health practitioner to gain a better
sense of the changes occurring in the field. It offers the program
planner justification for the dollar value of preventive efforts and
a blueprint for system change. For the graduate student and others,
it provides an excellent review of the political and social evolution
of children's health care in the United States. We hope this material
will be put to use to develop a system of care in which the needs of
children are met.

Reference

Gullotta, T. P., & Noyes, L. (1995). The changing paradigm of community health:
    The role of school-based health centers. *Adolescence, 117,* 108-115.

Acknowledgments

With this volume, the Child and Family Agency relationship with Sage comes to an amicable end. The next volume in this series will be with another publisher. Endings are inevitably a time for reflection. In this regard and speaking for the agency and myself, we leave with good memories. I would like to recognize the production, copyediting, and marketing staff at Sage who in every dealing have been helpful, friendly, and professional. In developing volumes for this series, C. Deborah Laughton and Eileen Carr have been the perfect soulmates. I will miss them both.

Dedication

Across the decades, the Child and Family Agency has been successful because a devoted group of volunteers has made the mission of the agency—children—their principle concern. This volume honors all of these remarkable people who have served this agency so well for twenty years or more. Thank you for your concern for the needs and wants of children.

Child and Family Agency Auxiliary
20 year members

Ager, Ginny
Allingham, Mary
Barry, Harriett
Bartholet, Anne
Barton, Jean
Belcher, Pat
Bell, Jane Ann
Benoit, Helen
Berry, Pat
Bevan, Betty
Bill, Sally
Boos, Peggy
Brennan, Joyce
Brewster, Helen
Brouwer, JoAn
Brown, Hetsy
Brown, Mac
Callahan, Peggy
Cantner, Linda
Castle, Joy
Cathcart, Dorothy
Cedio, Pinky
Chambers, Dee
Chapman, Betty
Clark, Anne
Connor, Carol
Cramer, Jeanne
DeBiasi, Mary
Deren, Ann Marie
Dickinson, Jane
Donnell, Jane
Douglass, Marilyn
Dovey, Louise
Dunning, Isobel
English, Debbie
Erb, Lillian
Escher, Mary Louise

Everett, Joyce
Flaherty, Kathleen
Francis, Celia
Freye, Virginia
Fritzsche, Patsy
Fuller, Kay
Gegenheimer, Shirley
Goode, Mary Lee
Graves, Carol
Greenberg, Alva
Greene, Nita
Harreys, Barbara
Hartmann, Liz
Haughton, Elaine
Higgins, Emily
Hill, Sally
Holmes, Pat
Holmstedt, Anne
Hoops, Barbara
Hoye, June
Hughes, Janet
Jackson, Becky
Jacobsen, Betty
Jalbert, Dorothy
Jamison, Eleanor
Jensen, Nancy
Keck, Barbara
Kitchings, Margaret
Kowenhoven, Regina
Kraska, Joanne
Lena, Jeanne
Letz, Beverly
Lovelace, Judy
Lyon, Claire
MacDougall, Lefty
Mackey, Virginia
MacMorrow, Marilyn

Marrion, Grace
Marshall, Patsy
McCarter, Claire
McConnell, Susan
McDonald, Louise
McDonald, Mary
Moore, Elizabeth
Moore, Marguerite
Morris, Judy
Morrison, Ellie
Moukawsher, Patricia
Murphy, Loretta
Myers, Sally
Nielsen, Claudia
O'Donnell, Betty
O'Donnell, Susan
O'Shea, Margaret
Ott, Gertrude
Page, Kathleen
Peterle, Joy Lee
Pfeil, Terry
Pullen, Mary
Read, Mary
Reilly, Kathie
Richartz, Nancy
Rivard, Lois
Robe, Charlotte

Roberts, Mary Ellen
Rogerson, Pat
Ryan, Pam
Ryland, Cemmy
Schaaf, Judy
Schwartz, Flo
Sergeant, Anne
Shickel, Valerie
Snyder, Martha
Southwick, Anne
Sproul, Martha
Stark, Ann
Stockwell, Helen
Thayer, Nika
Thomson, Bette
Towers, Chevy
Traub, Wendy
Trimble, Irene
Tuneski, Barbara
Turner, Ainslie
Turner, Roberta
Umberger, Dorothy
Williams, Linda
Wills, Gloria
Wimpfheimer, Louise
Ziegler, Patricia

• CHAPTER 1 •

Children and Health Care in the United States: Past, Present, and Future

JOHN G. DAY

Walton Hamilton once noted that the "organization of medicine" cannot be studied in isolation: "It is an aspect of culture whose arrangements are inseparable from the general organization of society" (Hamilton, 1932). The same can be said for how one pays for medicine, whether it is through private or public entities or in a pluralistic or centralized setting. This summary attempts to provide the essential historical and social context advocated by Hamilton.

Not surprisingly, children's health care and how it has been funded over the years has been heavily influenced by the general evolution of medicine and health insurance. At the same time, children's health care often proceeded in unique directions that ultimately determined today's structure and will no doubt influence how children will receive care in the future.

For example, doctors specializing in healing children have tended to look at the entire child, while other medical specialties have concentrated on specific or related body parts or organs. In addition, pediatricians have historically had a propensity to collaborate and identify with social activists, a trait shared by few other specialties. As a result, pediatricians early on have tended to be concerned about developmental as well as physical issues faced by children and in particular poor and abandoned children. This

holistic outlook results in an expansive view of the child's total
environment, including nutrition, education, and housing, as well
as the child's mental health and cognitive skills. Over time, this
perspective naturally leads to a "wellness" model of treatment
intervention (i.e., treatment, not just when sick, but also for prevention) long before practitioners in other areas began to embrace
this long-range view of medicine.

   Government policy regarding child health also has proceeded in
some unique directions. For example, a serious and sustained
federal focus for children came into being around the turn of the
20th century, long before it was thought appropriate that the
federal government support vulnerable segments of the population.
Prior to 1965 and the advent of Medicare and Medicaid, the health
care assistance received by children, though modest, exceeded the
help extended to the elderly.[1]

   Since 1965, children have been treated differently in terms of
government support even though children and the elderly have
similarities that warrant public intervention. Both can be identified
by age alone and have defined developmental vulnerabilities. Both
have a level of dependency that often requires assistance from
others, such as the family or government (Grayson & Guyer, 1995).
Some argue that the only reason for today's disparate treatment of
these vulnerable groups is the simple fact that children can't vote
and must rely on others to plead their case. Others point to a
number of other complex factors, such as public attitudes toward
single parents and welfare assistance, changing attitudes regarding
the responsibilities of children for the needs of their elderly parents,
an aging population, and real or perceived limits regarding society's
resources (Axinn & Stern, 1985).

   While there is much disagreement regarding the origins and
efficacy of government policy toward different population groups,
it is clear that today's health care system did not unfold in a
systematic way. Instead, the system "Grow'd like Topsy." Each
component was the result of a complex congruence of different
societal views of deserving populations, the appropriate role of
government, short-term political needs, various interest group pressures, and changing public and private priorities. Despite the complexity of the system and its heavy dose of capriciousness, there are
some discernable themes that one can see better from afar than

close up. That is why a very general historical summary—even at the risk of oversimplification—can provide useful insights into how the system evolved and its probable future direction.

The following history unfolds in chronological order, focusing on periods of U.S. history starting with the Colonial era. It highlights the major trends during each period regarding the role of children in society; society's perception of children's health and development; advances in medicine generally; the way children's health care is paid for; and the major economic, technological, and historical events that create and often change society's priorities. For ease of exposition, events and trends have been grouped into selected time periods somewhat arbitrarily. The grouping or categorization of periods also has been influenced by those used by Bremner (1970-1974) in his seminal five-volume work *Children and Youth in America: A Documented History.*[2] This chapter concludes with some thoughts about the future.

The Colonial Period Through the American Revolution: 1600-1776

Throughout much of the 17th century, the United States largely is composed of small frontier towns, farms, and villages. Society's basic social control, education, and economic production unit is the family (Beales, 1985). Children are treated like adults; they are integral parts of the family workforce and essential to its survival. A parent's reciprocal obligation to children is to prepare children for a calling. Occupational training is done directly through the family, especially for girls, or through an apprenticeship or indentured servant program for boys. Both parents and children expect that the grown children will care for their parents in old age (Beales, 1985; Bremner, 1970-1974).

During this period, American society is poor but not destitute. Pauperism is not widespread. Poor adults and poor and abandoned children are dealt with on an individual basis, usually through vendue, that is, the auctioning or bidding out for work and room and board on neighborhood farms. Where adults or children are not capable of work because of age or mental or physical disability, they are sent individually to private homes at public expense. The vendue approach works reasonably well in a colonial society, reflecting a belief that child development, as opposed to the character reformation of older errant citizens, is best done in the context of a family structure and hard work. Vendue also meets the needs of a scarce labor market and the reality that resources for separate public institutions are very limited (Trattner, 1979).

During this period, medicine is primitive and undisciplined. In fact, anyone can practice medicine. In addition, illness is viewed as a form of moral depravity reflecting God's displeasure. Cures range from various forms of penance, exposure to the elements, hard work, and folklore remedies, such as bleeding, blistering, and herbal medicine (Bremner, 1970-1974).

During the early 18th century, things begin to change. The frontier economy evolves into two different economies. Towns along the Eastern seaboard grow dramatically and become complex, dynamic centers of trade and commerce. In these eastern urbanized communities, social classes begin to develop, including a diverse middle class composed of merchants, professionals, and independent farmers (Shultz, 1985). Labor becomes more specialized. While children continue to be essential to the family business, there are signs that work roles in some families begin to change. For example, in the upper middle class, mothers become the managers of the home, and in this environment the child changes from a unit of economic production to one of consumption. Yet, a few miles to the west the world remains very much as it did for much of the 17th century. Frontier life is hard and dangerous. Survival requires a tight family unit with economic production roles for everyone, including children (Bremner, 1970-1974).

Infant and maternal mortality rates are very high. Epidemics of diphtheria and smallpox are common. Obstetric care is primitive (Bremner, 1970-1974). Although the prevailing theory of disease has a moral emphasis, there is a growing recognition in urban areas that there is too much "quackery" and that things can be improved by using the modest medical advances that are occurring on the European continent, especially with respect to obstetrics (Bremner, 1970-1974; Starr, 1982). During the mid to late 18th century some effort is made to structure and formalize the practice of medicine. For example, physician licensing and licensing exams are established in New Jersey in 1792 and New York City in 1760 (Bremner,

1970-1974; Starr, 1982). Even so, virtually anyone can still practice medicine and provide midwife services.

The forerunners of hospitals begin to emerge. Some of the almshouses in the larger cities start to set up special departments to care for the sick. These are America's first hospitals. Hospital charters are granted for Pennsylvania Hospital in 1751 and for New York in 1775. These original hospitals were built on the English model, where the primary purpose is isolation and maintenance, not cure (Temin, 1988). The hospital is financed through taxes (public hospitals), charity (private hospitals, usually with some religious affiliation), and, to a very limited degree, fee-paying patients. Most physicians who provide hospital services do so on a "pro bono" basis in exchange for clinical experience and the development of a reputation that will further their private practice (Halpern, 1988). Most people, however, are treated in their homes and pay physicians out of their own pocket. The less fortunate are treated in the special health section of almshouses or public hospitals (Day, 1996-1997).

The smallpox vaccine is discovered by Jenner in 1798. This discovery demonstrates the value of science, and some say the discovery contributes to an attitude change regarding the need for a more disciplined approach toward disease and medicine (Bremner, 1970-1974). Medical schools start to be established at this time, such as the College of Philadelphia in 1765 and Harvard in 1782 (Bremner, 1970-1974). A few practitioners begin to focus on child care and obstetrics. For example, in 1765, a private school of midwifery, affiliated with the University of Pennsylvania Hospital, is established, and in 1796 the first monograph on pediatrics is prepared as a dissertation for a medical degree. In addition, the University creates a separate department for in-hospital deliveries ("lying-in") in 1803 (Bremner, 1970-1974).

In this setting, the child, for the most part, is not viewed as any different from an adult for purposes of medical treatment. Medicine has not transformed itself into a science or developed to any significant degree the social and legal structures that make it a profession. There is no formal financing or pooling mechanism for care other than the very limited public expenditures for maintenance. Most institutional care for the poor relies on philanthropy by the well-to-do and medical providers. Those who can pay do so, and virtually all care is received in the home.

The American Revolution and the
Early Years of the New Republic: 1776-1810

Clearly, the major defining event during the early period of America's history is the establishment of a new, independent republic. The Constitution of the new republic is ratified in 1787. It is the end result of a complex give and take among many different economic interests and political views, especially toward concentrated government power. The Constitution explicitly recognizes that the federal government has limited powers: The union is between "autonomous" individual states, and all powers not expressly reserved to the federal government belong to the states (Bowen, 1986). Although the respective spheres of power between the state and federal governments wax and wane over the years, this historical view of limited federal power, coupled with the country's focus on rugged individualism and self-sufficiency, inhibits the intervention of the federal government in many areas, including social welfare and health care. This trend persists throughout the 19th and into the early 20th century (Trattner, 1979).

Another important development, both pre- and postrevolution, is society's changing attitude toward education. The needs of a growing and complex urban, professional, and rural economy during the mid-18th century requires the creation of a more focused and structured grammar school, which is called "The Academy" (Shultz, 1985). Over the next century, more than 300 academies are established, often with government charters and assistance (Bremner, 1970-1974). The Revolution itself creates new attitudes about the importance of public education for a viable democracy and realization of each citizen's potential. The new Constitution gives states greater power to establish and encourage education. However, it takes another 175 years before these efforts evolve into the modern public school system, which not only plays a key role in children's education, but also becomes an important part of the health care delivery system for children during the early 20th century.

The Start of the Industrial Revolution:
Rapidly Increasing Immigration and Urbanization
and the Rise of the Middle Class: 1800-1850

The first half of the 19th century is a pivotal transition period for the country. However, it is difficult to describe its significance because the trends accompanying the country's structural transition from an agrarian to an industrial economy were in their infancy and not clearly discernable. Even so, these forces culminate in the late 1800s in a new societal view that children have developmental needs different from those of adults and that special institutions are required to deal with these needs. This period is also the time when medicine starts to move from a discipline based on folklore to one of observation and science. Each of these topics is discussed below.

Are Children Different?

Many of the obvious differences between adults and children are concepts that are not suddenly discovered during the first half of the 19th century. People always have been aware that children require special oversight. However, the precise way to deal with a child's needs and the commitment to do so varied greatly over the years, depending on the prevailing economic, demographic, cultural, and social trends.

One of the more pervasive influences during this period is the Industrial Revolution, which begins in Europe and spreads to the United States in the emerging construction, iron, and textile industries. Although most children continue to work in the family business, an increasing number of women and children work in the factory. By 1816, approximately 90% of the textile factory workforce are women and children. In many mills, over 50% of the workforce are children, in part because their small hands and nimble fingers are well suited to working in the nooks and crannies of the new textile machinery (Bremner, 1970-1974).

Immigration also increases to unprecedented levels during this period. Between 1815 and 1860, over 5 million immigrants enter the United States. By 1860, the U.S. population triples (Trattner, 1979). In search of jobs, most of the immigrants congregate in the eastern ports of entry or move to the new textile centers in the Northeast. Many of these immigrants are children. Urban congestion is exacerbated by the increasing numbers of young men and women who leave the farm in hope of a better future in the cities (Clement, 1985).

New, emerging industries and growing domestic and international commerce create many economic opportunities and new job growth, although often in harsh and difficult environments. However, this job growth cannot keep up with the number of new immigrants from abroad and domestic migrants from the farms. As a result, already crowded cities became populated with many destitute and homeless adults and children. In the large cities, large groups of children roam the streets or congregate in certain areas of the city, creating fear of increased crime and possible civil unrest (Trattner, 1979).

The sheer volume of the destitute and abandoned population overwhelms the traditional ways for dealing with paupers, that is, labor in almshouses in the larger cities and the widespread use of vendue ("binding-out") and modified forms of apprenticeship outside of the urban areas (Bremner, 1970-1974). At the same time, direct aid in the form of money, food, and other necessities (usually referred to as "out-door" relief) increasingly falls into disfavor, because many believe it encourages and reinforces dependency (Bremner, 1970-1974; Clement, 1985). In addition, a growing number of reformers believe that relief should focus on children rather than adults, because children are more deserving, as they are not responsible for their condition, and because they are more likely to respond positively to society's efforts to educate and inculcate desired behavior (Finkelstein, 1985; Trattner, 1979). Reformers also believe that effective reformation can only be accomplished by separating children from sources of "social pollution" and placing them in a structured and disciplined environment. Accordingly, many social leaders have a distinct bias for institutional relief specifically designed for children. However, foster homes (an extension of "binding-out") continue to be another popular option (Trattner, 1979).

Because of these concerns, efforts are made to segregate dependent children from the adults and criminal youth in almshouses (Clement, 1985; Trattner, 1979). Efforts are also made to transfer children from almshouses to private orphanages and foster homes (Clement, 1985). However, these initiatives proceed gradually because of economic resource constraints and do not gain real momentum until the 1880s and 1890s (Clement, 1985).

Prompted by a humanitarian concern for children, the growing public safety concerns regarding large numbers of unattended children, and the growing distaste for public institutions as a place to deal with children, private philanthropists begin to establish private refuges or orphanages, especially after the 1880s. For example, New York has only two orphanages in 1825. By 1866, the number grows to more than 60. New York's orphanage population increases from 3,000 in 1847 to 26,000 in 1866 (Bremner, 1970-1974; Trattner, 1979). Although these institutions are very spartan, they are a significant improvement over the public almshouses. Because of the "public" service provided by the private orphanages, grateful state and local governments often supplement their charitable support with public funds (Bremner, 1970-1974).

At the same time, many object to institutional care of any kind for children. One of the more vocal and effective critics is Charles Brace of the New York Children's Aid Society. Mr. Brace argues that there is no viable substitute for a family in providing the nurturing, educational, and social control needs of children. Accordingly, he advocates that children be placed in foster homes, preferably in the West, some distance from the evils of the cities. In addition, scarce labor encourages foster parents to accept children (Bremner, 1970-1974; Clement, 1985). Importantly, the foster home concept is different from "binding-out" in that either party, the child or the foster parent, can end the arrangement. Both the institutional and foster home movement continue to grow during the remainder of the 19th century.

Although there are major differences between the institutional and foster home movements, both recognize that children are different from adults, with special vulnerabilities and needs. Both schools of thought also recognize that society should respond to these special needs. Meanwhile, the same realization is occurring in the context of other social institutions, such as family law, criminal law, and education. Each discipline draws from and reinforces the others (Cravens, 1985). Medicine is no exception.

Medicine Between 1800 and 1850

During the first half of the 19th century, medicine increasingly relies on observation. Traditional remedies, such as purging and bleeding, decline in popularity (Bremner, 1970-1974). This changing emphasis is especially true in urban areas, as the concentrations of sick people and their caretakers facilitate the collection of data and the sharing of clinical experience. It is during this period that medical practitioners begin to organize and to recognize the clinical and economic utility of a highly structured education and training program for physicians (Day, 1996-1997; Halpern, 1988). The

American Medical Association (AMA) is founded in 1847. Also, clinical "internships" begin at this time (Bremner, 1970-1974).

For some time now, most cities have had special isolation or "pest" facilities for the mentally ill, almshouses for the poor, and refuges and orphanages for dependent children. In many of these facilities separate space is dedicated within the facility to care for the sick. The almshouse's separate space is the forerunner of the public hospital. Similarly, health departments in refuges and orphanages are the forerunners of the children's hospital, the first of which are chartered in New York and Philadelphia during the 1850s (Halpern, 1988).

For the most part, those with financial means continue to be treated in the home. Urbanization, however, creates a new type of "homeless" person with financial means. As many individuals in cities often live in rented facilities far from their original home and family, they need a facility for treatment and recuperation. This need gives rise to a new institution: The voluntary hospital (Zuckerman, Thomas, Schneller, & Hall, 1993).

Care for the poor and for dependent children is paid through taxes or charity. Physicians working in almshouses, refuges, or orphanages do so free of charge or for a very modest stipend (Halpern, 1988). Those with financial means pay the hospital and physicians directly. Many medical practitioners perform a "Robin Hood" role by socializing their fees, charging the affluent more in order to treat the poor for less or for free.

Although children's health is not yet viewed as a distinct specialty, considerable public and private attention is given to child health and hygiene. Specific papers on child diseases are published with increasing frequency (Renn, 1987). Children's hospitals are established. Practitioners begin to suspect a connection between sanitary conditions and health, especially that of children. For the same reason, public health also receives increasing attention in literature and government studies (Renn, 1987).

Despite clinical and institutional improvements, infant mortality has not improved over the very high levels that existed in 1790 (Bremner, 1970-1974). The chief causes of death among children are diarrhea and enteritides, that is, inflammation of the intestines (Bremner, 1970-1974). It is not until the late 1880s that these maladies are linked to unsanitary food and milk.

Medicine Transforms Itself Into a Science,
Children's Health Becomes a Distinct Category
of Medicine, and Pediatrics Finds Common Cause
With Social Reformers: 1850-1900

During the last half of the 19th century, child health becomes a legitimate and distinct subject of inquiry. Although child health care is heavily influenced by the development of medicine generally, the evolution of pediatrics is different in several respects. For example, child health practitioners tend to be more holistic than other practitioners (Halpern, 1988). They tend to look at the entire child. Child health practitioners gain much of their experience in institutions that were originally designed to educate and nurture dependent children. As a result, they more readily recognize the relationship between a child's health and the child's physical and emotional environment. These practitioners also tend to be more involved in and influenced by the social reform movements of the day (Halpern, 1988). These differences are the direct result of a number of interrelated themes that characterized the last four decades of the 19th century: (a) continued and rapid urbanization and industrialization, (b) scientific medical advances that change the direction of medicine, and (c) 19th-century child welfare reform initiatives. These reform initiatives are the precursors of the Progressive Movement, which changes society's view about the role of government toward vulnerable populations and influences the direction of child health care from the 1890s through World War I.

Urbanization and Industrialization

The social and economic change occurring during the last half of the 19th century is unprecedented. The Civil War stimulates the spread of industrialization. The end of the war frees up significant human and economic resources that increase the growing economy's already strong momentum. The population of urban areas triples between 1870 and 1900. During the same period, existing urban centers grow rapidly and new urban centers emerge in the Midwest and South (Clement, 1985).

Immigration that ballooned in the 1840s continues and is supplemented by the so-called new immigration. More than 300,000 new immigrants arrive in 1886 alone. This influx increases annually into the next century. By 1905, the annual number of immigrants surpasses 1 million (Cohen, 1985; Wilson, 1989). As before, these new arrivals tend to congregate in the already congested areas of the Northeast, but this time they also fuel the growth of new urban areas in the north central United States (Cohen, 1985).

Living and working conditions in the cities are deplorable and very visible. In New York and other cities, houses are torn down and replaced with multistory tenements. Many of these structures have no windows or plumbing. Sanitation is sorely inadequate. Disease is widespread, and epidemics are not uncommon. Tuberculosis ravages both the old and young. In some areas, infant mortality exceeds 50% (Karger & Stoesz, 1990). The number of dependent children requiring help increases as children are left without parents because of the Civil War, disease, and industrial accidents. The number of working children between the ages of 10 and 15 increases from 750,000 in 1870 to over 1.7 million in 1900. It is estimated that 40% of these children work in factories and mills (Clement, 1985).

Not surprisingly, many middle-class city dwellers, and women in particular, begin to view these conditions with increasing anxiety. Society appears to be out of control and change is necessary. Reform initiatives during the last decades of the 19th century focus on many diverse issues, such as political corruption, immigration and sanitation, and women's and child labor. A common theme running through many of these issues is the well-being of children, whom many perceive to be the future of the country (Hawes & Heiner, 1985). Many of the leaders of the Progressive Movement form their views about what needs to be done in the settlement houses that are established in poor immigrant neighborhoods during the late 1800s (Karger & Stoesz, 1990; Trattner, 1979). These various reform efforts culminate during the last decades of the 20th century in the juvenile court system, public education, and a host of institutions for various types of dependent children, such as orphanages and institutions for the deaf, blind, and disabled.

Medicine Becomes a Science

During the last half of the 1800s, medicine makes a number of conceptual and scientific breakthroughs enabling the reformers to achieve some of their objectives. For example, Pasteur develops the germ theory of disease, which highlights the need for an antiseptic surgery setting and the importance of sanitation in everyday work and living environments generally. Anesthetics and clinical experience gained during the Civil and Crimean Wars expand treatment options and refine surgical techniques. In turn, support for the new technology and the need for a sanitary treating and healing environment require a centralized institutional setting, support staff, and specialists. These needs begin to solidify the central treatment role of the hospital, as well as the importance of hospitals to physicians (Day, 1996-1997).

Dr. Pasteur's insights lead others to discover the cause of many diseases during the 1880s, including tuberculosis, cholera, diphtheria, tetanus, and bubonic plague. These discoveries further confirm the relationship between sanitation and health. As vaccines are not available, the focus of medicine and the public is on prevention, which in turn drives a number of new public health initiatives. For example, 16 years after the creation of the U.S. Sanitation Commission, which focused on the sanitation needs in Civil War camps, 14 states create health departments. New York City establishes the first real municipal Board of Health, and other cities quickly follow suit (Trattner, 1979).

The American Public Health Association is established in 1872. Local public health associations are also established. These associations facilitate the exchange of information and the creation of new professional journals dedicated to public health issues (Bremner, 1970-1974).

The professionalization of medicine generally and the development of specialties evolve in a similar fashion. This evolution has three basic steps: (a) The practitioners recognize a division of labor and knowledge, and they create associations that permit the dissemination of this special knowledge to other practitioners in the discipline; (b) these interactions permit the development of a professional ethos and paradigm for this type of practice; and (c) the new "organized" discipline establishes training and other entry requirements for the practice, reflecting the values of the profession and its views on how to do its work (Friedson, 1970; Halpern, 1988).

Pediatrics as a recognized specialty begins to evolve. Between 1850 and the early 1900s, general practitioners build careers as partial specialists. Often, they affiliate with the health care facilities or clinics located in or aligned with the growing number of asylums, orphanages, and in children's hospitals. As is the case with other practitioners at this time, treatment within these facilities or specialized hospitals is usually performed at no charge. The affiliation, however, is not without its economic benefits for the doctor. The affiliation permits the practitioner to gain practical experience and expertise in the diseases of children, which, in turn, enhances the doctor's reputation and, thereby, generates referrals of paying patients and consultation fees from "non-specialist" practitioners (Halpern, 1988).

In 1880, the Pediatric Section of the American Medical Association (AMA) is created by Abraham Jacobi, the pioneer of American pediatrics. Four years later, the *Archives of Pediatrics,* the first English-language journal devoted to children's diseases, is published. During the same year, Luther Holt, who teaches pediatrics at Columbia, publishes *The Care and Feeding of Children: A Catechism for the Use of Mothers and Children's Nurses.* Holt's compilation of existing knowledge and advice goes through seven editions between 1884 and 1915, and stimulates and reinforces the public's growing interest in how best to care for children and provide maternal and child hygiene (Bremner, 1970-1974). In 1888, the American Pediatric Society is established. Institutions are established specifically to provide child health care. By 1895, most cities have at least one children's hospital (Bremner, 1970-1974).

Pediatrics and the Child Welfare Movement

One of the initial areas of pediatric focus is infant feeding, and this issue illustrates the interdependency between pediatrics and child welfare advocates. The child welfare movement intuitively senses that maternal and child hygiene have some relationship to infant mortality. Philanthropists and reformers support better mother education sessions and related activities. In 1880, a number of scientific papers confirm what Dr. Jacobi surmised earlier: There is a direct correlation between unpasteurized cow's milk and children's health. Once this relationship is established by science, child welfare advocates, philanthropists, and municipalities establish milk stations across the country where safe milk is sold at cost or even given away. This program becomes a fixture in city life until pasteurization is mandated by law in the early 1900s. There is little doubt that these milk programs play a critical role in reducing infant mortality (Halpern, 1988).

Starting in the 1870s, the public school—another creation of child welfare reformers—starts to be transformed into a health agency of sorts by having students undergo medical exams at school. These exams are designed to identify and isolate children with contagious diseases and to identify specific problems early. Over time, this congruence of public health concerns and public institutions leads to the creation of the school nurse, whom many now take for granted, and reinforces the need for municipal health departments (Bremner, 1970-1974; Wilson, 1989).

As the century ends, there is clear focus on children. Many efforts are under way to develop tailor-made responses to the plight of children in many different disciplines, for example, education, penology, and medicine. While pediatrics is recognized as an area of specialization, its development is not as far along as are other medical specialties. In addition, the field of pediatrics is resisted by many general practitioners, who view the family as their patient base. As a result, some believe that pediatrics suffers from an inferiority complex regarding other practitioners and that this insecurity drives pediatricians to affiliate or ally with the more visible social activists. Others believe that this relationship is mutually beneficial as reform objectives are legitimized by medical science and the value and respect of pediatricians is enhanced (Black, 1988; Halpern, 1988).

The Progressive Movement, Federal Intervention in Children's Health Care, and Pediatrics Comes of Age: 1900-1930

Federal Intervention

Immigration and urbanization continues its momentum. Between 1885 and 1915, the U.S. population increases from 57 to 100 million. Almost 15 million immigrants arrive between 1905 and 1915. As in the past, new immigrants tend to settle in urban areas. The migration from farms to cities also is relentless. In 1890, the rural population is double that of urban centers. By 1910, the rural and urban populations approach parity and by 1920, more people are living in cities than on the farm (Cohen, 1985).

The economy and heavy industry also grow at an unprecedented rate. The nation's gross national product (GNP) doubles between 1890 and 1915. Employment in heavy industry triples, with more than half of the new jobs in factories employing 500 or more (Clement, 1985). Despite this economic growth, new job creation cannot keep up with the growing population. The disparity between rich and poor increases. Poverty becomes widespread across the country. This poverty promotes slums, disease, and crime, especially in the cities, a trend that, in turn, increases the momentum of ongoing reform efforts. New reform efforts are stimulated to deal with industry's oppressive and often unsafe labor practices, especially for women and children.

These reform efforts, which are supported by large segments of society, become known as the Progressive Movement. The Progressive Movement plays an influential role in local and national politics between 1900 and World War I. The movement is credited with reforms in many areas, such as natural resource conservation, civil service reform, the regulation of transportation, antitrust laws, child labor laws, and mother's aid or pension laws. While some debate whether the Progressive Movement was motivated by humanitarian or social control concerns,[3] there is little debate that child welfare plays a key, if not a central, role in the movement, and that government intervention to protect the vulnerable is now accepted as a legitimate use of government power, at both the state and federal levels.

Although the importance of infant feeding and sanitary milk continue through the first two decades of the century, there is a growing awareness that children's health is directly related to their living and working environment. One influential assessment attributes 40% to 80% of early childhood deaths to "bad conditions" (Wilson, 1989).

In 1906, the federal legislation for a Children's Bureau is first introduced in Congress. The Bureau's purpose is not to provide medical services, but rather to investigate the conditions in which children live. Its mission is to collect and publish data regarding the impact of these conditions on the health and development of children and to compile, publish, and distribute educational materials for the general population (Wilson, 1989).

The concept of a Children's Bureau receives widespread support from women's groups, as well as major elements within the Progressive Movement and President Theodore Roosevelt. In 1909, the president convenes the first White House Conference on Children, and one of its key recommendations is the creation of the Children's Bureau. Opposition to the Bureau centers over the degree to which the Bureau's activities may interfere with states' rights. There is also concern about the efficacy of using the federal government for activities the Bureau would undertake, and fear that once established, the Bureau's authority would be difficult to limit. Those opposed to its creation include industrial interests that rely on child labor and, to a more limited degree, child welfare reformers who feel the Bureau would intrude upon or duplicate their philanthropic activities (Wilson, 1989).

After considerable debate, legislation creating the Bureau is approved in 1912. The Bureau's staff views its mission "aggressively" and looks first at infant mortality. Because of sketchy birth records, the Bureau enlists the help of local women's clubs to collect birth data in specific localities. The data show a direct correlation between infant mortality and family income, the employment of mothers, and maternal health and hygiene (Wilson, 1989). The Bureau also publishes educational materials on a wide range of subjects, including infant mortality, child labor legislation, and the need for mothers' pensions. Its first pamphlet, *Prenatal Care,* receives national acclaim, and its publication *Infant Care* becomes the most widely distributed publication of the Government Printing Office (Wilson, 1989).

This publicity and education regarding infant mortality and the importance of prenatal care provide a new issue for the child welfare reform movement now that sanitary milk is available. The combination of these forces, along with the strong general thrust of the Progressive Movement, provides the conceptual framework and grass-roots support for a more direct form of federal intervention through grants-in-aid to the states. Widespread public support, along with the ratification of the 19th Amendment giving women the vote, is crucial in overcoming the formidable and often vitriolic opposition (Costin, Bell, & Downs, 1991). Once again, opposition centers over the legitimacy of federal intervention, the sanctity of states' rights, and now a somewhat new twist: Opponents charge that legislative grants to the states would be the precursor of socialized medicine. Although the AMA maintains a low profile during the fight over the creation of the Children's Bureau, it aggressively lobbies against the proposed Maternity and Infancy Protection Act, which is known as the Sheppard-Towner Act. Members of the AMA Section of Childhood Diseases support the law, however. After an acrimonious, internal fight, the AMA refuses to publish the position of the Section. This refusal prompts a walk-out by Section members and leads to the creation of the American Pediatric Society (APS; Halpern, 1988).

The Sheppard-Towner Act becomes law in 1922. It is a 5-year program that provides matching funds to states for the purpose of establishing child hygiene or welfare bureaus to improve health care for mothers and children. The Children's Bureau administers the program. For the most part, the program involves educational activities through a variety of methods, such as bulletins, public nurse visits, consultation clinics, and "other suitable methods." Direct medical care is provided only where necessary, "especially in remote areas" (Wilson, 1989). The Bureau's focus on education reflects a deference to the general medicine practitioners, who at this time are increasingly concerned about growing competition from the emerging specialty of pediatrics and are apprehensive about potential competition from the government (Halpern, 1988).

The impact of Sheppard-Towner is profound. Between 1924 and its expiration in 1929 (it was extended for 2 years in 1927), the program is responsible for the creation of more than 3,000 child care clinics, over 4 million clinic exams, 3 million home visits, and 22 million educational brochures (Black, 1988). By 1926, 47 states have a child hygiene division. The number of public health nurses increases from roughly one hundred to more than ten thousand by 1929. Between 1906 and 1926, infant mortality decreases from 148 to 71 per 1,000 while overall life expectancy increases from 48 to 58 years of age. While these are significant accomplishments, the more enduring legacy of the Children's Bureau and the Sheppard-Towner Act is the precedent these initiatives establish for federal intervention in child welfare matters; the grant-in-aid concept, which balances federal and state interests; and the creation of a new institution called "The Wellness Conference," which transforms pediatrics and heavily influences how child care will be delivered in the future.

Pediatrics Becomes a Full-Time Specialty
and Helps Repeal the Sheppard-Towner Act

In 1926-1927, Congress and the country debate whether Sheppard-Towner should expire or be continued in perpetuity. The
debate is as intense as it was in 1921-1922. However, the opposition from organized medicine is stronger. Of even greater importance, the pediatric community is not united. Many pediatricians
oppose the extension because of the potential economic impact on
their practice, which is an index of the major changes that have
occurred in pediatric practice over the preceding 10 years. Ironically, these changes were the end result of the Sheppard-Towner
programs that the pediatricians originally supported.

In the early 1900s, child health specialists, for the most part, are
part-time private specialists and are affiliated with a charity, academic, or research institution. Often, the part-time specialists practice general medicine and have teaching responsibilities. General
practitioners, on the other hand, provide most child care. Pediatricians are primarily consultants. Pediatrics also gives child welfare
reform groups scientific legitimacy, but the pediatricians do not yet
control the reform agenda.

By the end of the 1920s, pediatrics is well along in its transition
to a full-time specialty that renders services in private offices as well
as in clinics. Between 1912 and 1929, children's health care shifts
its focus from treating disease and sanitation issues to prevention
and routine checkups for healthy children. This change begins with
the local infant welfare clinic and education program funded by
federal and state money under the Sheppard-Towner Act. A principal feature of the new approach is frequent, periodic medical
consultations, usually with medical professionals (either doctors or
nurses) for the purpose of evaluating how the child's development
is progressing. These consultations become known as the "Wellness
Conference." Participating physicians (usually part-time child specialists, through the local pediatric associations, state agencies, and
the Children's Bureau) develop systematic procedures for the Wellness Conference and periodically refine their definition of physical
and mental norms against which to measure a child's progress. In
time, the American Pediatric Society (APS) develops guidelines for
well-child techniques. Medical schools change the pediatric cur-

riculum to emphasize disease prevention and child-rearing advice
and to require a certain amount of clinical experience as a prereq-
uisite to practice (Halpern, 1988).

As a result, a strong demand for periodic medical consultations
is created, whether or not a child is sick. As the middle-class
demand increases, consultations migrate from the clinic, where
they are free, to the private office, where a fee is charged. The
office-based specialty practice becomes viable on a full-time basis.
No longer does a practitioner have to wait for referrals based on a
reputation developed through pro bono work at children's clinics
or hospitals. At the same time, there is growing resistance by the
pediatric specialist against clinics providing free consultations to
those that can afford to pay. Clearly, the mood of many pediatricians has changed considerably between 1920 and 1929. In 1920,
most pediatricians supported Sheppard-Towner and even formed
the APS in part to separate themselves from the AMA's opposition
to the legislation. Nine years later, the APS is divided on whether
to extend the law. In addition, a significant number of APS members
require in exchange for their support that the legislation expressly
prohibit the federal government from competing with fee-for-service medicine (Halpern, 1988).

This ideological schism among pediatricians foreshadows the
future direction of health care financing: that is, a system where
those who can afford it have private voluntary insurance coverage
or pay for care out-of-pocket, while those who cannot afford to pay
receive care through public or philanthropic programs. This approach is quite different than that of many other industrialized
countries that rely on a comprehensive universal health care system.
Understanding why the United States proceeds in its unique direction provides some insight into why the United States responds the
way it does to the future health care needs of children.

Health Insurance in the United States During the First Three Decades of the Twentieth Century: 1900-1930

Broad-based insurance coverage is important for access to health
care, especially for vulnerable populations such as the elderly and
children. The linkage between the availability of care and insurance

becomes even stronger in an industrialized economy and the increasing cost of treatment.

For these reasons, most industrial countries, by 1920, have compulsory insurance programs for both income protection and health care expenses. By contrast, the United States has limited piecemeal public programs and virtually no private medical expense insurance (Somers & Somers, 1961).

For example, in 1920, some 37 states have workers' compensation laws, which provide income protection and limited medical benefits for industrial accidents. In addition, mothers' pension aid provides sporadic income protection for single mothers and their children. Similarly, Sheppard-Towner monies fund wellness clinics that stress "education" and, in rural areas, some direct treatment.

Private health insurance, as we know it today, is non-existent. A limited number of prepaid and salaried physician group health practices serve workers in certain hazardous industries, such as lumbering, mining, and railroads. Several hospital-based group practices also serve some communities. In addition, small mutual benefit and fraternal sickness funds often provide limited benefits, usually for funeral expenses and modest income protection. Although price data are lacking, most believe that only a fraction of the population receives such protection (Starr, 1982). Women and children are an exception, however, with many receiving some focused public and philanthropic support, especially for preventive care and hygiene (Davis, 1934). One often-cited reason why the United States did not follow the other industrial countries regarding compulsory universal health coverage is the United States' historical bias against federal involvement in public welfare matters during the late 18th and early 19th centuries. Many also point to the opposition of the medical profession, the insurance and pharmaceutical industries, and, on occasion, organized labor (Applebaum, 1961). They also point to the absence of strong, cohesive, and broad middle-class support for compulsory health insurance (Applebaum, 1961; Starr, 1982). In this regard, middle-class wage-earners during the early 1900s are more concerned about the risk of lost income than the risk of large medical expenses, in part because the cost of medical care is still affordable on an out-of-pocket basis for much of the population. Medical specialization, technology, and the emerging central role of the hospital starts driving up health care costs between 1910 and the 1920s, but the impact of these increasing costs on the middle class builds slowly. In addition, when the support for compulsory health care coverage gains momentum, as it does between 1915 and 1920, public attention and resources are diverted by overreaching geopolitical events, such as World War I (Applebaum, 1961; Starr, 1982).

Private insurance coverage does not fill the vacuum for many of the same reasons. The limited number of health financing mechanisms that do exist (e.g., prepaid group practices) are vigorously opposed by organized medicine. Labor is also suspicious of employer motives in establishing and supporting group disability, life, and health insurance protection (Applebaum, 1961). Insurance companies and mutual benefit and fraternal societies start to experiment with disability and some health coverage during early 1900s. They experience disastrous financial results, however—largely because they do not yet have accurate data regarding medical and disability utilization and the abnormally high disability experience during the economic recessions of the first several decades of the century (Applebaum, 1961).

The early experience with disability and medical expense makes the private insurance sector "gun-shy," reinforcing traditional perceptions regarding what is and is not an insurable risk. For example, many in the insurance industry believe that an insurance company should insure only clearly defined and quantifiable risks, because ambiguity regarding covered losses prevents accurate pricing of the insurance coverage—a key to assuring the company's solvency (Vaughn, 1989). Insurers and regulators also are concerned about the related concepts of "moral hazard" and "adverse selection."[4] These concepts, which have their genesis in more simplistic times and evolve primarily in the context of individual coverage, heavily influence the private insurance industry's approach toward the emerging new risks of an industrial and urban society during the 1930s.

As late as 1915 many insurers and regulators are very cautious about group insurance despite its clear cost efficiencies and the better-than-average experience of full-time workers compared to the rest of the population (Starr, 1982). Part of this caution is driven by competitive concerns of companies and agents that sell individual insurance. This caution is also based on the fact that all individuals in the group are eligible for coverage; there is little or no individual underwriting to protect against adverse selection. Regulators, in response to employer pressure and the obvious efficiencies of group coverage, respond by allowing only employer groups to provide group coverage because these groups are not created for the purpose of obtaining insurance. For the same reasons, regulators also insist upon 100% employee participation if employers pay the entire cost of group coverage, which increases the odds of a mix of both good, average, and bad risks. For the same reasons regulators also insist upon at least 75% employee participation if employees do not pay the entire cost. These attitudes slow the expansion of group coverage to other groups, such as professional and fraternal associations or benefit associations sponsored by unions.

Many insurers also are reluctant to move beyond income protection (e.g., life and disability), which can be defined in specific dollar amounts, to medical expense coverage. These insurers believe that appropriate medical treatment and its duration are difficult if not impossible to measure (Cunningham & Cunningham, 1997; Somers & Somers, 1961). Even during the 1920s, insurers have an intuitive sense that appropriate medical care is highly judgmental and heavily influenced by consumer expectations and provider-induced demand. We also shall see that the industry's views about what is and is not an insurable risk heavily influences how early health insurance coverage is designed and the degree to which children and maternity care are covered, especially during the 1940s.

Equally, if not more, important are the changing attitudes of the middle class toward the risk of large medical expenses, which is directly related to medical technology and scientific advances that increase the number of serious diseases that now can be treated. These advances often involve expensive equipment and diagnostic options that are done in the hospital setting. Although most illnesses can still be treated at home by general practitioners and the cost of home diagnosis and treatment is roughly the same as it was 10 to 20 years earlier, the cost of treatment for an increasing number of diseases has become much more expensive, especially those requiring hospitalization. According to one estimate, only one sixth of all illnesses in the late 1920s are "serious" in nature. Yet, the treatment costs of these illnesses accounts for 50% of the total amount spent by families on health care (Davis, 1934).

One manifestation of this growing middle-class anxiety and an example of the medical profession's concern regarding structured financing is the Committee on the Cost of Medical Care, which is funded by a number of health-oriented foundations in 1926 (Starr, 1982). Composed of over 45 physicians, economists, and public health specialists, the Committee for the first time quantifies how much the United States spends on health care. The Committee documents that the medical cost for a serious illness represents a significant and increasing percentage of a family's income (Davis, 1934). While careful not to advocate a compulsory health insurance system, a substantial majority urge the promotion of voluntary "prepayment" or health insurance plans, where the cost of health care is spread over large populations, rather than absorbed by individuals or their families (Cunningham & Cunningham, 1997; Starr, 1982). Committee members say this "insurance" or prepayment is analogous to an individual budget for needed care, and then propose the payment for it through fixed, periodic voluntary private "prepayments," taxes, or both (Cunningham & Cunningham, 1997; Starr, 1982).

A nine-member minority strenuously objects to the recommendation. This minority, eight of whom are physicians, reflects organized medicine's concern that any program of this kind has the potential to become an intermediary between the doctor and patient, and thereby has the potential to limit the profession's clinical and economic autonomy over that relationship. Shortly after the release of the Committee's recommendation, the AMA embraces the minority's view and characterizes the majority's position as "socialism and communism" and tantamount to "inciting revolution" (Starr, 1982).

As the decade ends, there is a growing public desire for protection against health care costs associated with serious illness. Many in the provider community agree, but many do not and are adamant in their views. Providers and insurers that ponder the efficacy of pooling health care risks are cautious. Their reticence, however, is short-lived.

In 1929, the Great Depression leads to a decrease in the money for patient care, forcing hospitals with large fixed costs to move quickly and doctors to rethink their position. A few hospitals lead the way and create provider controlled insurance companies—the so-called Blue Cross plans. Much to the surprise of many, the market demand for the new hospital benefits is overwhelming. It does not take long for the nonprovider insurance companies (known as commercial insurers) to enter the market and to devise ways to overcome their historic concerns that medical expenses are not insurable (Cunningham & Cunningham, 1997).

The Great Depression and World War II: The Catalysts for Major Federal Social Legislation and the Start and Rapid Growth of Voluntary Employed-Based Health Insurance: 1930-1950

During the 1930s and 1940s, the major change agents are the Great Depression and World War II. The resulting social and political demands created by these cataclysmic events force the federal government to undertake several initiatives that permanently involve the federal government in social welfare matters. These same demands and resulting federal policy changes stimulate the growth of private group health insurance, expanded medical research and new treatment advances and, during the late 1940s, a significant expansion in hospital capacity. These federal and private sector initiatives establish the foundation for today's mixed public and private health insurance system. In addition, the combination of new treatment opportunities, expanding hospital capacity, and insurance sets the stage for unprecedented medical cost inflation that ultimately forces a restructuring of the medical delivery and financing system during the closing decades of the century. This restructuring impacts how everyone, including children, receive and pay for health care.

The New Federal Health and Related Programs

In 1929, the same year the Sheppard-Towner Act expires, the stock market crashes, signaling the start of the Great Depression. By 1932, over 6 million people are unemployed. More than half a million are looking for work in Chicago alone, and over a million are doing so in New York City. The gross national product (GNP) drops by 50%, and manufacturing output is down 54%. For the first time in U.S. history, more people leave the United States than immigrate to it. Soup and relief lines became a familiar fixture in every city (Ashby, 1985; Bremner, 1970-1974).

Private charity and municipal relief agencies are overwhelmed and their resources are soon exhausted. President Franklin

Roosevelt is inaugurated in 1933, and he institutes a wide range of banking and economic reforms along with public work programs. One of the New Deal's most significant undertakings is the Social Security Act of 1935. The Act has three basic components: (a) an old-age pension program; (b) a federal unemployment system; and (c) federal grants for maternal and child-welfare services, relief for dependent children, and vocational rehabilitation for handicapped children. President Roosevelt removes national health insurance from the package at the last minute because of concern that AMA opposition could jeopardize the entire program (Sardell, 1988).

The last of these programs, Title IV and Title V, are distinctly different programs but are often confused. Title V resembles the Sheppard-Towner Act by providing federal grants-in-aid to stimulate child and maternal health programs, such as family planning, children and youth projects, and dental services. It is a means-tested program that concentrates on discrete populations, especially mothers and young and crippled children. Initial appropriations for the Title V programs are twice those for Sheppard-Towner. Title V programs also are administered by the Children's Bureau (Bell, 1965).

Not much attention is paid to Title IV, which is titled "Grants to States for Aid to Dependent Children." It is designed to enable the family to remain together under the moral guidance and nurturing of the mother. Title IV is the logical extension of the Progressive Movement's widow's pension or mother's aid. The original mother's aid laws were not effective because they were voluntary and inadequately funded by the states (Bell, 1965; Leff, 1973; Trattner, 1979). Adequate state funding becomes an even greater problem during the Depression. Title IV tries to remedy these problems by creating a uniform national program, with more adequate funding through the use of federal money to match state appropriations. Title IV is administered at the state level (Bell, 1965).

Although the AMA is very vocal in 1929 regarding the Sheppard-Towner extension, it does not openly voice its concern for Title V because a viable Title V program may reduce the political need for comprehensive health care reform that many believe will be part of President Roosevelt's social security package (Wilson, 1989). Instead, the AMA makes an attempt to have Title V administered by some agency other than the Children's Bureau. While this effort is unsuccessful, a significant change for Title IV does occur, which may or may not have been due to organized medicine's lobbying efforts. At the last minute in House and Senate negotiations on Title IV, its administration is moved from the Children's Bureau to the newly created Bureau of Public Assistance (later renamed the Bureau of Family Services) under the Social Security Administration (Wilson, 1989). Separating Title IV from the Children's Bureau shifts Title IV's focus from children to poor relief and assures that Title IV will become embroiled in future ideological controversies regarding welfare and single-parent families. In 1935, no one understands the long-term significance of this change. By 1965, Title IV grows into the largest and most controversial of our welfare programs, that is, Aid to Families with Dependent Children (AFDC). AFDC also becomes a major eligibility condition for health care coverage for poor children.

World War II creates its own demands for increased maternity and medical benefits, especially for the wives and children of men serving in the armed forces. Early efforts by the Children's Bureau to provide this coverage through Title V are inadequate because the Bureau does not have enough resources. As a result, Congress, in 1943, unanimously enacts the Emergency Maternity and Infant Care Act (EMIC), which provides direct payments for medical nursing, maternity, and first-year infant care for the dependents of every serviceman in the lowest four service grades. Financial need is not a requirement. Between 1943 and 1948, Congress appropriates $133 million for the program and over 1.5 million recipients receive care. At EMIC's zenith, one out of every seven births in the United States is covered (Ashby, 1985; Strickland & Ambrose, 1985).

Contemporaneous with and maybe in part because of EMIC, there is some movement in Congress for a national compulsory health insurance system funded by business and individual taxes. The Wagner-Murray-Dingell bill is introduced in 1943. It is subsequently reintroduced with President Truman's support in 1945 and 1947. It provides for a compulsory system funded by a social security-type payroll tax (Bremner, 1982). Proponents argue that such legislation is necessary to address access problems that have been created by the high cost of medical care (Bremner, 1982). President Truman's 1945 message to Congress in support of the legislation points to EMIC and other federal hygiene and disease control measures as precedent for federal involvement. The president also invokes the need to care for children as the primary reason for the proposal, because it is necessary to make sure "that our health programs are pushed most vigorously with the youngest segment of the population" (Truman, 1961). The Children's Bureau, however, is more interested in perpetuating EMIC or some other child-specific legislation (Starr, 1982). In support of the Bureau's approach, Congressman Pepper introduces legislation that would appropriate $100 million annually for grants to the states for maternity care, medical care for children, services for crippled children, and child welfare services. Although Congress does not approve either bill, the 1946 Social Security Amendments almost double the appropriations for Title V programs. Additional Title V increases are authorized during the 1950s.

The Start of Voluntary Employer-Based Private Health Insurance

Prior to 1929, hospitals have trouble keeping up with public demand. After 1929 and the start of the Great Depression, the environment changes dramatically. Over one third of all hospital beds are now empty, and hospitals face severe cash flow problems.

A number of individual hospitals and eventually the American Hospital Association devise the so-called Blue Cross solution. Blue Cross is a not-for-profit pooling arrangement controlled by the local medical community and covers hospital expenses for all hospitals in a "service area," usually a city and surrounding towns or a major metropolitan area. Blue Cross coverage is available for *all* hospitals in the service area in order to avoid giving one hospital a competitive advantage over another (Day, 1996-1997). Blue Cross negotiates "service" agreements with the local hospitals—that is, a per diem price for all hospital services provided to a patient and for a specified number of hospital days—and then sells this package to subscribers for a monthly or annual premium. The Blue Cross plan covers only hospital services. It does not cover the fees charged by physicians and surgeons who treat patients in the hospital. Although Blue Cross plans are committed to providing individual coverage, they have a distinct bias for group employer-based coverage because of the more favorable and predictable health experience of a working population compared to communitywide experience (Cunningham & Cunningham, 1997)

The success of Blue Cross hospital coverage is immediate. In 1933, there are six plans nationwide covering 55,000 members. Two years later there are 17 plans nationwide with a membership of 215,000. Enrollment climbs to 4.4 million in 1940, 15.7 million in 1945, and 27 million by 1947 (Cunningham & Cunningham, 1997). This success is not lost on doctors or commercial insurers.

Although physicians are financially impacted by and concerned about decreased cash flow during the Depression, they are more anxious about the prospect of some third-party entity (even one under their control) negotiating fee levels, as Blue Cross does under its service arrangements with hospitals (Starr, 1982).

At the same time, the financial benefits and stability of pooled financing are alluring. In 1934, the AMA relents and embraces third-party financing provided that the financing system incorporates certain key principles. The most important of these principles is that every aspect of medicine, including its financing, "must be under the control of the medical profession," and no third party can come between the patient and the physician (Day, 1996-1997). The AMA also borrows a concept from the property and casualty insurance industry called "indemnity" insurance in order to minimize the intrusion of third-party insurance into the doctor-patient relationship. Under the indemnity approach, there is a strict separation between the financing and the delivery of care. The insurance contract reimburses (or "indemnifies") the patient for all or part of what the patient owes the doctor. The choice of doctor is solely up to the patient, and treatment and fee decisions are solely between the doctor and patient (Day, 1996-1997).

Despite AMA endorsement of third-party financing under these very specific conditions, many doctors are cautious. In 1935, there are over 200 different pilot programs sponsored by local medical societies. It is not until 1939 and the threat of a government program in California that the first physician-controlled *surgical* insurance plan becomes operational. It is called Blue Shield and not surprisingly provides for indemnity rather than Blue Cross service-type coverage (Cunningham & Cunningham, 1997). And in 1943, the AMA, concerned about the prospect of state or federal compulsory insurance, formally encourages the formation of and participation in Blue Shield plans. Even so, by 1944, Blue Shield has only

1.8 million members. This increases to 3.6 million in 1946 and to only 6.5 million by 1950 (Cunningham & Cunningham, 1997).

Commercial insurance companies (i.e., private stock and mutual insurance companies) are impressed by Blue Cross's success. In 1934, the commercial carriers start to market hospital indemnity insurance only. By 1940, the commercial insurers cover 3.7 million people. By 1950, enrollment increases to almost 40 million, just 2 million members less than Blue Cross. In 1952, commercial membership exceeds that of "the Blues." Although the Blues and the commercial insurers favor employer-based groups, a considerable amount of individual coverage is also sold to those who can afford it (Somers & Somers, 1961).

The dramatic growth of the commercial insurers is due, in part, to their enhanced multistate capability, which is attractive to multistate employers. In addition, the commercials are somewhat more distanced than the Blues from the influences of local medical societies. As a result, the commercial issuers start to market surgical indemnity coverage several years before the first Blue Shield plan is up and running (Somers & Somers, 1961).

World War II economic policy also stimulates the demand for health care coverages and does so in a way that strengthens the link between private health care insurance and the workplace. For example, a key component of managing a war economy is a wage and price freeze. In order to ameliorate the harshness of the wage freeze, employers are allowed to provide employee benefits without having these benefits considered wages. In 1949, the U.S. Supreme Court upholds a National Labor Relations Board decision that makes employee benefits a legitimate subject for collective bargaining. Collectively bargained health benefits expand rapidly, and these benefits by their nature are employer-based and can be best realized through group coverage. Union contracts also stimulate nonunion employers to emulate union negotiated benefits (Somers & Somers, 1961). The federal tax laws are also clarified to make sure that employee health care benefits are not considered taxable income to employees.

The resurgence of collective bargaining also influences benefit design. Before World War II, unions focus on the worker's dignity and wages. After World War II, organized labor's focus shifts to family security, which translates into expanding fringe benefits, including health care coverage not only for their workers but also their dependents (Barnard, 1982; Somers & Somers, 1961). As a result, the number of people covered by group plans grows dramatically. For example, in 1940, commercial insurers alone provide group health coverage to 2.5 million people. By 1950, the number increases to over 22 million people. When combined with Blue Cross and Blue Shield, the total number of covered individuals increases from 12 million in 1940 to 76.6 million in 1950 (HIAA, 1996).

Patterns of Early Insurance Coverage and Its Implications for Children

Health expense coverage provisions are very diverse. Yet patterns exist and are influenced by the traditional insurance views regarding what insurers believe are insurable risks and organized labor's focus on family security.

For most of the 1940s, both the Blues and commercial insurers limit coverage to care in the hospital, rather than in the doctor's office. This reticence represents some deference to physician concerns about third-party financing. It is also due to widely held views that an insured is less apt to "subject himself to unnecessary surgical operations just to collect an insurance benefit which must be turned over to the doctor" and the feeling that "there is little danger of doctors performing surgical operations merely to collect fees through insurance" (Fitzhugh, 1951). For the same reasons, the commercial insurers and Blue Shield tend to use deductibles and co-payments to thwart any potential moral hazard (Brill, 1956). Blue Cross, on the other hand, provides first-dollar coverage because of its service agreement with the hospitals (Cunningham & Cunningham, 1997). These moral hazard concerns also explain why expansions of coverage beyond the hospital, such as major medical health insurance, does not make its appearance until the next decade.

Early health insurance coverage also tends to be limited to the individual purchasing coverage or the covered worker rather than to their dependents. Dependent coverage is worrisome because nonworkers have "no obligations, they don't have to go to work, they would just go to the hospital and lie down" (Cunningham & Cunningham, 1997). Despite these concerns, the labor movement's focus on family security results in collective bargaining agreements that expand coverage for dependents. Many nonunion employers follow this example.

Many insurers also are cautious about in-hospital maternity benefits other than for complications of pregnancy because maternity care is, in effect, hospitalization of a "planned incidence" and "a matter of choice." More often than not, the Blues and the commercials treat maternity differently than other health expenses, either by excluding it from coverage or by providing for a lump sum or special dollar limits. For these same reasons and the historic inclination to limit coverage to care in the hospital, neither the Blues nor the commercials cover prenatal or well-baby visits. In addition, maternity coverage often involves a waiting period (Cunningham & Cunningham, 1997).

The early Washington, D.C., Blue Cross plan for federal employees illustrates these coverage patterns. Under the federal employees' plan only federal employees, rather than their dependents, are covered. Maternity benefits are offered for female workers but only after a 10-month waiting period (Cunningham & Cunningham, 1997).

The Ascendancy of Employer-Based Health Insurance, the Parallel Growth of Federal Government Programs for Vulnerable Populations, and Emerging Gaps in Health Insurance Coverage: 1950-1960

Much of the 1950s are characterized by unparalleled prosperity, public confidence, and optimism. There is a sense of resource abundance that influences virtually all aspects of government policy from highways to hospital construction (Madrick, 1995).

Although the absolute incidence of poverty decreases dramatically between 1940 and the late 1950s, there is a growing awareness that not everyone is doing well. As the decade ends, an increasing number of scholars and observers "discover" significant pockets of hard-core poverty composed primarily of the elderly, minorities, and single-parent (often female) households (Galbraith, 1958; Harrington, 1962). A deep recession in the late 1950s ends the post-World War II economic expansion. The recession makes more visible the plight of the poor and reminds all Americans that prosperity cannot be taken for granted.

The first 3 years of the decade are also a time of war. The Korean conflict erupts in 1950, and it is a war that the United States does not quite win. America's confidence is also shaken by the USSR's *Sputnik,* as well as the USSR's growing economy and presence in the world. The Cold War is under way. The "shadow of atomic annihilation" and the shaken American confidence bring the issue of "personal security" to the forefront, which gets reflected in increasing attention to working conditions and employee benefits (Barnard, 1982).

These cross-currents of optimism versus pessimism and affluence versus poverty help drive the rapid expansion of private health insurance for the middle class, as well as the expansion of government programs for the poor. However, the interrelationship of these public and private programs is not seamless. There are gaps in coverage, which become more apparent during the 1950s.

The following will look first at the expansion of private group health insurance for the middle class. It will then summarize the incremental but important changes in federal and state health programs for vulnerable populations, such as poor children and the elderly, that set the stage for massive federal intervention during the following decade.

Employer-Based Voluntary Health Care Comes of Age

The forces that encourage the growth of private group health coverage continue throughout the 1950s. For example, health care costs continue to increase, and people worry about the cost of unexpected illness. Government tax and labor policies supporting employee-based coverage remain in place (Day, 1996-1997). In addition, continued economic growth and prosperity enable employers to finance expanded employee health benefits (Somers & Somers, 1961). The Korean conflict also enhances the growth of collective bargaining for fringe benefits through the imposition of new wage and price controls as well as a ruling by the Wage Stabilization Board that employer contributions to employee benefit plans will not be offset against other wage limits (Applebaum, 1961). As a result of these forces, employer-based voluntary health insurance increases dramatically over the next several decades, in terms of both the number of people covered and the scope of covered treatment.

Between 1940 and 1960, the number of individuals with private health insurance increases from 12 million to 122.5 million, or from 9% to 68% of the total civilian population (HIAA, 1996; U.S. Census Bureau, 1993). Between 1950 and 1960 alone, the number of covered individuals almost doubles, from 76 million to 122 million (HIAA, 1996). Approximately 75% of these individuals receive coverage through group insurance, which for the most part is employer-based insurance (Somers & Somers, 1961).

Although 70% of all employee benefit plans are established by employers unilaterally, organized labor has a profound influence on the growth and content of all fringe benefits, including health insurance (Somers & Somers, 1961). Labor's post-World War II focus on family security makes both the dependent coverage and employer contribution to the cost of health benefits a priority. As a result, large corporations start to pay all or a substantial portion of the cost of negotiated health care benefits. Smaller companies often pay smaller amounts. In addition, nonunion companies follow the trend established by the union-negotiated plans. Insurance company underwriting standards also encourage employer contribution because they evidence employer commitment and mitigate against antiselection by encouraging broad employee participation (Beam, 1991). By 1960, it is estimated that manufacturers on average pay 21% of their payroll for fringe benefits. In the finance, insurance, and real estate industries, the proportion approximates 25% (Barnard, 1982).

Dependent coverage expands during the 1950s and 1960s. While data are somewhat sketchy, it appears that by the mid-1960s approximately 1.7 dependents are covered by group insurance for every covered employee (HIAA, 1968-1970).

For many years, insurers resist coverage for "routine medical visits and other miscellaneous medical expenses because such expenses are more a matter of budgeting than the sharing of any substantial risk" (Fitzhugh, 1951). Yet market demand and collective bargaining force insurers to provide "regular medical" insurance, meaning coverage for *in-hospital* physician services other than that provided by the surgeon (Somers & Somers, 1961). Moreover, in 1952, "major medical" or "catastrophic coverage" makes its appearance. This insurance covers all kinds of medical care both in and outside the hospitals. By 1959, major medical is the fastest growing health insurance product and covers some 22

million people. Insurers have become more comfortable covering
nonhospital health care, especially when done through employer-
based group coverage with its benefit of above-average risks and
the use of significant co-pay and deductibles to guard against moral
hazard (Brill, 1956).

The Balkanization of the Insurance Risk Pool

Competition between the Blues and commercial insurers also
influences the design of health insurance packages. Commercial
insurers "experience-rate" the group business. That is, the rate is
set to reflect the actual experience of each employer's working
population. The Blues, on the other hand, charge a community rate
that reflects the experience of the entire community, not just that
of the working population. The Blues use community rating both
for ideological and sometimes for regulatory reasons (Beam, 1991).
In addition, many Blue Cross/Blue Shield plans often believe their
broad "social" mission requires them to provide access to everyone
despite the obvious risk of adverse selection. This risk is reduced
by limiting acceptance of new insureds to a set period once a
year—the "open enrollment" period or Minneapolis Plan. Commercial carriers, however, are not subject to these requirements and
can freely underwrite coverage (Cunningham & Cunningham,
1997).

As the commercial insurers gain market share, the Blues begin to
emulate the commercials on a number of fronts. The Blues move
away from service arrangements and toward specific dollar indemnity benefits. The Blues also embrace experience rating. Over the
next several decades, this transformation of the Blues eventually
results in the loss of their special tax exemption at the federal level
(Cunningham & Cunningham, 1997).

The use of experience rating, however, is much more than an
interesting footnote in the history of the Blues and commercial
health insurance. Employer-based coverage reflects the experience
of the relatively healthy population of workers and their families.
As a result, the nation's community risk pool becomes fragmented,
making it more difficult for better-than-average risks to subsidize
below-average risks. Larger employers often are able to use expe-

rience rating. Smaller employers in the aggregate should have a
comparable advantage, but a small employer does not have the large
numbers of employees to smooth out random fluctuations of adverse experience. Similarly, those buying individual coverage tend
to have below-average risk compared to that of the working population. Thus, those individuals who are poorer insurance risks
increasingly have access and affordability problems as experience
rating expands. These access and affordability issues build during
the 1950s and 1960s, prompting government intervention targeted
at improving access to insurance for smaller businesses and individuals in the 1980s.

Experience rating also motivates employers, especially those that
contribute to employee health plans, to have a direct employer
interest in controlling health care costs. As Paul Starr (1982) noted,
"as benefit packages expanded, this interest [of employers] was to
become one of the most powerful new elements in the politics of
American health care."

Federal Assistance for the Indigent, the
Unemployed, the Aged, and Their Dependents

As private health insurance increases during the 1950s and
1960s, the plight of those who have no coverage and are separated
from the workforce becomes more glaring. Although various federal programs are proposed for the specific categories of uncovered
individuals, and in particular the aged and children, few major
programs are enacted into law. In fact, few ever make it out of
Congressional committee (Bremner, 1982). Instead, Congress and
the executive branch make only incremental changes. While these
changes pump some additional dollars into the health care system,
these resources barely keep up with the increasing demand.

For example, Congress repeatedly increases the authorizations
for Title V programs (maternal and child health, crippled children,
and child welfare services). However, with the exception of 1958,
actual funding falls below the authorized funding level (Bremner,
1982). Title V undergoes the most change in its smallest program,
namely, child welfare. Here the new appropriations permit the
states to build an administrative infrastructure to deal with homeless, abandoned, and abused children, especially in rural areas
(Bremner, 1982).

During the late 1940s and the 1950s, Title IV, as opposed to Title V, eligibility is periodically expanded. One change of special note occurs in the early 1950s, setting the stage for future controversy. Congress expands Title IV grant eligibility beyond children to mothers and other caretakers (Bremner, 1982). This expansion, however, precludes assistance whenever an able-bodied adult male lives in the household. This limitation, which remains in place until 1961, has its genesis in the fear that unrestricted aid would encourage illicit sex and desertion (Bremner, 1982). This fear (which is later revealed to be grossly overstated) is reinforced by the continued growth of single-parent families headed by females and expanding ADC enrollments (Bremner, 1982). As federal eligibility expands, many states restrict eligibility through "suitable home" and "access to the house" rules. Although the number of ADC families decreases between 1950 and 1955, this trend is short-lived. Starting in 1955, the number of ADC recipients increases annually. By 1960, the number of individuals receiving aid approximates 3 million (some 850,000 more than in 1950) while the number of children for every 1,000 of the under-18 population that receive aid remains the same (Bremner, 1982).

Equally important to children is the income protection provided by Old Age, Survivors and Disability Health Insurance (OASDHI). Although this program is originally limited to retired workers in the 1940s and 1950s, it is expanded to cover dependents of the worker, including widows, widowers, and children. In addition, the program expands over time to cover more and more workers. By 1960, 9 out of 10 mothers and young children have survival protection in the event a covered worker dies. Over 1 million children, representing two thirds of all fatherless children, receive benefits under the program (Bremner, 1982; Patterson, 1982). Although the OASDHI and ADC provide income protection rather than health insurance coverage, these monies provide important financial support to maintain family structure, thus indirectly providing some means for medical care and a healthier environment.

As the 1950s close, there is a growing consensus that more needs to be done for the indigent and the aged. In 1956, the Social Security Act is amended to allow states more flexibility in using OASDHI monies for health care for the "needy aged." California and Colorado institute their own programs.

In 1958 and 1959, Congressional hearings are held on the Forand Bill, which provides funds for hospital and surgical care for the aged built around OASDHI and funded through a 0.5% increase in the employer and social security tax. The AMA opposes the legislation, citing the "dangers of socialism" (Bremner, 1982).

As the decade closes, Secretary of Health, Education and Welfare Flemming and a Social Security Advisory Board conclude that there is no evidence that women bear illegitimate children in order to get benefits under ADC. Secretary Flemming opposes the states on "suitable home" Title IV restrictions, and his efforts finally culminate in legislation in 1961 permitting aid to children in homes when one caretaker is an able-bodied male. Only one half of the states take advantage of this new federal flexibility regarding eligibility (Bremner, 1982).

Although infant mortality continues to decrease during the 1950s, the rate of decrease slows compared to the 1940s. For certain pockets of hard-core poverty, however, the rate remains stable or even goes up, especially for urban blacks (Bremner, 1982).

Filling the Gaps: Medicare and Medicaid, the War on Poverty, and the Great Society: 1960-1970

The era of the Great Society and the War on Poverty is an important decade for children's health care. It is an even more important decade for the future direction of how all Americans pay for and receive health care.

Growing concerns about systemic social and economic discrimination of the poor and minorities and the related "vicious cycle of poverty" culminate in the civil rights movement and significant social legislation. Major pieces of legislation, such as the Civil Rights Act of 1964 and 1967 and the Voting Rights Act of 1965, are aimed at eliminating discrimination in public facilities, the political process, education, and employment. The Kennedy and Johnson administrations also focus on programs to create job opportunities and to upgrade the labor skills of the poor (Davis & Schoen, 1978). Many of these programs are holistic in their outlook, including, for example, job training for poor teenagers, as well as nutrition and preschool programs, and health care for migrant workers, pregnant women, children, and the elderly.

Of special significance are two large federal health care initiatives, known as Medicaid and Medicare. Medicaid provides health coverage to many poor children and their caretakers. Medicare, which provides health insurance to people 65 years or older, also has an important but indirect impact upon children's health because Medicare provides coverage for many elderly caretakers and disabled children who do not qualify for Medicaid. In addition, both Medicaid and Medicare initially use the fee-for-service reimbursement methodology, which "accommodates" the medical profession's desire for clinical and economic autonomy (Starr, 1982).

These federal programs inject a significant amount of new purchasing power into the system. When combined with private health insurance, approximately 80% of the population now has health coverage. Many believe the expansion of public and private insurance is a major reason for increased utilization and rising medical costs.

The following will summarizes the evolution of Medicare and Medicaid. It then looks at these major initiatives of the War on Poverty and the Great Society that directly impact children.

The Federal and State Governments Become Major Purchasers of Health Care

In part because of the increasing cost of health care, pressures build during the 1950s for compulsory coverage for the "deserving" elderly and to a lesser degree the poor. At the same time, Congress is wary about massive reform because of fiscal concerns and potential opposition from organized medicine (Marmor, 1973). Congressman Mills and Senator Kerr attempt to defuse the issue for the elderly by proposing a federal-state matching grant program for the "elderly poor." This proposal, which becomes law in 1960, gives the states an option to participate in the program. Critics say the program won't achieve its objective of providing a meaningful "safety net" for the elderly. By 1964, most agree that the program is a failure. As a result, pressure for a more comprehensive elderly program picks up momentum. This is also the same time period that the Kennedy and Johnson administrations begin to implement programs designed to allow the poor to help themselves. An integral part of the latter initiatives is better health care for the poor.

In response to the growing pressures to cover the elderly and the poor, the AMA and House Republicans propose a voluntary insurance plan for physician services to complement President Johnson's proposal to cover hospital care. Three different but related concepts are being debated by the Congress: hospital and physician care for the elderly and poor; the appropriate federal and state roles in protecting these vulnerable populations; and compulsory or voluntary health insurance for the general population. These three concepts are melded together into two closely related programs known as Medicaid and Medicare. Medicare provides for compulsory hospital insurance (Part A) and voluntary physician insurance (Part B) for the elderly. Part A is funded by dedicated payroll and employer taxes, while Part B is funded through a combination of premiums and general tax revenues. Medicaid is a federal-state matching grant program covering both hospital and physician care for the poor. Although there are many differences between these two federal programs, they are similar in that they maintain the existing medical professional paradigms of the freedom to choose one's physician, physician discretion regarding appropriate treatment, and fee-for-service reimbursement (Marmor, 1973).

Medicaid becomes particularly important for children and pregnant mothers. Although states are given the option of covering certain categories of individuals, Medicaid also requires that certain other categories of people must be covered. One mandatory category is those who receive financial assistance under the federal-state Aid to Families with Dependent Children (AFDC) welfare program. AFDC, the expanded successor to Title IV's ADC program, provides cash benefits to low-income children who have an unemployed, incapacitated, or absent parent. Assistance is also given to other so-called caretakers in the household in order to sustain the family unit (Karger & Stoesz, 1990). States are also given the option to cover low-income pregnant women and children who meet AFDC income limits but do not qualify for AFDC payments because both parents are at home. Most states exercise this option. Although Medicaid is not limited to AFDC children and qualifying members of the child's family, mothers and children are by far the major beneficiaries of the program (Davis & Schoen, 1978).

However, many are critical of the Medicaid program. They claim the program does not fulfill its "entitlement" potential or vision. Reasons often given for this failure include the tying of Medicaid eligibility to welfare cash assistance, and giving states, which have limited financial resources, the *option* of expanding coverage beyond the minimum mandate (Rosenblatt, Law, & Rosenbaum, 1997). Despite these limitations, there is little question that Medicaid is in large part responsible for a sharp increase in use of medical services by the poor of all ages, including children (Davis & Schoen, 1978).

Medicare and Medicaid pour large amounts of money into the health care system. Five years after their effective date, both programs cover some 41 million people and pay out over $14.7 billion annually (HIAA, 1996). The cost of both programs is far in excess of the original estimates (Wing, Jacobs, & Kuszler, 1998).

The War on Poverty and the Great Society

The 1960s are characterized by a renewed interest in contemporary social problems. One key focus is the plight of poor children and the importance of children's health (Wilson, 1989).

For example, in 1960, the White House Conference on Children and Youth celebrates its Golden Anniversary by reaffirming the 1909 White House Conference's Charter of Children. Two years later, President Kennedy recommends and Congress approves an expansion of the National Institutes of Health by the creation of a National Institute of Child Health and Human Development (Aguilar, 1995; Wilson, 1989).

In 1963, Congress enacts the Maternal and Child Health Act, which increases Title V appropriations for prenatal care for low-income and high-risk mothers. It is hoped that this expansion of Title V will have a significant impact in reducing the risk of mental retardation, bacterial meningitis, asthma, and diabetes (Wilson, Bartels, & Rubin, 1988). Over the next 10 years, appropriations for these focused programs increase from $5 million to $73 million annually. By 1973, Congress is funding over 100 Title V projects in 36 states (Aguilar, 1995).

The national problem of hunger, combined with business interest in stimulating demand for agricultural products, combine to produce the Food Stamp Act of 1964. This law provides low-cost coupons for both the working and nonworking poor to redeem for food. In addition to enhancing the diet of the poor, it equalizes to some degree the varying AFDC benefit levels among the states (Dickinson, 1995).

In 1967, Medicaid is given additional responsibility for preventive health services to low-income children and adolescents. The program is called the Early and Periodic Screening, Diagnostic, and Treatment Program (EPSDT). Under this program, states are required to screen all eligible children through age 21 for actual or potential handicapping or disabling conditions. Once such conditions are identified, Medicaid must pay for the treatment and correction of these conditions (Sardell, 1988). Though this program is supported by the American Academy of Pediatrics, many local pediatricians are concerned that publicly funded EPSDT services will adversely impact their practice (Sardell, 1988).

Neighborhood health centers also receive federal funds on a demonstration basis (Sardell, 1988). Located in poverty areas in order to facilitate access, these health centers concentrate on clinical and social medicine, such as nutrition, housing, and sanitation. By the early 1980s there are over 800 such centers, in both rural and inner-city areas (Sardell, 1988). These neighborhood health centers primarily treat woman and children (Sardell, 1988). Other significant initiatives include nutrition counseling, and food for pregnant and lactating women and children up to age 5, known as the Women, Infant and Child Program (WIC); the school lunch program; and preschool education (Project Head Start). All of these programs have a beneficial impact on access to health care, neonatal mortality, maternal and infant mortality, and improved child development (Costin et al., 1991; Starfield, 1985).

Despite these improvements, the precursors of change emerge. In 1967, the Children's Bureau, which has provided a federal focus for the needs of children for over 50 years, loses much of its power. Its Title V administrative responsibilities are transferred to the Public Health Administration and other functions go to other departments. In addition, the Children's Bureau itself is moved to the Office of Child Development in the Department of Health, Education and Welfare (Davis & Schoen, 1978; Sardell, 1990a). As a result of these changes, the federal focus on children becomes more diffused.

By the late 1960s it is increasingly clear that the impact of the substantial federal resources dedicated to children is diluted by the piecemeal and disjointed roll-out of these social programs and the myriad number of agencies responsible for their implementation. Efforts to assure greater coordination, such as the Federal Panel on Early Childhood and the Office of Child Development, have little impact (Bremner, 1970-1974). The dispersion of responsibility for children's programs sets the tone for the retrenchment of government support for children that occurs over the next 15 years. Equally important, health care policy for the poor, including children, increasingly gets caught up in the growing interdependency between work and welfare policy and idealized views of appropriate family structure and life (Axinn & Stearn, 1985; Wilson, 1989).

Changing Health Care Priorities: From Expanding Health Care Access to Cost Containment and the Start of "Managed" Care: 1970-1980

Although few significant structural changes occur in the U.S. health care system during the 1970s, the decade is a watershed period regarding U.S. health care policy and the future evolution of the U.S. health care system. It is during the 1970s that government policymakers and business leaders change their views regarding the nation's health care priorities. Prior to 1970, health care access and expanded medical capacity is of prime importance. As a result, both government and the private sector support programs designed to expand hospital capacity, medical research, medical education, and public and private health insurance coverage (Starr, 1982).

During the 1970s, the focus of government and business shifts away from expanding access to ways of containing the rising cost of health care because of the adverse impact these rising costs have on federal and state budgets and the cost of doing business. Although the 1970s are a period of abnormally high inflation, health care costs continue to increase significantly faster than inflation generally and the growth of the U.S. economy (Day, 1996-1997; Wing et al., 1998).

The rising cost of health care is especially troublesome because it impedes the ability of government and the private sector to maintain or expand existing levels of protection. Affordability of coverage is even more critical for individuals and small businesses. Children are especially vulnerable because they receive coverage through the private sector as dependents, a coverage status that is often adversely impacted more than other coverages by cost constraints or hard economic times. Similarly, the other major source of coverage for children, Medicaid, is often one of the first targets whenever government revenues become tight. In addition, changing U.S. demographics and, in particular, increasing teenage pregnancy and single-parent families, who for the most part are poor, put added pressure on existing government safety nets, such as Medicaid.

Initial government responses to increasing medical costs experiment with direct regulation aimed primarily at providers in the hope that existing levels of care will either be done in less costly settings or that providers will continue to provide care at reduced reimbursement rates. Disillusionment with the spotty success and even counterproductive impact of these regulatory efforts lays the foundation for increased reliance on financial incentives during the 1980s (Melhado, 1988).

The private sector focuses on incremental benefit design changes that stress utilization review and increased cost sharing by employees, which begins in the late 1970s. Employers also start to change how they finance benefits in order to avoid state mandated benefits and premium taxes.

All of these efforts are done on a piecemeal basis and any "savings" realized in one sector are often transferred to another. Although much effort is expended, health care costs in the aggregate continue to increase but do so in a way that exacerbates the affordability problem for those that do not have coverage. In addition, efforts to control health care costs by all payers start to dismantle the informal safety net that grew up along side third-party coverage (Iglehart, 1988). This informal safety net exists in many large hospitals in major metropolitan areas that, because of their size and revenue streams, permit "excess" reimbursements from private payers to cover the costs of the uninsured poor who often seek care in their emergency rooms. As a result of these interrelated trends, the uninsured population that had remained relatively stable over the past decade slowly begins to grow, which puts further pressure on the system.

Even though the forces that are put into play by the changing attitudes toward cost containment proceed slowly, their cumulative impact over time, like gravity, has an enormous influence on the evolution of the health care system and how many children receive health care. For this reason it is important to review briefly the magnitude of medical cost inflation in the 1970s and how the public and private sector respond to it.

Medical Cost Inflation
Between 1950 and 1980

Between 1950 and 1970, national health expenditures (NHE) increase 586% (from $12.7 billion to $74.4 billion), while the GNP increases by only 347% (from $288 billion to $1 trillion). Between 1970 and 1980, this disparity moderates somewhat, but the pattern continues: NHE increases 2.6 times to $280 billion while the GNP increases 1.5 times to $2.7 trillion (HIAA, 1996). Similarly, personal consumption of health care dollars as a percentage of total personal consumption increases from 4.6% in 1950 to 8.69% in 1970. By 1980, the percentage approximates 10.3% (HIAA, 1996).

These cost increases are accompanied by an even more dramatic increase in the number of people covered by public and private third-party coverage. Between 1940 and 1970, the number of people having public and private health insurance grows from 12 to 198 million, or by 1,550%. During the same period, the U.S. population increases by only 64% (Day, 1996-1997). Claims and benefits paid from public and private coverage increase from $29.4 billion in 1970 to $136.3 billion in 1980 (HIAA, 1996; Wing et al., 1998).

Equally important, especially from a political perspective, the cost of Medicare and Medicaid is now far in excess of the initial projections (Wing et al., 1998). This sticker shock is compounded by the fact that these costs are a significant and growing component of federal and state budgets. For example, the government's share of national health expenditures increases from $10.8 billion to $27.8 billion between 1965 and 1970 (Starr, 1982).

Increased utilization resulting from the growth of third-party coverage is in part responsible for increasing medical costs, especially during the 1960s and 1970s. Another important reason is the increased cost of treatment and diagnosis. Medical advances before and during World War II involved relatively inexpensive drugs and therapies. After World War II, medical advances, largely funded by government research dollars, involve sophisticated and expensive equipment and procedures. These advances also multiply with great rapidity (Starr, 1982). Hospitals, whose capacity has been expanded considerably by federal Hill-Burton grants and loans since World War II, are uniquely suited to provide the organizational structure, personnel, and capital necessary to purchase, operate, and spread the units of costs of the new technology. Equally important, the economic interests of hospitals and physicians continue to be aligned. Hospitals charge on a "cost basis," which complements the physician fee-for-service system. More volume means more revenue and profit for both physicians and hospitals (Day, 1996-1997).

In addition, this alignment is reinforced by the asymmetry of information between the doctor and patient, which means that treatment demand often is defined more by physicians than patients (Renn, 1987). As a result, physicians are the dominant source of hospital patient referrals. Since hospitals view doctors rather than patients as their primary customers, a technological "arms race" develops between hospitals as each tries to outdo the other to attract doctors, the source of fee-paying patients (Temin, 1988).

Not surprisingly, hospital care, as it did in the 1930s and 1940s, represents the largest and fastest growing component of health care expenditures. Between 1950 and 1980, hospital care as a percentage of personal health expenditures increased from 4% to 44% (HIAA, 1996).

Early Government Responses to Medical Cost Inflation: Direct Regulation and the Demise of Passive Third-Party Financing

Most health care cost-containment strategies that are familiar to us today were developed and even implemented here and there before the 1960s. However, sustained and widespread momentum for cost containment does not materialize until the late 1960s (Institute of Medicine, 1989; Somers & Somers, 1961). One of President Nixon's first initiatives is to deal with the escalating cost of Medicare and Medicaid. The Nixon administration characterizes the issue as a "massive crisis" and warns that unless corrective measures are taken, the entire medical system will "break down" (Starr, 1982). This urgency is shared by the business community. As a result, there is a flurry of federal and state legislative and regulatory activity during the first half of the 1970s. Most agree that these activities have little impact on increasing medical costs other than laying the foundation for the so-called market-based initiatives during the 1980s (Wing et al., 1998).

Initial regulatory efforts emphasize direct regulation of providers through utilization review, physician reimbursement rate schedules, hospital rate review, and limits on hospital facility expansion. Some of these efforts have limited success, while others have a counter-productive impact. Several illustrations convey the sense of urgency and frustration associated with these early regulatory efforts.

The 1966 Medicare law provides for hospital utilization peer review of the appropriateness and the necessity of hospital treatment paid for by Medicare. However, it does not work well. The sheer volume of cases, after-the-fact review, the vagueness of diagnosis, and the community of interest among hospital staff physicians prevent it from working as many hoped it would. The program is beefed up in 1972 and again in 1982 to give the reviewers of care more independence and focus (Furrow, Greaney, Johnson, Jost, & Schwartz, 1995). Even the improved versions get mixed reviews (Furrow et al., 1995).

In 1973, and again in 1982, Medicare reimbursement to participating physicians is limited to prevailing charges in their practice area, subject to annual Medical Economic Adjustments. Cost concerns result in rates lower than prevailing rates and a decline in physician participation in the program. Complaints from physicians and medical beneficiaries force somewhat more realistic adjustments in the 1980s (Furrow et al., 1995). Similarly, a number of states institute Medicaid fee schedules, which are set much lower than what physicians are paid for Medicare and much lower than usual and customary rates to private patients. In addition, these physicians are not allowed to balance-bill. As a result, many physicians decline to participate in Medicaid or else do so on a selective basis (Wing et al., 1998; Yudkowsky, Cartland, & Flint, 1990).

Probably the most successful regulatory effort involves state experimentation with hospital rate regulation. These early state efforts provide the conceptual foundation and experience for far-reaching rate reform in the 1980s (Furrow et al., 1995). In addition, state and federal efforts to restrain hospital expansion through certificates-of-need laws appear to have had some beneficial impact (Furrow et al., 1995; Wing et al., 1998), though others disagree

(Phelps, 1997). Federal funding for these programs is reduced during the late 1970s and then repealed altogether during the 1980s. Even so, many states keep these laws in place, especially in the eastern United States (Furrow et al., 1995).

By the mid-1970s, most state insurance regulators have abandoned their earlier position of enforcing a strict separation between those who deliver care and insurance companies that pay for much of it (Day, 1996-1997). Regulators begin to encourage and often require commercial carriers and the Blues to implement a variety of utilization controls, such as hospital precertification and elective surgery second-opinion requirements. State regulators also encourage benefit changes that limit what care is covered (e.g., "medically necessary" and "experimental limits") and the greater use of deductibles and co-pays (Day, 1996-1997). Insurance companies are also urged to be aggressive in negotiating hospital rates and to pay only "usual, reasonable and customary" physician fees (Day, 1996-1997). Many states also force the Blues to limit the number of medical providers on their Boards of Directors in order to dilute any provider influence that might impede the aggressive pursuit of cost containment (Cunningham & Cunningham, 1997).

Because of the disappointing results of direct, public-utilities-type regulation, many begin to look at market-based options. In the early 1970s, President Nixon turns to the prepaid group practice concept, what is now called a Health Maintenance Organization (HMO), as an alternative to fee-for-service medicine (Starr, 1982). In order to encourage HMO growth, President Nixon enthusiastically proposes and the Congress enacts the Health Maintenance Organization Act of 1973. The new law eliminates many of the legal restrictions that organized medicine created at the state level to thwart the growth of prepaid group and HMO plans (Day, 1996-1997). The new law also provides for start-up grants, subsidized financing, and, under certain circumstances, even mandates that employers make HMOs part of their benefit package (Day, 1996-1997). Simultaneously, the National Association of Insurance Commissioners (NAIC) develops its own model HMO law, which makes it clear that an HMO can deliver and pay for health care without violating the prohibition against the corporate practice of medicine (Day, 1996-1997).

While the Nixon administration predicts that 1,700 HMOs will be up and running by the end of the decade, HMO growth is very

slow during the 1970s because HMO networks are capital intensive, and individuals and employees are slow to abandon the traditional systems that permit the "free choice" of one's physician. Even
so, there is a general recognition that HMOs are here to stay (Starr,
1982).

As HMOs slowly gain market share, another network designed
to realize cost savings begins to emerge: the Preferred Provider
Organization (PPO). In its purest form, the PPO is a group of
providers that agree to discounted fee-for-service rates for services
rendered in exchange for patient referral or volume (HIAA, 1995).
Originally, PPO networks are established by insurance companies
in response to increasing employer and regulatory concerns about
rising health care costs. Insurers that offer PPOs use deductibles
and co-payments to encourage employees to use the PPO network
(Beam, 1991). In addition, the PPO often is more attractive than
the HMO to many employers and employees because the PPO
provides more provider choice and more flexible product pricing.
For example, the PPO structure allows patients to go to non-PPO
doctors if they pay a deductible or higher co-pay. PPOs can also
fund coverage on an experience-rating basis, while most HMOs
cannot (Potanka, 1989).

Because of the PPO's flexibility it becomes the main platform for
the growth of network care during the 1980s. However, organized
medicine does not pay much attention to PPOs during the 1970s,
probably because the PPO still embraces the fee-for-service concept
and PPOs do not have sufficient market share to significantly
impact existing doctor-patient relationships or referral patterns
(Day, 1996-1997). This ambivalence changes in the mid-1980s as
PPOs become a major building block in the emerging new health
care system.

Private Sector Response: Increased
Employee Cost Sharing and Increased
Use of Experience Rating

Employer pressure is one of the reasons why state insurance
regulators actively encourage insurance companies to play a more
active role in utilization review of claims and the increased use of
deductibles and co-pays. In addition, employees are asked with
increasing frequency to pay for the cost of employer-based health

coverage. For example, in 1980 the Health Insurance Institute reviewed a large sample of new group cases in the low and mid market (Spencer, 1981). One third of these cases were noncontributory, 8% required employees to pay the total cost of coverage, but the great majority involved a sharing of costs by employers and employees (Spencer, 1981). Of particular importance from our perspective is the pattern of employee contributions. In most contribution plans, the employer pays for all of the employee's coverage, while the employee pays all or a portion of the premium for dependent coverage (Spencer, 1981).

Of even greater significance, an increasing number of employers move to a more aggressive form of experience rating known as minimum premium plans. Although a minimum premium plan is still insurance in that the insurance company continues to assume the risk, a substantial portion of the claims are paid out of the employer's operating revenues as the claims are incurred. This arrangement permits the employer, rather than the insurance company, to obtain the benefit of the interest "float" on claim dollars and reduces the base on which premium taxes are calculated. Other employers go one step farther and "self-insure" their health benefit programs. Under these arrangements the employer assumes the entire risk. Here the insurance company or a third-party administrator administers the program for a fee. These self-insurance programs are called Administrative Services Only or ASO plans (Day, 1996-1997). Employers realize even more savings under these plans because ASO is not insurance and, therefore, both claim dollars and administrative costs are not subject to state insurance premium taxes and state mandated benefits, which by the late 1970s can amount to between 15% and 20% of the insurance premium (Gabel & Jensen, 1989). In 1974, Congress enacts the Employee Retirement Income Security Act (ERISA), which stimulates the trend toward self-insurance by providing that self-insured employee benefit plans are beyond the reach of state insurance regulators and the state tax laws (Day, 1996-1997).

The growth of ASO coverage and aggressive experience rating, such as minimum premium plans, accelerates the fragmentation of the community risk pool that started 10 to 15 years earlier when traditional experience rating was first introduced. As a result, those that remain in the community pool are increasingly above-average risks. Those that cannot experience rate or self-insure, usually small businesses, the self-employed, and individuals, often find health coverage unaffordable. Because the antiselection potential is greater for these risks, insurers also have trouble pricing the coverage and are more selective in their underwriting. These access and affordability issues for the small employer and individuals prompt regulatory intervention during the late 1980s.

Health Care for Children

Children's health care coverage improves somewhat during the 1970s. With the possible exception of small employer groups, employment-based insurance coverage continues to grow, although at a much slower rate. Dependent coverage, including that for maternity and child care, becomes more commonplace but is by no means universal. Traditional attitudes toward maternity coverage still prevail. However, this is one of the few areas where coverage expands because of the growing number of women in the workforce, as well as gender discrimination concerns. For example, in 1978, Congress amends Title VII of the 1964 Civil Rights Act to prohibit age and sex discrimination. As a result, employers with more than 15 employees must treat pregnancy as they would any other illness or disability (Beam, 1991). Many states enact similar legislation for employers with less than 15 employees (Beam, 1991; Casey, 1994).

Prior to 1970, it is also common for insurance to cover newborns from their day of birth, but only if they are healthy. By the end of the 1970s, most states require newborn coverage irrespective of the newborn's health status (Casey, 1994).

Because of adverse economic conditions and inflation, the poverty population between 1970 and 1980 increases from 24.6 to 29.3 million, an increase of 20%. As cost pressures mount, the states make incremental reductions in optional Medicaid AFDC eligibility categories and reduce provider reimbursement well below that provided by Medicare and private coverage (Rosenblatt et al., 1997; Wing, 1983). As previously pointed out, low physician reimbursement results in significantly reduced physician participation in the Medicaid program (Rosenbaum, 1992; Yudkowsky et al., 1990). Hospital shortfalls are made up from other payers, which further increases the cost of private insurance coverage. This phenomenon is called "cost shifting" and highlights the interrelationship of all parts of the complicated health care system and the difficulties of dealing with its imperfections on a piecemeal basis.

Despite the serious concerns about Medicaid's growth and a growing Congressional tolerance toward permitting state cutbacks, Congress in 1972 federalizes the Supplemental Security Income (SSI) program, which provides benefits to the needy aged, blind, and disabled (Oberg & Polich, 1988). As a result, states are required to administer and share in the cost of SSI, although they have no flexibility regarding benefit levels as they do for AFDC recipients. This change inadvertently shifts the direction of Medicaid toward expensive skilled care nursing and intermediate care facilities rather than poor mothers and children. By the end of the decade, Medicaid expenditures have increased by some 15.5%. At the same time, there is a growing disparity between the benefits provided to traditional AFDC categories and to SSI beneficiaries. For example, in 1980, Medicaid covers some 21.6 million people. Of this total, SSI beneficiaries, namely the aged, blind, and disabled (primarily adults), approximate only 6.2 million or 29%. Yet these beneficiaries receive 72.9% of the total benefits paid out under Medicaid, much of it going for nursing home care for the elderly. AFDC recipients, on the other hand, approximate 14.1 million or 65.1% of the total number of covered beneficiaries and most of these are children. However, AFDC recipients account for only 28.1% of the total Medicaid benefit dollars (Wilson et al., 1988).

This shift or bias toward institutional care or nursing home care may reflect the fact that there is no visible spokesperson for children at the federal level. The Children's Bureau continues to exist but is buried in the federal bureaucracy. Support for children's programs increases, but this support is increasingly provided on a fragmented basis through programs that are dispersed throughout the federal and state governments. In 1980 there are over 260 federal programs alone that relate to children, and these programs are administered by over 20 different agencies (Grayson & Guyer, 1995; Wilson, 1989).

Despite this lack of coordination, infant mortality continues its downward trend, although the rate of decline slows toward the end of the decade. In 1976, the Bicentennial Assessment of the National Council of Organizations for Children and Youth concludes that while there has been "progress in child health and well-being," there are also a number of "discouraging and puzzling changes" (National Council, 1976). Major concerns include (a) a growing proportion of poverty children relative to the total population, although the absolute number is decreasing; (b) an increase in the number of single-parent families without the "economic equality or social supports necessary to provide for the development of their children"; and (c) the meager progress that has been made regarding handicap deaths and illnesses caused by poverty, malnutrition, and inadequate prenatal care (National Council, 1976).

As the 1970s end, a number of trends are discernable. Third-party payers are becoming increasingly aggressive in negotiating and even regulating provider reimbursement rates and in imposing increasingly stringent utilization oversight. No longer does business or government defer to the norms of the medical profession to the same degree it did in the past (Wing et al., 1998). Large employers increasingly move to self-insurance. They also increasingly rely on network delivery of care, especially PPOs, because of the ability of these networks to negotiate volume discounts and to provide utilization review. Cost-containment initiatives, coupled with reduced government reimbursement rates, subject institutional providers to increasing economic pressure, which limits their ability to cross-subsidize uncompensated care. All of these trends become much more visible during the 1980s.

The Ascendancy of Managed Network Health Care, New Financial Incentives for Health Care Providers, and President Reagan's "New Federalism": 1980-1990

Despite the state and federal regulatory cost-containment efforts described in the preceding section, medical cost inflation continues to outpace the Consumer Price Index (HIAA, 1996). Health care costs are now the fastest growing component of federal and state budgets. In 1965, federal and state governments paid 22% of all health care expenditures. By 1980, government pays 40% (Sardell, 1988).

Business is confronted with the same problem. Between 1965 and 1987, business's share of national health expenditures (NHEs) increases from 17% to 30%. In the 1960s, health care benefits account for 14.3% of what employers spend on employee benefits.

By the end of the 1980s, health benefits account for 38% (Employee Benefit Research Institute [EBRI], 1997a).

Public and private sector cost-containment efforts that started in the 1970s gain increasing momentum through the 1980s and 1990s. Private payers are able to consolidate their purchasing power through PPOs and, to a more limited extent, HMOs. These new purchasing entities control significant patient volume and are able to negotiate attractive reimbursement rates with hospitals and doctors. In addition, these purchasers, including federal and state governments, rapidly begin to move away from the traditional fee-for-service reimbursement system because of its incentives to provide more care and the difficulty of controlling utilization through direct regulation alone. As a result, hospitals, doctors, and health insurance companies are forced to redefine themselves or go out of business.

The coupling of utilization review and new reimbursement incentives is reinforced by new insights into the efficacy of much treatment prescribed by doctors. Studies are now showing that such treatment has little or no scientific basis and that much of it is unnecessary.

Other important changes unfold as medical costs continue to increase. In particular, the post-Vietnam era is characterized by very high inflation, a sluggish economy, and a changed societal view of resource availability. These changes result in decreased public support for many social welfare programs. Because Medicaid and related programs are especially vulnerable, poor children and pregnant mothers are victims of this retrenchment during the first half of the 1980s. Almost immediately, infant mortality rates begin to deteriorate. Reaction to this deterioration restores and even improves government support for children and pregnant mothers during the last half of the 1980s.

The following section describes the sea change in society's view regarding the science of medicine and how this changed perception encourages the integration of health care utilization review and new financing incentives into new network delivery systems. The resulting concentration of purchasing power of the new integrated networks puts immense economic pressure on traditional health care delivery institutions and forces major changes in how care is delivered and funded. This economic pressure also reduces the ability of hospitals to subsidize uncompensated care.

New Economic Incentives for
Health Care Providers

Medical researchers and epidemiologists, such as Jack Wennberg, document with increasing frequency that physician practice patterns vary greatly from area to area for no apparent reason other than different medical philosophies of what is appropriate care ("practice style") and without dramatically different outcomes. The costs for these different treatments vary widely even when adjusted for regional economic differences (Wennberg, 1989). Other studies show that a significant amount of unnecessary care is being delivered (Meyers & Schroeder, 1981). Research also confirms that practice decisions often are influenced by economic considerations. For example, the amount of treatment and number of tests under fee-for-service reimbursement often is greater than under prepaid care and without any apparent difference in outcome (Gray, 1997).

These studies tend to reinforce one another and give rise to a growing consensus that hospitals and doctors are the main drivers of medical cost inflation and that there is a broad range of acceptable treatment for many conditions and at varying costs, with little or no difference in outcomes. It also appears that clinical decisions are often influenced by how one is paid, rather than the efficacy of treatment. If these perceptions are correct, they validate the view that medical costs can be "managed" without sacrificing quality though utilization controls and economic incentives (Day, 1996-1997). This growing consensus is reflected in a number of government and private cost-containment initiatives.

In 1981, Medicare changes its previous "cost plus" hospital reimbursement system to a prospective payment (DRG) system. Here, hospitals are paid a set fee based on the average cost of a particular illness (i.e., a diagnostic related group or DRG). Under DRGs, more efficient hospitals get more revenue, while inefficient hospitals get less. DRGs not only encourage more efficient hospital care, they also start to dismantle the economic alignment that exists between hospitals and physicians. Hospitals now are forced to reduce unnecessary long hospital stays. Physicians, on the other hand, retain much of their traditional autonomy over medical diagnosis and treatment. This autonomy coupled with the fee-for-service system pushes in the opposite direction (Day, 1996-1997).

However, prospective payment for children's hospitals is delayed for 8 years because DRGs are based on adult experience. Pediatricians and child advocates argue that children are not just "little adults," and their average experience, especially for chronic and serious conditions, may be quite different from that of adults. Regulators are also concerned that children's hospitals will have greater difficulties than traditional hospitals with the new economic incentives because of their heavy dependence on Medicaid and their disproportionate share of uninsured patients (Green, 1989; Payne & Restuccia, 1987).

Notwithstanding these concerns, a number of states begin to move toward prospective payment for all hospitals, including those that care for children. By 1989, 29 states use some form of prospective payment and 17 states use DRGs (Furrow et al., 1995). The tensions between hospital administrators and staff physicians grows. As the decade progresses, hospitals increase their oversight of clinical matters, including more stringent reviews of physician utilization patterns and the use of "economic" credentialing (Day, 1996-1997). Technology also permits physicians to treat outside the hospital, which puts increased economic pressure on the hospitals. In effect, physicians become competitors with the hospital (Stoeckle, 1995). Capitation rates create similar incentives for HMOs to provide cost-effective health care through the negotiation of favorable hospital per diem rates, utilization review, and the monitoring of practice patterns.

During the 1970s, both the federal and state governments start to pay doctors through fee schedules that are set at levels designed to reduce the cost of these programs. As a result, Medicare and Medicaid pay physicians at a rate well below the norm. This results in many physicians refusing to participate in the program. In 1986, Congress responds to provider complaints by memorializing into law an old regulation that requires the states to set provider rates at a level sufficient to assure service for covered benefits to the same extent as the general population. The new law also provides a special focus on obstetrics and pediatric services (Rosenblatt et al., 1997). Because of these same concerns and the importance of Medicaid to children, HCFA starts to review annually the adequacy of state reimbursement rates for obstetricians and pediatricians (Furrow et al., 1995).

The Ascendancy of HMOs and PPOs:
New Networks That Combine Both
the Financing and Delivery of Care

While HMO growth is slow during the 1970s its membership increases rapidly during the 1980s, from 9 million to 34 million in 1989. PPO membership also increases during the decade from 12.1 million to 34 million members. As PPO market share grows, the medical profession becomes increasingly concerned that the financial incentives used to channel employees to network doctors violate the old freedom-of-choice and corporate practice of medicine laws. In response to these issues, as well as continued pressure from private employers concerned about cost containment, state insurance regulators develop and implement the NAIC's 1986 model PPO law. The model law places some limits on the use of financial incentives to channel patients to network providers. At the same time, it explicitly makes PPOs a legitimate arrangement for the financing and delivery of care. The model law also gives PPOs great flexibility in how the PPO is structured. As a result, PPOs aggressively add to utilization review capabilities, primary care physician gatekeepers, and even capitation payments. As a result, PPOs can operate much like HMOs, while still offering employers the ability to experience rate or self-insure (Potanka, 1989). PPOs also have more flexibility than HMOs regarding new product innovations, such as point-of-service "HMOs," where a network member can opt out of the network and receive treatment elsewhere as long as he or she pays a higher deductible or co-payment (Potanka, 1989).

As HMO and PPO network market shares increase, they enhance their bargaining position. In addition to economic concessions, such as per diem and discounted rates, networks implement more aggressive utilization review programs. During the 1980s utilization review of some sort is extended to most providers, even for treatment reimbursed under traditional fee-for-service indemnity contracts. In addition, the private sector tends to be more aggressive than government regarding pretreatment and concurrent utilization review as opposed to posttreatment utilization review. Pretreatment and concurrent review, by definition, introduce a party other than the treating physician directly into the ongoing medical decision-making process (Day, 1996-1997). A new utilization review industry emerges to satisfy the widespread demand for utilization review from self-insured employers and PPO networks that do not have their own in-house utilization capabilities. As provider concerns regarding utilization review increase, many states start to license and regulate utilization review organizations (Furrow et al., 1995).

With the growth of managed care networks and utilization review, hospitals find it more difficult to pass along or "cost shift" Medicare and Medicaid shortfalls to private payers. The elimination of cost shifting starts to dismantle the informal hospital safety net for the uninsured, including children, that emerged after the 1940s (Iglehart, 1998). As cost shifting becomes more difficult, many hospitals start to turn uninsured patients away, including pregnant women who are in labor. In 1986, Congress responds to this "patient dumping" with the Emergency Medical Treatment and Labor Act. Hospitals receiving Medicare reimbursement are now required to stabilize patients and make appropriate arrangements for their transfer to public facilities (Furrow et al., 1995).

In response to these economic pressures, hospitals begin to focus more on cost-efficient care and to seek out new sources of revenue. For example, not-for-profit hospitals are forced to embrace many of the entrepreneurial attitudes, marketing practices, and diversification strategies that characterize their for-profit counterparts. They do this through consolidations, mergers, alliances, joint-ventures, and the aggressive marketing of their services. In addition, significant amounts of new capital are needed both to expand a hospital's market share through acquisition of other delivery systems and for the development and installation of the expensive information and monitoring technologies necessary to operate in a managed care environment. Many hospitals and a number of Blue Cross/Blue Shield plans go one step farther and convert to for-profit operations in order to raise this needed capital (Fubini & Antonelli, 1996; Gray, 1997). Teaching hospitals also have a hard time adjusting to these new pressures, in part because of their research mission, their dependence on government reimbursement, and managed care's emphasis upon primary rather than specialty care (Blumenthal & Meyer, 1996).

The Impact of Health Care's
Destructuring on Children

Children's hospitals, which for the most part are teaching hospitals, have less flexibility in dealing with the changing environment than their adult-oriented counterparts. For example, children's hospitals are more dependent on Medicaid, which unlike Medicare does not reimburse hospitals for medical education activities (McEachern, 1995; Nemes, 1993). In addition, a significant proportion of pediatric subspecialty treatment is done in the office, and new technology is rapidly accelerating this migration away from the hospital (Green, 1989; Leslie, Sarah, & Palfrey, 1998). Today's declining birthrate only reinforces the declining number of children requiring acute care facilities.

Equally important, pediatrics' successes over the past 20 years regarding extreme premature births and congenital anomalies are shifting future disease patterns away from tertiary and secondary care to the monitoring of chronic disabilities that can be done in the home and school setting (Leslie et al., 1998). This shift is reinforced by the increasing importance of environmental, cultural, and lifestyle influences on child and adolescent development (Evans & Friedland, 1994).

Like many other physicians, pediatricians will be subject to increasing cost pressures and changing patient referral patterns. Pediatricians, both generalists and subspecialists, are affiliating with one another into group practices (usually a vertical integration) in order to enhance their bargaining power, assure patient volume, and facilitate the interdisciplinary team approach required by the changing disease patterns of children (Leslie et al., 1998). Many pediatricians also affiliate with children's hospital (PHO) networks (Fitzgerald, 1994). Others believe they are better off joining community hospitals that have a more diverse patient mix as well as a large number of affiliations with different managed care organizations (Cleary, 1994). The increased focus on the monitoring of health status and the treatment of chronic conditions, as well as early intervention for prenatal and perinatal care, also requires that the new networks work closely with the myriad agencies and groups that comprise community-based health care (Leslie et al., 1998). These cost pressures and disease pattern changes will also require the increased use of allied professionals, a task that should be much easier in child health care because children are not preoccupied with the credentialing differences between a nurse practitioner and a doctor.

These new demands upon pediatric generalists and subspecialists require a revamping of the residency curriculum and the provision for more diverse training locations in order to reflect the emerging realities of increased ambulatory care, out-reach clinics, cross-cultural issues, and collaboration with ancillary providers and public health and social agencies (Leslie et al., 1998; Williams, Stein, & Leslie, 1998).

President Reagan's "New Federalism"

As the private medical sector undergoes massive change, President Reagan in 1980 announces a new view of government and labels it the "New Federalism." Under the New Federalism, government, especially the federal government, is viewed as the cause of or at least a contributing factor to many societal ills, rather than a solution. In addition, when government intervention is appropriate, this intervention can best be done at the state level (Sardell, 1988). This view of government has a significant impact on Medicaid and health care coverage for poor mothers and children as described below (Costin et al., 1991).

The Omnibus Budget Reconciliation Act of 1981 gives the states more leeway in defining and funding Medicaid eligibility at the state level. The new law creates four block grants for 24 programs that previously were funded separately, and it also reduces the aggregate funding by 25%. One of the new block grants is the Maternal Health Care Block Grant, which combines eight independent programs for mother and children services. Also, the states are given more discretion regarding provider reimbursement rates and can apply for waivers from Medicaid's free-choice requirement. These last changes set the stage for implementing mandatory Medicaid managed care in the 1990s (Wilson, 1989; Wilson et al., 1988).

These changes have their intended impact. Between 1981 and 1983, some 440,000 families, including some 700,000 persons under the age of 21, lose their Medicaid coverage (Sardell, 1990, p. 279). Adjusted for inflation, maternal and child health funding is reduced by 18%. Appropriations for food stamps and school lunch programs also are reduced. In addition, Title V's comprehensive maternal and infant care programs, children and youth projects, family planning, and dental services are eliminated. Attempts are also made to eliminate WIC and EPSDT, but Congress refuses to go along (Costin et al., 1991).

The states also reduce physician reimbursements further, and the number of physicians and pediatricians that accept Medicaid patients continues to decline (Rosenbaum, 1992; Wilson, 1989; Wing, 1983). Infant mortality rates start to decline at a substantially lower rate than they have since 1965. Anemia in pregnant women is seen more frequently, and the number of low-birth weight babies increases (Sardell, 1990).

Children's advocacy groups and others publicize this deterioration in the general health status of children. Similarly, the American Academy of Pediatrics urges that the Children's Bureau be given "new" responsibilities to investigate and publicize the impact of federal programs on children (Wilson, 1989). In 1983, the House of Representatives establishes the Select Committee on Children, Youth and Families, which partially fills the former role of the Children's Bureau, to investigate children's issues and create public awareness regarding the plight of children. As a result of increased publicity and the revelation that the United States will not meet the Public Health Service's 1990 infant mortality objectives, Medicaid coverage is expanded six times for pregnant mothers and children between 1985 and 1990. These changes sever the link between Medicaid eligibility and AFDC welfare cash assistance. Also, states are required to cover all pregnant women and children up to age 6 with family incomes at or below 133% of the poverty level and to provide phased-in coverage for poverty-level children up to age 19. These changes also simplify Medicaid's enrollment process; require access to nonphysician specialists, state licensed nurse-midwives, and pediatric nurse practitioners; and require coordination with other federal programs aimed at children and mothers (Congressional Research Services, 1993).

It is interesting to note that even in the context of widespread public concern regarding the growing federal deficit, which manifests itself in the Balanced Budget and Emergency Deficit Control Act of 1985 (Gramm-Rudman), programs such as AFDC, Medicaid, food stamps, and WIC are excluded from across-the-board budget cuts (Sardell, 1990). In part because of the Medicaid expansions between 1985 and 1990, the Medicaid population and the cost of the program resume their upward growth. Between 1985 and 1990, the number of Medicaid recipients increases from 15.3 to 17.2 million. However, the benefits paid nearly doubles from $9.2 to $17.2 billion (HIAA, 1996). Children are the largest group of beneficiaries. Infant mortality and related indicators of child health stabilize and by 1990 reflect the pre-1980 rate of improvement (Congressional Research Services, 1993).

Even so, the imbalance between AFDC and SSI recipients continues to grow. In 1989, roughly two thirds of Medicaid's beneficiaries are in AFDC families but account for only 25% of Medicaid expenditures. SSI recipients, on the other hand, primarily adults and the elderly, comprise one third the covered beneficiaries but receive some 75% of the benefits (Sardell, 1990).

Uninsured Children and the Interrelationship Between Public and Private Coverage: 1987-1993

Despite state, federal, and private efforts to make public and private health coverage more accessible and affordable through cost containment, expanded government coverage, and insurance reform, the uninsured population continues to grow at a rate faster than the non-elderly (under age 65) population.[5] For example, between 1987 and 1993, the uninsured increased from 31.8 million or 14.8% of the non-elderly population to 39.3 million or 17.3% (Fronstin, 1997a). Children, especially poor and minority children, make up roughly a quarter of the uninsured population, from a high of 26.7% in 1987 to a low of 22.7% in 1992 (Fronstin, 1997a).

The continued growth of the uninsured population (and the much harder to measure "under-insured" population) is a source of great concern to policymakers and a major impetus behind most health reform proposals. For many, these concerns are premised on egalitarian and redistributive justice principles. For others, cost containment and efficient resource allocation are just as important. Studies show that the uninsured usually get care only when they are sick and when they do so, the care is often less effective than it would have been had they received regular periodic checkups (Employee Benefit Research Institute [EBRI], 1995). In addition, this care is usually provided in an acute care setting, irrespective of whether an acute care setting is appropriate, because the hospital emergency room is the most convenient or only point of access. Uninsured individuals also are less apt to seek relatively inexpensive systematic preventative treatment, such as immunizations, which can realize huge long-term cost savings (EBRI, 1995). It is also well established that systematic and preventive care produce significantly greater long-term benefits for children and pregnant mothers than for many other population groups (Evans & Friedland, 1994; Rosenbaum, 1992).

Many believe that a major reason for the growing number of uninsured is directly related to the rising cost of health care relative to the economy as a whole and the ongoing economic restructuring. For example, as the cost of health care insurance increases, employers, especially the smaller ones, are less likely to provide health care benefits or, at a minimum, require additional employee contributions. In recent years, even large and mid-size employers shift more coverage costs to employees through increases in employee contributions, deductibles, and co-pays. As employees shoulder these costs, real wage growth since the 1970s has steadily declined (Fronstin & Snider, 1996-1997; Haveman & Wolfe, 1993; Madrick, 1995). As a result, more and more employees are less likely to participate in an employers's plan even when a plan is available (Cooper & Schoen, 1997). Employers also appear to be cutting back on dependent coverage or increasing the amount that employees must pay for it (Fronstin & Snider, 1996-1997; Meyer & Naughton, 1997).

Other probable reasons for the increasing number of uninsured include the restructuring and downsizing of American industry in the manufacturing sector in the mid-1980s and the service sector in the 1990s (Fronstin & Snider, 1996-1997). Restructuring results in the elimination of jobs. As jobs are lost, many employees lose their health coverage and often find it hard to get comparable coverage or coverage that is not subject to a preexisting condition limitation. This coverage dislocation prompts government intervention, such as the 1986 federal (COBRA) and state continuation of insurance legislation that allows terminated employees to maintain their coverage for a certain period of time at their own expense without an employer subsidy (Furrow et al., 1995).

Restructuring also results in a shift from a manufacturing to a service economy that traditionally has not provided health care benefits due to workforce demographics and less union presence (Fronstin, 1997b). Employer attitudes regarding employee benefits also starts to change from one of "paternalism" to one that stresses "individual choice" and "responsibility" (Salisbury, McDonnell, & Rheam, 1996).

The demographics of the uninsured population reflect these trends. For example, roughly 80% of the uninsured, including children, live in families headed by a person who works on a full- or part-time basis. Roughly half of these workers are self-employed or work for small employers (i.e., less than 25 workers) and have a family income level at or below 200% of the poverty level. Over 80% of the uninsured live in families with incomes of $20,000 or less. In addition, most of the working uninsured work in the service and related sectors (Fronstin, 1997a).

These trends also explain why the percentage of the non-elderly population covered by employer-based health care steadily decreases between 1987 and 1993: from 69.2% to 63.5%. Employer-based coverage for dependents, including children, also declines from 35.4% to 30.7%. The percentage of children covered by employer plans relative to *all* children declines from 66.7% in 1987 to 58.6% in 1993 (Fronstin & Pierron, 1997).

Despite these declines, the number of uninsured children in absolute numbers (ranging from a high of 9.6 million to a low of 8.5 million) and as a percentage of all children (ranging from a high of 13.6% to a low of 12.7%) remains relatively stable. Many attribute this stability to Medicaid's ability to absorb these children, which was made possible by the expansion of Medicaid in the late 1980s. Between 1987 and 1993, Medicaid's child population increases from 10 million to 16.5 million or from 15.5% to 22% of all children in the United States (Fronstin & Pierron, 1997).

This correlation between the expanding Medicaid population and the declining employer-based coverage leads some to hypothesize that the existence of expanded government coverage may be another reason why employees decline employer-based coverage: they or their dependents can obtain "free" coverage from Medicaid (Culter & Gruber, 1997; Fronstin & Pierron, 1997). Policymakers are cautioned to keep this "crowding-out" phenomenon in mind in formulating future changes in the health care system.

Although the number of uninsured children during the late 1980s remains somewhat stable, many feel that additional action is necessary. In 1989, Congress creates a National Commission on Children. This bipartisan Commission is designed to serve as a "forum on behalf of the children of the nation." In June 1991, the Commission presents its final report to the president, titled *Beyond Rhetoric: A New American Agenda for Children and Families* (National Commission, 1991). The 34-member Commission is unanimous on the need for a "bold" new national policy where children and the family have a top priority. The Commission also unanimously declares that there are too many uninsured children and pregnant women and that this coverage gap should be closed. In addition, all members agree that expanded medical care and insurance are only a part of the overall solution to improving the health status of children and that families and communities must become the guardians of children's health.

The only significant area of disagreement centers over how to expand coverage for poor mothers and children. Twenty-five members advocate universal and comprehensive coverage for pregnant women and for children through age 18 to be implemented either through a public (employer tax) or private (employer mandate) system. The majority also recognize the need for cost containment and embrace both managed care and global budgeting as vehicles for keeping medical costs in line (National Commission, 1991). The minority recommends a market-driven solution that resembles "managed competition"[6] (National Commission, 1991). The Commission's report, which reflects significant ideological differences on a number of important issues, demonstrates that a broad consensus exists regarding the need to improve children's health and that this can be realized only through a holistic view of the child's total environment and support systems.

As the 1980s end, there are a number of clear-cut trends. Health care costs continue to increase faster than wage growth and general economic inflation. Network delivery of care and managed care are expanding rapidly and putting economic pressure on all providers, including children's hospitals and pediatricians. Many medical specialists, including obstetricians and pediatricians, attempt to distinguish their discipline from the rest of medicine in an effort to preserve their traditional role in the new health care system. Some providers even see the restructuring as an opportunity to enhance their discipline's position relative to other medical specialties. More and more employers assume the risk of health care inflation and utilization through self-insurance. Employers also shift more of the cost of health care their to employees through deductibles, co-pays, and premium contributions. The percentage of the non-elderly that are covered by employer-based care continues on a steady decline that started a decade earlier. The percentage of dependents covered by employment-based insurance also declines. Conversely, the number of uninsured individuals continues to grow, and a significant number of the uninsured are children.

All of these trends are publicized in the popular media and Congressional hearings and extensively in academic journals. There is a pervasive feeling across the nation that health care is in a state of crisis.

Comprehensive Health Care Reform, the Shift to Incremental Reform, and the Managed Care Backlash: 1990-1998

Although the last decade of the millennium is not yet over, it has already proven to be one of extremes. For example, infant mortality statistics—an index of the health status of children—shows both positive and negative trends. Between 1950 and 1991, infant mortality declines rapidly (at an estimated 3% per year) and reaches an all-time low in 1994 of 7.9 infant deaths per 1,000 live births (National Center of Health Statistics, 1995). If the trend continues, the number of infant deaths should reach the Public Health Service's goal of 7 deaths per 1,000 live births by the year 2000. However, the rate of decline is far greater for white babies than it is for blacks, and this disparity is increasing rather than decreasing. Between 1950 and 1991, the ratio between black and white babies increased from 1.6 to 2.2, and it now appears that the mortality decline for black babies will fall far short of the national goal (National Center for Health Statistics, 1995).

The decade also is one of contrasts regarding health care reform and regulation. The first 4 years of the 1990s are characterized by alarm and hyperbole both for and against comprehensive reform. The next 4 years eschew radical change. During the first 4 years of the decade, managed care is praised for restraining health care cost inflation without sacrificing quality. Managed care is also the cornerstone of President Clinton's comprehensive health care reform plan. Many states also embrace managed care as the way to deliver Medicaid benefits. During the following 4 years, managed care is criticized by the public, the medical community, and eventually by the president himself. Market regulation, which is still in ascendancy during the early 1990s, is second-guessed with increasing frequency during the last half of the decade, and arguments are made for various forms of direct regulation.

These vacillations are not surprising when viewed in the context of the massive restructuring and change under way in the world, the national economy, and the health care industry. These stops and starts also illustrate the difficulties of realizing fundamental as opposed to incremental change.

Initial Health Care Reform Efforts, Culminating With the Demise of the Clinton Plan

By 1990, health care reform is receiving considerable attention. Over 30 bills have been introduced in Congress, covering the entire spectrum of reform options from single-payer government systems to the use of tax incentives (Shiels & Wolfe, 1992). Various interest groups develop their own preferred approaches. Pediatricians and advocates for children are no exception, although most reform proposals would extend greater coverage to pregnant mothers and children in some manner. For example, several proposals contemplate special pediatric standards for "medical necessity" and "experimental" coverage limits, because adult criteria cannot be used to evaluate the efficacy of the special physical and development needs of children (Wehr & Jameson, 1994). Physicians in a number of medical specialties, such as obstetrics, argue that they should be allowed to be "primary care physicians" under managed care because of the unique nature of their specialty (Fox-Grage, 1991; Uhlman, 1997).

The American Academy of Pediatrics (AAP) is also active. In 1991, the AAP unveils a proposal for universal comprehensive coverage for pregnant women and children up to age 21 (AAP, 1993). The AAP proposal would require employers to provide coverage for working, pregnant employees; pregnant spouses of employees; and the dependents of employees. Women and children not covered by the employer mandate would be covered by a new government program that replaces both AFDC and pregnant mothers' and children's coverage under Medicaid (AAP, 1993).

While most reform proposals focus on expanding coverage to the uninsured, concern about how health care is delivered and financed reaches far beyond the uninsured. Many believe that the economic slowdowns during the 1980s and early 1990s represent a fundamental restructuring of the economy rather than a cyclical downturn; that is, the transition from a post-industrial to an information economy. In addition, the end of the Cold War accelerates the redeployment of domestic resources. *Downsizing* and *out-sourcing* became familiar terms, and this time the phenomena extend to the "white-collar" service and financial sectors. Those who lose their jobs, often lose their health insurance. Also, many of the new jobs do not provide employee benefits, or benefits are available at reduced levels (Long & Rogers, 1995). Although COBRA and state continuation requirements provide some relief, one must pay for continuation coverage without the benefit of an employer contribution. Affordability is an issue for many.

Public uncertainty regarding the changing economy is reinforced by the dramatic restructuring under way in the health care industry. A general unease spreads throughout the population. Public opinion polls reflect a 90% approval rating for the proposition that the health care system needs to be changed significantly (Hacker, 1996).

It is in this environment that a special election in 1991 becomes a catalyst for comprehensive reform, at least in the minds of politicians, their advisors, and the media (Blendon & Szalay, 1992; Hacker, 1996). Traditional wisdom holds that the major obstacle to major health care reform is the difficulty of convincing the middle class to embrace fundamental change that benefits relatively few, while radically changing how the middle class receives and pays for its health care (Starr, 1991). Opinion polls and the media coverage convince policymakers and their advisors that the middle class may be ready to go the distance (Edwards, Blendon, & Leitman, 1992). On a health reform platform, a relatively unknown candidate, Harrison Wofford, campaigns for the Senate seat vacated by the untimely death of Senator Heinz of Pennsylvania. Wofford's unexpected 55% victory over nationally known, seasoned candidate Richard Thornberg generates considerable optimism among reform advocates.

The Democratic presidential nominee, Governor Clinton (whose campaign advisors also worked on Wofford's campaign) makes health care reform a major campaign issue (Hacker, 1996). President Clinton is elected in 1992. His victory is attributed in large part to the economic recession and middle-class unease about the economy and, to a lesser degree, health care. President Clinton makes health care reform his top priority. After 18 months of work, the Health Security Act of 1994 (HSA) is unveiled. The HSA is a detailed, top-to-bottom revamping of virtually every aspect of the existing U.S. health care system. The proposal resembles the German system, with numerous adjustments to deal with unique American public and private institutions and the concerns of many interest groups (CCH, 1993).

Initial reactions to the Clinton plan are favorable. There is a widespread desire to see the current health care system improved, especially to assure continued coverage for those who already have it, in a rapidly changing economic environment. However, support for the proposal dissipates quickly. Within 6 months it is clear that Congress will not approve the Clinton plan. Many reasons are given for the demise of the proposal. Major ones are its sheer complexity, its heavy reliance on government, and the far-reaching impact it would have on the entire health care system. Others also cite our system of government, which stresses checks and balances and makes fundamental change very difficult (Morone, 1992). Also, it is an era of "sound-bite" media communications that amplify the power of interest groups both for and against the proposal (Hacker, 1996).

In 1994, the Republicans capture both houses of Congress, in part because of the public's aversion to the "big government" character of the Clinton health plan. The Republicans place on the national agenda a more focused version of President Reagan's New Federalism that attacks government directly, especially at the federal level. The Republicans also believe that the public is increasingly willing to reexamine entitlements even though this issue is viewed as controversial, if not more controversial than health care reform. A Bipartisan Commission on Entitlement and Tax Reform, chaired by Senators Kerry and Danforth, concludes that unless there is either a major change in our entitlement programs or new taxes, virtually all tax revenue will go for entitlements by the year 2010 (Bipartisan Commission, 1995). The Republican Congress aggressively pushes the issue of entitlements, but back-tracks during the 1996 presidential campaign, especially with respect to Medicare. President Clinton wins the election. The Republicans retain control of both houses of Congress. Because of the president's narrow reelection margin, the number of close Congressional races, and the Republicans' reduced majority in the House, there is a strong consensus in both parties that radical change that impacts the middle class is both nonproductive and politically dangerous.

The Shift to Incremental Reform

After the election, the president moves to the middle of the political spectrum. In addition, both the president and Congressional leaders are committed to show the public that they can work together. A number of proposals are enacted by the 104th Congress and signed by the president that indicate a possible future pattern regarding health care reform. Key characteristics of the new direction include: (a) incremental change rather than dramatic reform; (b) increased use of employer mandates rather than government funded programs, which avoid or reduce the need for new tax revenues; (c) employer coverage mandates applicable to *all* employers, both the insured and those who self-insure coverage for their employees; and (d) targeted government programs that focus on politically sensitive groups. Another recurring theme centers on the need to eliminate the link between employers and health care coverage and to find a substitute for the employer.

The first example of this new direction is the Health Insurance Portability and Accountability Act of 1996.[7] This law reflects a bipartisan effort to address middle-class concerns regarding the portability of health coverage from job to job and the ability to obtain coverage, if coverage is unavailable through an employer. The law applies to *all* employers, both insured and self-insured, and to all insurers. The law limits the use of preexisting conditions. It also requires insurance companies in the small group market to insure any employer and to guarantee the renewal of such coverage. In addition, the new law puts pressure on the states to create insurance facilities to assure the availability of health care coverage for everyone, including high-risk individuals. Although the law deals with access, it does not address the issue of affordability, except to the extent that rates for coverage through state safety-net market facilities can be subsidized, either through general state revenues or, more likely, the insurance industry and employers. In this regard, several decisions of the U.S. Supreme Court in 1995 and 1997 indicate that ERISA's restrictions on state action may not be as broad as previously thought and states may have some leeway to impose general taxes on all third-party payers, including self-insured employers. These taxes can be used for purposes such as reimbursement to hospitals for uncompensated care or to subsidize state high-risk or residual market pools for the uninsured (Day & Wade, 1995).

One important part of the new portability act is a pilot program for Medical Savings Accounts (MSAs)—a form of IRA that enables individuals to accumulate money for medical expenses not covered by catastrophic insurance that must be purchased when one sets up an MSA. Since the catastrophic coverage only covers medical expenses in excess of $4,000 annually, this coverage would cost much less than normal first-dollar health care coverage. Savings estimates range anywhere from 40% to 50% less. The MSA concept is vociferously opposed by many, including those who support comprehensive universal health coverage. They view the MSA as a way to fragment the middle class further and to "skim" off healthy risks from the community pool. Supporters of the MSA see the concept as a way to make employer-based coverage more affordable. Some even view it as a way to eliminate the link between employment and health care coverage. Ironically, many MSA advocates have the same goal as those who support universal coverage, although the latter would replace the employer with government rather than the individual.

A second example of incremental reform appears in the national debate over the deficit and entitlements and, in particular, Medicaid and welfare reform. Congress enacts legislation that radically changes Medicaid by eliminating all Medicaid entitlements and caps federal contributions at the existing level. The law is vetoed by the president. The reasons for the veto include the need to keep existing social programs in place and to build upon them. At the same time, the president and the Congress develop and implement the Personal Responsibility and Work Opportunity Reconciliation Act of 1996. The new welfare law replaces AFDC, the JOBS program, and Emergency Assistance with a "non-entitlement" block grant called Temporary Assistance to Needy Families (TANF). TANF requires the states to impose strict work and time limits on the availability of welfare benefits. With the exception of children receiving Supplemental Security Income (usually the disabled) and legally resident aliens, Medicaid appears to have been left intact for young children and pregnant women. However, the law now permits the states to eliminate Medicaid for any household head who does not cooperate with or meet state work requirements. In addition, the new law is complicated. Many are concerned that those eligible for coverage will not understand whether they are covered or not and, if not, how to obtain coverage under alternative eligibility paths (Rosenblatt et al., 1997).

The potential adverse impact of TANF upon children is ameliorated by the 1997 federal budget, which provides for significant additional federal funding for the State Children's Health Insurance Program (Children's Program). The Children's Program is justified in this climate of fiscal conservatism on the grounds that early intervention for children avoids or minimizes more expensive care later in life (General Accounting Office, 1996; National Governor's Association, 1997). In addition, the average cost for a child's health care coverage is much less than for an adult. Finally, children are one of the few vulnerable populations that evoke widespread public sympathy.

The program receives bipartisan support, is supported by the National Governor's Association, and is passed by large majorities in both houses of Congress. As a result, the states receive some $40 billion over 10 years to expand health care for low-income uninsured children (in families with income up to 200% of the poverty level). States also are given great flexibility in how to distribute the money. Some will use it to expand Medicaid. Others will create or supplement "Kid-care" programs in order to underscore the "non-entitlement" nature of these new benefits (Rosenbaum, Johnson, Sonosky, Markus, & DeGraw, 1998). States are also encouraged to reach out to the estimated 3 million children who are eligible but not enrolled in Medicaid (Selden, Banthin, & Cohen, 1998).

At the same time that the legislation is being debated and passed by Congress, public opinion polls show that health care's coverage for children doesn't even make the top 10 public concerns relating to children. These polls shock child advocates and health care policymakers, who now feel that the public needs to be educated about the importance of expanded health coverage for children (Colburn, 1997).

These successes and the pattern of what does and does not work is not lost on the administration. In September 1997, the president says he will seek health care reform on an incremental basis and that the possible next targets for "reform" are early retirees and the unemployed (BNA, 1997a).

The Managed Care Backlash and the Rethinking of Market Regulation

"Managed care" comes under increasing scrutiny during the last half of the decade. In large part, this backlash is the consequence of managed care's successes. It is now the dominant form of health care delivery (Fubini & Antonelli, 1996). During 1996, HMO enrollment is above 60 million members and is projected to increase to over 100 million members by the year 2000 (HIAA, 1996). Also, managed care is credited for reducing health care inflation. Health care costs between 1994 and 1996 are essentially flat, although many believe this price stability is only temporary (Fronstin, 1998). In addition, managed care is now mandated for Medicaid in many states, and the federal government is encouraging managed care options for Medicare (Day, 1996-1997). Some go so far as to say that managed care, despite its blemishes, has saved the existing health care system (Brink, 1998; "Patients or Profits?" 1998).

However, managed care realized its cost-containment successes by radically changing how health care is delivered and financed in the United States. Importantly, it limits one's choice of provider and often results in changed doctor-patient relationships whenever an employer selects a new carrier. In addition, a few highly publicized bungled care decisions by some managed care organizations reinforce public and provider concerns regarding quality. Government and employer reaction comes quickly.

The president, who made managed care the cornerstone of his 1994 Health Security Act, now openly criticizes managed care and establishes a Presidential Advisory Commission on Consumer Protection and Quality in the Health Care Industry. The Commission is charged with developing appropriate consumer safeguards and regulatory oversight. In November 1997, the Commission recommends a Consumer Bill of Rights, and the president pushes for its early enactment into law. The proposed safeguards include strengthened appeals and grievance procedures for benefit and utilization decisions, including an independent, external review. Seventy-four percent of Americans endorse the president's proposal provided that these safeguards would not raise costs or cause employers to terminate coverage (Pham, 1998). In February 1998, the president, by executive order, requires the implementation of the recommendation for all government medical programs (BNA, 1997b). The president also urges the private sector to adopt the proposals voluntarily.

Many states do not wait for the Commission's recommendations. During the 1996-1997 legislative session, over 8,000 anti-managed care bills are introduced, and some 150 separate pieces of legislation are enacted into law. For the most part, these laws focus on utilization practices for specific diseases or provide for the external review of utilization decisions. In addition, employers shift their attention to quality assurance and disclosure of health plan practices and procedures now that cost inflation appears to be under control (Lippman, 1997). The academic literature increasingly focuses on for-profit health care and questions market-based regulation (e.g., Carleton, 1997).

Although organized medicine continues to be very fragmented, the profession is united over the need for more professional control or input into practice guideline and utilization review decisions. The profession also supports legally sanctioned collective activity by doctors to enable greater professional influence over the new networks without violating the antitrust laws (Day, 1996-1997). Providers also want to form provider-owned networks so they can deal directly with the purchasers of care. They also seek less stringent regulation for their own networks, especially with respect to solvency (BNA, 1997c).

Regulators at the federal level feel increasing pressure to revamp or refine the traditional rules regarding antitrust, provider fraud, and kick-back laws, as well as not-for-profit tax rules. These rules inhibit the development of provider-owned networks and the ability of providers to negotiate collectively with managed care organizations, at least on terms that providers deem acceptable. State regulators also seriously begin to examine how they have regulated managed care in the past and how it should be regulated in the future.

After 1994, public opinion polls continue to show that substantial majorities (70%-80%) believe the health care system needs to be fixed. Many have concerns about managed care and for-profit medicine. Unanimity evaporates when the questions focus on specifics, although a majority feel that there is a role for government (Blendon & Brodie, 1995). A 1997 poll, on the other hand, appears to show somewhat less concern: 52% believe the government should intervene and regulate managed care entities, while 40% do not believe government intervention is worth the resulting increase in cost. Eight percent say they do not know what makes sense (Bowman, 1997). Similarly, anti-managed care referendums, which in early 1997 looked like winners when first placed on the ballot, are defeated in Oregon and Washington. It begins to appear the public may be more comfortable with a middle position that includes regulated managed care.

Recent data also suggest that the historic decline in employer-based coverage may be reversing, although it is too soon to reach definitive conclusions (Fronstin, 1997c; Pearlstein, 1997). Some believe that the number of employers offering coverage has increased, but that the percentage of participating employees continues to decline (Cooper & Schoen, 1997; Goldstein, 1997). Meaningfully, the number of uninsured children also appears to be increasing and seems to coincide with a decline in the percentage of children covered by Medicaid (Fronstin & Pierron, 1997). However, these numbers do not reflect the impact of the 1997 children's legislation, the new welfare law, and the degree to which these changes and accompanying confusion will exacerbate Medicaid's traditionally slow "take-up" rate, that is, how many Medicaid eligibles will actually apply in the new environment.

Where we go from here is anybody's guess. However, there are some recurring themes and ongoing social and economic trends that will heavily influence the future evolution of the system, and these themes and trends provide some insight regarding what may happen.

Conclusion: Some Observations
and a Prognosis for the Future

Just how children will fare under the U.S. health care system of the next century is dependent upon a complex amalgam of fundamental American values that are reflected in recurring themes throughout our history, as well as a number of recent but enduring demographic and economic trends.

Over the past 250 years there have been three particularly important recurring themes regarding U.S. social policy and children. First, American citizens distrust government, especially centralized government. This distrust is reflected, for example, in our Constitution, the long-standing reticence to have the federal government involved in social welfare, and more recently, President Reagan's New Federalism. Our distrust of strong central government, coupled with our "checks-and-balance" structure, leverages the ability of entrenched interests to block systemic change. As a result, broad-based reform has been stymied in many areas, while change on an incremental basis has become the rule. Exceptions to this general proposition are for the most part driven by significant social, political, and economic dislocation, such as the Civil War, the Great Depression, and World War II.

Second, the attitudes of policy elites and the general population toward social welfare have repeatedly emphasized the moral hazard of welfare programs rather than the benefits of such programs, such as political stability and social justice. The narrow scope of the mothers' pension laws during the 1920s and Medicaid's "suitable home" requirements are just two manifestations of this emphasis. This view of social welfare reinforces the public's traditional distrust of government intervention, especially at the federal level.

A third recurring theme is that policymakers and the body politic really do view children as different from the general population, both clinically and from a political perspective. While this theme is camouflaged by our bias in favor of senior citizens, especially since the 1930s, there is little question that children, more than most other population groups, have been and continue to be viewed as vulnerable and deserving of protection and public and philanthropic assistance (Haveman & Wolfe, 1993).

There are also a number of important recent trends that will influence how children will receive health care in the future. First and foremost is the aging of our population, which is a product of declining birthrates and increasing life expectancy. Unfortunately, the aging population will increase the demand for health services while decreasing society's ability to pay for this care. The second and related trend is a widespread belief that real wage growth has stagnated since the 1970s and that there are resource limits regarding what the country can or cannot do. A third important trend relates to how medicine will be delivered in the future. America is well along in a transition from an atomistic medical delivery system, composed of individual practitioners who generally provide treatment when one is sick (the so-called sickness model), to a more systematic approach that focuses on prevention and the coordination of care (the so-called wellness model). This transition is also accompanied by a movement toward cost-effective care that makes greater use of ancillary providers and, when appropriate, case management.

The following summarizes some probable interactions of these themes and trends with respect to children's health care.

The delivery of children's health care will be heavily influenced by the evolution of medicine generally. In particular, individual pediatricians and children's hospitals are in the midst of a painful and inevitable rationalization of professional relationships, practice styles, and institutional capacity as a result of changing economic, demographic, and clinical realities. Children's hospitals are forced to consolidate as the decreasing birthrate, technological advances, and cost concerns reduce the overall amount of tertiary care in the hospital setting. Pediatric generalists and subspecialists will consolidate into groups and networks that affiliate with one or more managed care organizations and community hospitals. Pediatric primary care physicians will treat an increasing number of maladies now treated by subspecialists and will refer only the more complicated cases to the subspecialist. It also is likely that ancillary providers will continue to evolve as an essential, respected, and increasingly relied-upon component of any viable practice.

Because of the changing nature of children's and adolescents' "disease" patterns (i.e., increasing chronic care), most pediatric practice will be outside the hospital and will focus on both prevention and wellness visits, as well as the monitoring and treatment of chronic conditions. Both well-baby care and the monitoring and treatment of chronic disease will use the same infrastructure and practice style. For example, local community presence and outreach capability will be essential. Also, social and physical environmental threats to children's health and the complex nature of chronic disease will require increased collaboration between interdisciplinary provider teams and public health and social agencies. In a practice environment of continuity of care and diverse disciplines, the pediatrician's role as the children's advocate will increase, with respect to both clinical treatment and social issues. In many ways, the new practice environment will resemble the pediatric practice environment of the early 1900s.

Our uniquely American culture, as well as economic and demographic changes, also will dictate how children's health care is financed. Absent some major cataclysmic economic or natural disaster, the U.S. health care system probably will continue on its present dual track of voluntary private coverage for those who can afford it and public financing for only certain categories of individuals who cannot afford coverage, such as the "deserving poor."

This dual track scenario is the most probable for a number of reasons. First and foremost, the sheer magnitude of up-front money needed to extend coverage to all of the uninsured (estimated to be $100 billion[8]) is not feasible, even on an incremental basis, in the existing and foreseeable climate of limited resources. Second, the transition to a compulsory universal health care system will not be easy, especially in a country that embraces entrepreneurial individualism rather than solidarity.[9] For example, universal coverage requires the use of socialized pricing or some form of community rate where the young and healthy "cross-subsidize" the cost of care for the old and sick. This socialization of risk also requires everyone to participate in the system. As a result, the cost of cross-subsidy would be shouldered by the working young and middle class, the self-employed, and employers—key constituencies needed to effect change. In addition, the aging population will undermine rather than enhance the willingness and the ability of the middle class to fund existing entitlements, such as Social Security and Medicare, much less new social programs, such as universal health care coverage. The significance of this demographic change is illustrated by the declining ratio of workers to retirees under Social Security. In 1945, there were 42.1 workers for every retiree. By 1990 the number of workers dropped to 3.8 and is expected to decrease to less than 3 by 2030 (EBRI, 1997a). Many predict Medicare's insolvency during the first decade of the 21st century unless changes are made, in large part because of these demographic trends (Bipartisan Commission, 1995). Interestingly, many universal health care systems in other industrial countries, including those that are held up as models for the United States, are experiencing similar fiscal and demographic strains (Iglehart, 1998; Morone & Goggin, 1995). In summary, an environment of decreasing resources, global competition, an aging population, and our past history makes it unlikely that the United States will develop a culture of solidarity necessary for a compulsory universal and comprehensive health insurance care system.

One can argue that health care for children is at risk in this environment because of the dependency of children and the fact that they cannot vote. While this risk exists, there are countervailing considerations. First and foremost, a broad spectrum of society, at least during this century, has viewed children as being different from most other vulnerable populations and therefore warranting more sympathy than other groups. While this sympathy on occasion has wavered or been reduced to benign neglect, a helping hand for children has been a rather consistent and remarkably reoccurring theme throughout the past 150 years, especially when considered in the context of the United States' preference for rugged individualism. Possibly because children are vulnerable and innocent and because they represent our future, children's causes have had widespread political appeal. These causes have often been a key unifying and key organizational influence for a variety of political and social movements. The Progressive Movement is a case in point. In addition, the Children's Bureau, the Sheppard-Towner Act during the 1920s, Title V of the Social Security Act, the Emergency Maternity program during World War II, the War on Poverty, the Congressional reaction against President Reagan's Medicaid cutbacks, and the recent bipartisan support for expanded child care are tangible evidence of a continuing empathy for children under a wide variety of different economic and social conditions.

Even though children can't vote, they, more than almost any other group, consistently evoke spontaneous and formidable support in both the public and the private sectors. In addition, child advocacy has a long and respected history as evidenced by the child welfare movement during the Progressive Era and more recently the broad coalition spearheaded by the Children's Defense Fund that forced the expansion of Medicaid during a period of fiscal austerity. Today, child advocacy and its history are an important part of a social worker's curriculum. The vitality of this type of advocacy is reflected in over 80 child advocacy organizations in 41 states as well as the National Association of Child Advocacy (Costin et al., 1991; Wagner, 1990).

Another countervailing force is that early medical and public health intervention makes a significant difference in infant mortality and adolescent development. While this relationship has been well accepted since the early years of the 20th century, it has become especially important in recent times because of fiscal constraints and the high cost of medical technology. The cost of early intervention through prenatal, neonatal, and postneonatal care is considerably less than that for the average adult. In addition, early care is extremely cost-effective. Reducing the number of low-birth weight babies greatly reduces the need for expensive neonatal care and the long-term costs associated with chronic disabilities such as cerebral palsy, autism, and retardation (Rosenbaum, 1992). The Institute of Medicine estimates that every 1 dollar of early care saves 3 dollars of care in later years (Institute of Medicine, 1985). The demonstrated benefits of early intervention for maternity care and children will bridge the ideological differences between proponents and opponents of distributive justice and thereby assure widespread support for keeping pregnant women and children in the "deserving" category. In fact, it is likely that the existing combination of Medicaid and the Children's Health Insurance Program will be expanded through outreach initiatives (to ensure enrollment of eligible children) and additional funding whenever possible, to assure universal coverage for expectant mothers and children.

Although universal health care coverage for children now appears to be attainable, there is a critical need to focus as well on other factors essential for the optimal development of children. This broadened focus, which goes well beyond the traditional concept of health care, is especially important for the increasing number of children that live in poverty (Brooks-Gunn & Duncan, 1997). These other factors include the provision of a safe and nurturing environment, adequate nutrition, income security, and education (Corcoran & Chaudry, 1997). Today there are myriad private, federal, state, and local initiatives to address children's needs in each of these areas. However, these programs, like the health care system, "Grow'd like Topsy" into a bewildering array of means-tested and age eligible, categorical, and disease-specific programs. This program diversity is testimony for the need to view children holistically. At the same time, there is little coordination among these programs. In addition, there are significant overlaps that result in redundant and costly administrative infrastructure. This complexity alone limits access and program effectiveness, which dilutes the impact of the considerable resources now devoted to children.

How best to allocate public and private resources for these essential efforts is not easy to discern. As two observers recently put it, "our knowledge of the full impact of both public sector and parental investment in children's attainment is more broad than deep" (Haveman & Wolfe, 1993). Despite this murkiness, there is an obvious first step: Most agree that there is an urgent need to rationalize and better coordinate existing public and private programs. However, there are differences in just how to do it. Some argue for a children's version of the "network on aging" at the national and community level, similar to the Older American's Act of 1965 (e.g., Grayson & Guyer, 1995). Others advocate a "multipronged" approach because of the interrelated nature of a child's environment and the uncertainty surrounding the relative benefits of the many programs (Haveman & Wolfe, 1993).

Interestingly, the emerging local and community health care infrastructure for children can play a key role in rationalizing existing children's programs at the state and federal level. This emerging system will provide committed leaders that have a grassroots advocacy capability and the knowledge and communication resources necessary to realize change. Similarly, this new leadership structure will provide the diverse perspectives necessary to evaluate what works and does not work for children in terms of health care and their overall development. This holistic consideration is essential if the United States is to conserve its most important national resource: its children.

Notes

1. Many correctly assert that the social welfare disparity between children and the elderly began in the 1930s with the enactment of Social Security and that this disparity accelerated with social security benefit increases and Medicare in the 1950s

and the 1960s. For one of the better analyses of the social, economic, and demographic influences on U.S. policy toward these two vulnerable population groups, see Axinn and Stern, 1985. See also Preston, 1984.

2. This work provides excerpts from *original* sources covering diverse topics as they relate to children, such as family structure, education, apprenticeship and labor, philosophy, religion, and health. It was published in 1970 and provides an essential starting point for anyone interested in the history of children in the United States.

3. Some revisionists believe the Progressive Movement had a conservative rather than humanitarian orientation in that it was designed to assert the dominance of government in society and politics during rapidly changing times. Others stress the humanitarian rationale. In all probability, both motivations were present (Clement, 1985).

4. Moral hazard is the tendency of people who have insurance either to be careless about the prevention of losses or to have a greater propensity than non-covered individuals to use the insurance benefits. Adverse selection is the tendency of individuals who pose an above average risk to buy and maintain insurance coverage to a greater degree than those who are average or below-average risks (Vaughn, 1989).

5. The elderly (over 65) are excluded because virtually all, at least 99%, are covered by Medicare.

6. This concept was first articulated by Alain Enthoven and Paul Elwood. Here the market would be restructured or regulated to permit individual consumers to choose between competing health plans on the basis of price and quality. Key ingredients would include standard health coverage, equal or no tax subsidy, consumers paying a significant portion of the premiums, and restrictions on risk selections and pricing by health plans (Enthoven, 1988).

7. Starting in the early 1990s, the National Association of Insurance Commissioners developed a number of small group reforms that formed the conceptual basis for the new federal legislation. A federal solution, however, was necessary to extend many of these concepts to both insured and self-insured plans.

8. This estimate assumes that the number of uninsured approximates 40 million and that the average annual cost of a comprehensive benefit package approximates $2,500.

9. Solidarity is a set of "informal norms and beliefs that express trust in our fellow citizens, obligations to help each other and a commitment to cooperation for the sake of collective well-being" (Stone, 1995) and is a concept upon which the social welfare systems in other industrial countries are based (Morone & Goggin, 1995).

References

Aguilar, M. (1995). Women and health care. In R. L. Edwards (Ed.), *Encyclopedia of social work* (pp. 2539-2551). Washington, DC: National Association of Social Workers.

American Academy of Pediatrics. (1993). *Pediatrics, 91,* 506-508.

Applebaum, L. (1961). The development of voluntary health insurance in the United States. *The Journal of Risk and Insurance, 28*(3), 25-33.

Ashby, L. (1985). Partial promises and semi-visible youths: The Depression and World War II. In J. M. Hawes & N. R. Heiner (Eds.), *The American childhood: A research guide and historical handbook* (pp. 489-532). Westport, CT: Greenwood.

Axinn, J., & Stern, M. (1985). Age and dependency: Children and the aged in American social policy. *Milbank Memorial Fund Quarterly, 63*(4), 648-670.

Barnard, J. (1982). American workers, the labor movement, and the cold war, 1945-1960. In R. H. Bremner & G. W. Reichard (Eds.), *Reshaping America: Society and institutions: 1945-1960* (pp. 115-146). Columbus: Ohio State University Press.

Beales, R. (1985). The child in 17th century America. In J. M. Hawes & N. R. Heiner (Eds.), *The American childhood: A research guide and historical handbook* (pp. 15-56). Westport, CT: Greenwood.

Beam, B. (1991). *Group benefits: Basic concepts and alternatives.* Bryn Mawr, PA: The American College Press.

Bell, W. (1965). *Aid to dependent children.* New York: Columbia University Press.

Bipartisan Commission on Entitlement and Tax Reform. (1995). *Final report.* Washington, DC: Government Printing Office.

Black, J. (1988). A sentimental market place: Who controls child health care? In E. M. Melhado, W. Feinberg, & H. M. Swartz (Eds.), *Money, power and health care* (pp. 209-232). Ann Arbor, MI: Health Administration Press.

Blendon, R., & Brodie, M. (1995). The public's contributions to Congressional gridlock on health care reform. *Journal of Health Politics, Policy and Law, 20*(2), 402-410.

Blendon, R., & Szalay, U. (1992). The politics of health care reform: The public's perspective. In R. Blendon & T. Hymans (Eds.), *Reforming the system: Containing health care costs in an era of universal coverage* (pp. 37-60). New York: Faulkner & Gray.

Blumenthal, D., & Meyer, G. (1996). Academic health centers in a changing environment. *Health Affairs, 15*(2), 200-215.

Bowen, C. (1986). *Miracle at Philadelphia: The story of the Constitutional Convention, May to September, 1987.* Boston: Little, Brown.

Bowman, K. (1997). *Health care attitudes today.* Washington, DC: American Enterprize Institute for Public Policy Research.

Bremner, R. (Ed.). (1970-1974). *Children and youth in America: A documented history: Vol. 1. 1600-1865; Vol. 2: 1866-1932; Vol. 3. 1933-1970.* Cambridge, MA: Harvard University Press.

Bremner, R. (1982). Families, children and the state. In R. Bremner & G. Reichard (Eds.), *Reshaping America: Society and institutions: 1945-1960* (pp. 3-32). Columbus: Ohio State University Press.

Brill, E. (1956). Group major medical expense insurance. *The Journal of the American Society of Chartered Life Underwriters, 10*(4), 310-323.

Brink, S. (1998). What is the value of a voice? *U.S. News and World Report, 124*(9), 40-46.

BNA, (1997a). Clinton floats trial balloons on expansion of health coverage. *Health Care Policy, 5*(37), 1441-1442.

BNA. (1997b). Clinton orders federal health programs to comply with "Consumer bill of rights." *Health Care Policy, 6*(9), 359-360.

BNA. (1997c). Provider coalition says insurers favor state PSO rules to dampen competition. *Health Care Policy, 5*(28), 1119.

Brooks-Gunn, J., & Duncan, G. (1997). The effects of poverty on children. *Children and Poverty, 7*(2), 55-71.

Carleton, S. (1997). Health reform rediscovers the patient. The state of health care in America [Special issue]. *Business Health.*

Casey, J. (1994). *State Mandates Health Benefits Letter* [newsletter] (pp. 1-11). Washington, DC: Capital Publishing.

Cleary, A, (1994). Kid-sized care. *Hospitals & Health Networks, 68*(15), 101-103.

Clement, P. (1985). The city and the child, 1860-1885. In J. M. Hawes & N. R. Heiner (Eds.), *The American childhood: A research guide and historical handbook* (pp. 15-56). Westport, CT: Greenwood.

Colburn, D. (1997, December 16). What worries Americans most about their children. *The Washington Post,* p. Z8.

Cohen, R. (1985). Child-saving and progressivism, 1885-1915. In J. M. Hawes & N.R. Heiner (Eds.), *The American childhood: A research guide and historical handbook* (pp. 415-488). Westport, CT: Greenwood.

CCH. (1993). *President Clinton's health care reform proposal and health security act.* Chicago: Commerce Clearing House.

Congressional Research Services. (1993). *Medicaid source book: Background data and analysis: A 1993 update.* Washington, DC: Government Printing Office.

Cooper, P., & Schoen, B. (1997). More offers, fewer takers for employment-based health insurance: 1987-1996. *Health Affairs, 16*(6), 142-149.

Corcoran, M., & Chaudry, A. (1997). The dynamics of childhood poverty. *Children and Poverty, 7*(2), 40-54.

Costin, L., Bell, C., & Downs, S. (1991). *Child welfare: Policies and practice,* White Plains, NY: Longman.

Cravens, H. (1985). Child-saving in the age of professionalism, 1915-1930. In J. M. Hawes & M. R. Heiner (Eds.), *The American childhood: A research guide and historical handbook* (pp. 415-488). Westport, CT. Greenwood.

Culter, D., & Gruber, J. (1997). Medicaid and private insurance: Evidence and implications. *Health Affairs, 16*(1), 194-200.

Cunningham, R., & Cunningham, R. (1997). *The Blues: A History of the Blue Cross and Blue Shield system.* DeKalb: Northern Illinois University Press.

Davis, K., & Schoen, C. (1978). *Health and the War on Poverty: A ten year appraisal.* Washington, DC: Brookings Institution.

Davis, M. (1934). The American approach to health insurance. *Milbank Memorial Fund Quarterly, 12,* 204-217.

Day, J. G. (1996-1997). Managed care and the medical profession, old issues and old tensions, the building blocks of tomorrow's health care delivery system. *Connecticut Insurance Law Journal, 3*(1), 1-78.

Day, J. G., & Wade, K. L. (1995). The political viability of health care federalism. *Connecticut Law Review, 28*(1), 151-160.

Dickinson, N. S. (1995). Federal social legislation from 1961 to 1994. In R. L. Edwards (Ed.), *Encyclopedia of social work* (pp. 1005-1013). Washington, DC: National Association of Social Workers.

Edwards, J., Blendon, R., & Leitman, R. (1992). The worried middle class. In R. J. Blendon & T. S. Hymans (Eds.), *Reforming the system: Containing health care costs in an era of universal coverage* (pp. 61-81). Washington, DC: Faulkner & Gray.

Employee Benefit Research Institute. (1995). *Sources of health insurance and the characteristics of the uninsured: Analysis of the March 1994 Current Population Survey* (EBRI Special Report SR-28). Washington, DC: EBRI-ERF Publications.

Employee Benefit Research Institute. (1997a). *EBRI databook on employee benefits* (4th ed.). Washington, DC: EBRI-ERF Publications.

Employee Benefit Research Institute. (1997b). Employment-based health insurance and the changing work force. *EBRI notes.* Washington, DC: EBRI-ERF Publications.

Enthoven, A. (1988). *The theory and practice of managed competition in health care finance.* New York: Elsevier Science.

Evans, A., & Friedland, R. (1994). *Financing and delivery of health care for children.* Background paper for the National Academy of Social Insurance Advisory Committee on Reforming American Health Care Financing: Policy and Administrative Choices, Washington, D.C.

Finkelstein, B. (1985). Casting networks of good influence: The reconstruction of childhood in the United States. In J. M. Hawes & N. R. Heiner (Eds), *The American childhood: A research guide and historical handbook* (pp. 111-152). Westport, CT: Greenwood.

Fitzgerald, J. (1994). PHOs on the rise at children's hospitals—Survey. *Modern Healthcare, 24*(36), 10.

Fitzhugh, G. (1951). Group accident and health insurance. *The Journal of the American Society of Chartered Life Underwriters, 6*(2), 144-145.

Fox-Grage, W. (1991). Widening the network: Specialty physicians as primary care providers. *State health notes* (pp. 3-6). Washington, DC: Forum for State Health Policy Leadership.

Friedson, E. (1970). *Profession of medicine: A study of the sociology of applied knowledge.* New York: Dodd, Mead.

Fronstin, P. (1997a). Health insurance portability: Access and affordability. *EBRI Issue Brief No. 173.* Washington, DC: EBRI-ERF Publications

Fronstin, P. (1997b). Sources of health insurance and characteristics of the uninsured: Analysis of the March, 1997 survey. *EBRI Issue Brief No. 192.* Washington, DC: EBRI-ERF Publications.

Fronstin, P. (1997c). *Trends in health insurance coverage* (Issue Brief). Washington, DC: EBRI-ERF Publications.

Fronstin, P. (1998). Features of employment-based health plans. *EBRI Issue Brief No. 201.* Washington, DC: EBRI-ERF Publications.

Fronstin, P., & Pierron, B. (1997). Expanding health insurance for children: Examining the alternatives. *EBRI Issue Brief No. 187.* Washington, DC: EBRI-ERF Publications.

Fronstin, P., & Snider, S. (1996-1997). An examination of the decline in employment-based health insurance between 1988 and 1993. *Inquiry, 33*(4), 317-325.

Fubini, S., & Antonelli, V. (1996). Restructuring the American health market—Separating myth from reality. *Health Trends Issue Brief* (pp. 1-48). Bethesda, MD: Health Trends.

Furrow, B., Greaney, T., Johnson, S., Jost, T., & Schwartz, R. (1995). *Health law.* St. Paul, MN: West.

Gabel, J., & Jensen, G. (1989). *The price of state mandated benefits.* Washington, DC: HIAA.

Galbraith, J. (1958). *The affluent society.* Boston: Little, Brown.

General Accounting Office. (1996). *Health insurance for children: State and private programs create new strategies to insure children.* Washington, DC: Government Printing Office.

Goldstein, A. (1997, November 10). More employees decline to pay for health plans, boosting number of uninsured. *Washington Post,* p. A-12.

Gray, B. (1991). *The profit motive and patient care: The changing accountability of doctors and hospitals.* Cambridge, MA: Harvard University Press.

Gray, B. (1997). Conversions of HMOs and hospitals: What's at stake? *Health Affairs, 16*(2), 29-47.

Grayson, H., & Guyer, B. (1995). Rethinking the organization of children's programs: Lessons from the elderly. *Milbank Memorial Fund Quarterly, 73*(4), 565-597.

Green, J. (1989). Children's hospitals, they're still growing, but their payment formula is about to be watered down. *Modern Healthcare, 19*(13), 18-23.

Hacker, J. (1996). National health care reform: An idea whose time came and went. *Journal of Health Politics, Policy and Law, 21*(4), 647-696.

Halpern, S. (1988). *American pediatrics: The social dynamics of professionalism: 1880-1980.* Berkeley: University of California Press.

Hamilton, W. (1932). Personal statement. *Medical care for the American people.* Chicago: University of Chicago Press.

Harrington, M. (1962). *The other America: Poverty in the United States.* New York: Macmillan.

Haveman, R., & Wolfe, B. (1993). Children's prospects and children's policy. *Journal of Economic Perspectives, 7*(4), 153-174.

Hawes, J., & Heiner, N. (1985). Introduction: The historiography of American childhood. In J. M. Hawes & N. R. Heiner (Eds.), *The American childhood: A research guide and historical handbook* (pp. 3-13). Westport, CT: Greenwood.

HIAA. (1968-1970). *Statistical information bulletin.* (Available from HIAA Library, 555 Thirteenth St. N.W., Suite 600 East, Washington, D.C., 20004-1109)

HIAA. (1995). *Managed care: Integrating the delivery and financing of health care.* Washington, DC: HIAA.

HIAA. (1996). *Source book of health insurance.* Washington, DC: HIAA.

Iglehart, J. (1998). Physicians as agents of social control: Thoughts of Victor Fuchs. *Health Affairs, 17*(1), 90-96.

Institute of Medicine. (1985). *Preventing low birthweight.* Washington, DC: National Academy Press.

Institute of Medicine. (1989). *Controlling costs and changing patient care: The role of utilization management.* Washington, DC: National Academy Press.

Karger, H., & Stoesz, D. (1990). *American social welfare policy: A pluralistic approach.* New York: Longman.

Lippman, H. (1997). Are employers missing the signs? *Business Health, 15*(12), 36-41.

Leff, M. (1973). Consensus for reform: The mother's-pension movement in the progressive era. *The Social Service Review, 47*(3), 397-417.

Leslie, L., Sarah, R., & Palfrey, J. (1998). Child health care in changing times. *Pediatrics, 101*(Suppl.), 746-751.

Long, S., & Rogers, J. (1995). Do shifts toward service industries, part-time work and self-employment explain the rising uninsured rate? *Inquiry, 32*, 11-16.

Madrick, J. (1995). *The end of affluence: The causes and consequences of America's economic dilemma.* New York: Random House.

Marmor, T. (1973). *The politics of Medicare.* New York: Aldine.

McEachern, S. (1995). Medicaid managed care: Hospitals need a "safety net." *Health Care Strategic Management, 13*(12), 1, 20.

Melhado, E. (1988). Competition versus regulation in American health policy. In E. Melhado, W. Feinberg, & H. Swartz (Eds.), *Money, power and health care* (pp. 15-102). Ann Arbor, MI: Health Administrations Press.

Meyer, J., & Naughton, D. (1997). Who's saying no to uninsured kids? *Business Health, 15*(3), 33-37.

Meyers, L., & Schroeder, S. (1981). Physician use of services for the hospitalized patient: A review, with implications for cost containment. *Milbank Memorial Fund Quarterly, 59*(4), 481-507.

Morone, J. (1992). The bias of American politics: Rationing health care in a weak state. *University of Pennsylvania Law Review, 140*(5), 1923-1963.

Morone, J., & Goggin, J. (1995). Introduction—Health policies in Europe: Welfare states in a market era. *Journal of Health Politics, Policy and Law, 20*(3), 557-569.

National Center for Health Statistics. (1995). U.S. infant and general mortality. Racial and social economic disparities. *1995 fact sheet.* Washington, DC: U.S. Department of Health and Human Services, Centers for Disease Control and Prevention.

National Commission on Children. (1991). *Beyond rhetoric: A new American agenda for children and families. Final report of the National Commission on Children.* Washington, DC: Government Printing Office.

National Council of Organizations for Children and Youth. (1976). *America's children 1976: A bicentennial assessment.* Washington DC: Author.

National Governor's Association. (1997). National governors adopt children's health policy. *Governors' Bulletin, 31*(11), 1-3.

Nemes, J. (1993). Reform may hurt pediatrics' ratings—S & P. *Modern Healthcare, 23*(19), 38-40.

Oberg, C., & Polich, C. (1988). Medicaid entering the third decade. *Health Affairs, 7*(4), 83-96.

Patients or profits? (1998). *The Economist, 346*(8058), 15.

Patterson, J. (1982). Poverty and welfare in America, 1945-60. In R. H. Bremner & G. W. Reichard (Eds.), *Reshaping America: Society and institutions, 1945-1960* (pp. 193-222), Columbus: Ohio State University Press.

Payne, S., & Restuccia, J. (1987). Policy issues related to prospective payment for pediatric hospitalization. *Health Care Financing Review, 9*(1), 71-82.

Pearlstein, S. (1997, November 13). As premiums grow, more workers decline health insurance. *Washington Post,* pp. E1, E10.

Pham, A. (1998). Health care "Bill of rights" popular—if it's free. *Boston Globe,* p. C5.

Phelps, C. (1997). *Health economics*. Reading, MA: Addison-Wesley.

Preston, S. (1984). Children and the elderly: Divergent paths for America's dependents. *Demographics, 21*(4), 435-457.

Potanka, E. (1989). Alternative health care delivery systems: A legal overview. *Association of Life Insurance Counsel Proceedings, 1988-1989, 28*, 101-205.

Renn, S. (1987). The structure and financing of the health care delivery system of the 1980s. In C. J. Shramm (Ed.), *Health care and its costs* (pp. 8-48). New York: Norton.

Rosenbaum, S. (1992). Rationing without justice: Children and the American health system. *University of Pennsylvania Law Review, 140*(5), 1859-1880.

Rosenbaum, S., Johnson, K., Sonosky, C., Markus, A., & DeGraw, C. (1998). The children's hour: The state children's health insurance program. *Health Affairs, 17*(1), 192-200.

Rosenblatt, R., Law, S., & Rosenbaum, S. (1997). *Law and the American health care system*. Westbury, NY: Foundation Press.

Salisbury, D., McDonnell, K., & Rheam, E. (1996). The changing world of work and employer benefits. *EBRI Issue Brief No. 172*. Washington DC: EBRI-ERF Publications.

Sardell, A. (1988). *The U.S. experiment in social medicine: The Community Health Center Program, 1965-1986*. Pittsburgh, PA: University of Pittsburgh Press.

Sardell, A. (1990). Child health policy in the U.S.: The paradox of consensus. *Journal of Health Politics, Policy and Law, 15*(2), 271-304.

Selden, T., Banthin, J., & Cohen, J. (1998). Medicaid's problem children: Eligible but not enrolled. *Health Affairs, 17*(3), 192-200.

Shiels, J., & Wolfe, P. (1992). The role of private health insurance in children's health care. *U.S. Health Care for Children, 2*(2), 115-133.

Shultz, C. (1985). Children and childhood in the eighteenth century. In J. M. Hawes & N.R. Heiner (Eds.), *The American childhood: A research guide and historical handbook* (pp. 57-110). Westport, CT: Greenwood.

Somers, H., & Somers, A. (1961). *Doctors, patients and health insurance*. Washington, DC: Brookings Institution.

Spencer, B. (1981). *Group benefits in a changing society*. Chicago: Charles Spencer & Associates.

Starfield, B. (1985). Motherhood and apple pie: The effectiveness of medical care for children. *Milbank Memorial Fund Quarterly, 63*(3), 523-546.

Starr, P. (1982). *The social transformation of American medicine*. New York: Basic Books.

Starr. P. (1991). The middle class and national health reform. *American Prospect, 6*(Summer), 7-12.

Stoeckle, J. (1995). The citadel cannot hold: Technologies go outside the hospital, patients and doctors, too. *Milbank Memorial Fund Quarterly, 73*(1).

Stone, D. (1995). Commentary: The durability of social capital. *Journal of Health Politics, Policy and Law, 20*(3), 689-694.

Strickland, C., & Ambrose, A. (1985). The baby boom, prosperity and the changing worlds of children 1945-1963. In J. M. Hawes & N. R. Heiner (Eds.), *The America childhood: A research guide and historical handbook* (pp. 533-586). Westport, CT: Greenwood.

Temin, P. (1988). An economic history of American hospitals. In H. E. Frech (Ed.), *Health care in America* (pp. 75-102). San Francisco: Pacific Research Institute for Public Policy.

Trattner, W. (1979). *From poor law to welfare state: A history of social welfare in America.* New York: Free Press.

Truman, H. (1961). Special message to the Congress recommending a comprehensive health program. November 19, 1995. *Public papers of the presidents of the United States: Harry S Truman, 1945.* Washington, DC: Government Printing Office.

Uhlman, M. (1997, June 15). Specialists' new role is in primary care. *Philadelphia Inquirer,* p. D1.

U.S. Census Bureau. (1993). Population and housing counts: 1790-1990. *1990 census of population and housing, table CPH-2-1.* Washington, DC: Government Printing Office.

Vaughn, E. (1989). *Fundamentals of risk and insurance.* New York: John Wiley.

Wagner, L. (1990). Children advocates seeking political clout to equal that of elderly. *Modern Healthcare, 20*(35), 26-27.

Wehr, E., & Jameson, E. (1994). Beyond benefits: The importance of a pediatric standard in private insurance contracts to ensuring health access for children. *The Future of Children, 4*(3), 115-133.

Wennberg, J. (1989). Hospital use and methodology among medicare beneficiaries in Boston and New Haven. *New England Journal of Medicine, 321*(13), 1168-1173.

Williams, R., Stein, L., & Leslie, L. (1998). Training pediatricians for the evolving generalist-specialist interface in the managed care era. *Pediatrics, 101*(Suppl.), 779-783.

Wilson, A. (1989). Development of the U.S. federal role in children's health care: A critical appraisal. In L. M. Kopelman & J. C. Moskop (Eds.), *Children and health care: Moral and social issues* (pp. 27-66). Boston: Kluwer Academic.

Wilson, P., Bartels, P., & Rubin, D. (1988). Providing medical care for the poor: Medicaid in a period of transition. In E. Melhado, W. Feinberg, & H. M. Swartz (Eds.), *Money, power and health care* (pp. 183-208). Ann Arbor, MI: Health Administration Press.

Wing, K. (1983). The impact of Reagan-era politics or the federal Medicaid program. *Catholic University Law Review, 33*(1), 1-91.

Wing, K., Jacobs, M., & Kuszler, P. (1998). *The law and American healthcare.* Aspen CO: Aspen.

Yudkowsky, B., Cartland, J., & Flint, S. (1990). Pediatrician population in Medicaid: 1978 to 1989. *Pediatrics, 85*(4), 567-577.

Zuckerman, H., Thomas, J., Schneller, E., & Hall, M. (1993). Principles of health care facility organizations and management. In M. Hall (Ed.), *Health care corporate law: Formation and regulation.* Boston: Little, Brown.

CHAPTER 2

Federal Involvement in Health Care Services: The Medicaid Program— A Safety Net for Low-Income Families and Children

CHRISTIE PROVOST PETERS

The Medicaid Program

The Medicaid program is the third largest source of health insurance in the United States—after employment-based coverage and Medicare. The largest program in the Federal "safety net" of public assistance programs, Medicaid provides essential medical and medically related services to people with limited means who are unable to acquire health care coverage. Designed to serve the most vulnerable populations in society, the Medicaid program covers millions of low-income women, children, aged, and individuals with disabilities.

The significance of Medicaid's role in providing health insurance coverage cannot be overstated. The proportion of the total U.S. population covered by Medicaid has increased from 8% in the early

AUTHOR'S NOTE: This chapter was written by Christie Provost Peters in her private capacity. No official support or endorsement by the Health Care Financing Administration is intended or should be inferred.

1970s to 13% in 1995 ("Health Insurance for Children: Many Remain Uninsured," 1995). In 1995, the Medicaid program served 18.7 million children, 7.6 million adults who care for these children, 4.4 million elderly, and 5.9 million blind and disabled individuals ("Health Insurance for Children: Many Remain Uninsured," 1995).

Medicaid coverage is particularly prominent among children. The 18.7 million children served by Medicaid in 1995 represented one out of every five children in the nation. About one third of all births each year in the United States are covered by Medicaid. Approximately 29% of all children between the ages of 1 and 5 and 22% of children ages 6 to 12 are covered by Medicaid (Henry Kaiser Family Foundation [Kaiser], 1997). Ninety percent of all children with HIV/AIDS are covered by Medicaid.

The Medicaid program has achieved success in reaching low-income children. The number of Medicaid beneficiaries under age 21 has risen from 9.8 million in 1985 to 18.7 million in 1995 (U.S. Department of Health and Human Services, 1997). This increase is predominantly due to changes in the program mandated by Congress and initiated by States over the years in efforts to expand coverage, improve health outcomes, and control program costs.

Although the Medicaid program has been successful in providing health insurance to many low-income children, the number of uninsured individuals continues to climb. It is estimated that there are approximately 10 million uninsured children (Kaiser, 1997). Furthermore, it is estimated that there are approximately 3 million children who are eligible for Medicaid but not enrolled in the program. As a result, many believe that further changes to the Medicaid program and the Federal government's role in providing health care are necessary.

This chapter highlights the Medicaid program, its role in providing health care coverage to low-income children and their families, and significant changes that have occurred in the program and other related Federal programs since Medicaid was enacted.

History

The Medicaid program was enacted in the same legislation that created the Medicare program—the Social Security Amendments of

1965 (P.L. 89-97). Prior to the passage of this law, health care services for the indigent were provided primarily through a patchwork of programs sponsored by State and local governments, charities, and community hospitals.

Before 1965, Federal assistance to the States for the provision of health care was provided through two grant programs. The first was established in the Social Security Amendments of 1950. Federal funds were provided to match State payments to medical care providers on behalf of individuals receiving public assistance payments (i.e., welfare payments). In 1960, the Kerr-Mills Act created a new program, called "Medical Assistance for the Aged." This means-tested grant program provided Federal funds to States that chose to cover the "medically needy" aged—elderly individuals with incomes above levels needed to qualify for public assistance, but in need of assistance for medical expenses (Congressional Research Services [CRS], 1993).

In 1965, Congress adopted a combination of approaches to improve access to health care for the elderly. The Social Security Amendments of 1965 created a hospital insurance program to cover nearly all of the elderly (i.e., Medicare Part A), a voluntary supplementary medical insurance program (i.e., Medicare Part B), and a expansion of the Kerr-Mills program to help elderly individuals with out-of-pocket expenses such as premiums, co-payments and deductibles, and costs for uncovered services (i.e., Medicaid). At the same time, Congress decided to extend the Kerr-Mills program, now the Medicaid program, to cover other populations—including families with children, the blind, and the disabled.

Like its preceding grant programs, the Medicaid program is targeted to populations traditionally eligible for welfare. The Medicaid program was designed to assist low-income single-parent families, aged, blind, and individuals with disabilities. Two-parent families with a working parent, single adults, and childless couples who are not aged or blind are not eligible to participate in the program. The law initially did not include an upper income limit for program eligibility, and States were allowed to provide coverage for higher-income individuals in traditional welfare categories. Congress later amended the law to cap the income levels for these higher-income "medically needy" groups to $133\frac{1}{3}\%$ of the maximum payment for a same sized family under Aid to Families with Dependent Children (AFDC; CRS, 1993).

In the first year, six States implemented programs. In 1966, 26 States implemented Medicaid programs, and in 1967 another 11 States did. Today, all States, the District of Columbia, and each of the Territories participate in the Medicaid program.

Federal Financing

State participation in the Medicaid program is voluntary. Federal Medicaid law does not require any State to participate in the program. However, if a State chooses to participate, it is entitled to receive Federal matching payment for its spending on covered services for eligible populations.

The Medicaid program is administered by the States with partial Federal funding. Because it is a Federal entitlement program, the Federal spending level is determined by the number of people participating in the program and program benefit levels. Federal spending for Medicaid comes from Federal general funds. There is no Trust Fund as there is for Medicare or Social Security.

The Federal government contributes between 50% and 80% of the payments made under each State program. This Federal Matching Assistance Percentage (FMAP) varies from State to State and from year to year because it is based on the average per capita income in each State. Relatively poorer States receive a higher matching rate.

The Medicaid program is the single largest source of Federal funds to the States. In fiscal year 1996, the Federal Medicaid matching payments to States totaled $92 billion. Of the $238 billion in total Federal grants-in-aid to the States, Federal payments for Medicaid represented nearly 40%. These Federal Medicaid payments were significantly greater than Federal payment for highways and mass transit ($25.2 billion), education ($13.3 billion), housing ($12.4 billion), food stamps ($29.8 billion), and welfare ($16.9 billion) (U.S. House of Representatives, 1997).

While Federal Medicaid payments are the largest source of Federal funds to the States, they constitute a relatively small portion of the Federal budget. In 1994, the Federal portion of Medicaid accounted for 6% of Federal outlays (Kaiser, 1997). This was less than Social Security (22%), defense (19%), and Medicare (11%) (Families USA, 1997b).

State Flexibility

State flexibility in the administration of the Medicaid program is an integral part of the Federal statute. The Federal law's inherent State discretion regarding eligibility, benefits, and reimbursement allows States to operate Medicaid programs that meet certain budget, political, and social parameters. State budgetary constraints, political philosophy toward welfare families, and the composition of the State's Medicaid population all contribute to the design and content of a State's Medicaid program (Holahan & Liska, 1997).

State discretion regarding program income eligibility criteria, services covered, and provider reimbursement has led to significant variations across State Medicaid programs. As a result, there are actually 56 different Medicaid programs—one for each State, the District of Columbia, and each of the Territories. State Medicaid programs differ in the beneficiaries covered, services provided, and the amount of State financing allocated to the program.

Eligibility

Medicaid policy for eligibility is complex and varies from State to State. A person who is eligible for Medicaid in one State might not be eligible in another State. Furthermore, eligibility requirements within one State can change during a year. In general, Medicaid eligibility is based on a combination of financial and categorical eligibility requirements.

Medicaid is a means-tested program. Beneficiaries have to be low-income and meet asset and resource standards. States determine the income thresholds and the asset and resource standards of their Medicaid programs within Federal guidelines. These standards vary from State to State and are different for each Medicaid-eligible population group within a State.

In general, financial eligibility for Medicaid is linked to receipt of Federally assisted income maintenance payments such as AFDC and SSI (Supplemental Security Income).[1] There are certain populations, however, where financial eligibility is based solely on income and resources. These populations—referred to as "poverty related groups"—were created in the late 1980s by Congress in an effort to expand Medicaid coverage of pregnant women and children by "delinking" Medicaid eligibility from receipt of AFDC.

Medicaid, however, does not provide medical assistance to all low-income individuals. Medicaid is available only to members of families with children and pregnant women, and to persons who are aged, blind, or disabled. Individuals not fitting these categories, such as single nondisabled adults or childless couples, cannot qualify for Medicaid—no matter how low their income is. Within these categorical groups further distinctions apply. For example, all the members of a single-parent family may receive Medicaid; in a two-parent family with one parent working full-time, the children receive continuous coverage, the mother is eligible only during pregnancy, and the father is never eligible (CRS, 1993).

There are certain populations that States are required to cover (i.e., "mandatory" or "categorical" groups) and other populations that States may choose to cover (i.e., "optional" groups). The Medicaid statute, Title XIX of the Social Security Act, identifies all mandatory and optional eligibility groups. Children and their families fall into both mandatory and optional Medicaid eligibility groups.

All States must provide Medicaid coverage to the following mandatory "categorically needy" eligibility groups:

- *AFDC-eligible individuals as of July 16, 1996:* States are required to provide Medicaid to individuals who meet the requirements for the AFDC program that were in effect in their State as of July 16, 1996.
- *Poverty-related groups:* States are required to provide Medicaid to certain pregnant women and children defined in terms of family income and resources. For example, States must cover all pregnant women and children below age 6 with family incomes up to 133% of the Federal Poverty Level (FPL).
- *All children born after September 30, 1983:* States are required to provide Medicaid to children born after September 30, 1983 with family incomes at or below the Federal poverty level. This requirement will result in the mandatory coverage of all children under the age of 19 with family incomes of 100% FPL by the year 2003.
- *Current and some former recipients of SSI:* In general, recipients of SSI are automatically eligible for Medicaid.
- *Foster Care and Adoption Assistance:* States must provide Medicaid to all recipients of foster care and adoption assistance under Title IV-E of the Social Security Act.

- *Certain Medicare beneficiaries:* States must provide Medicaid coverage
  to certain low-income Medicare beneficiaries.

States have the option to provide Medicaid coverage to other
"categorically related" groups. These optional groups fall within
the defined categories mentioned above but the eligibility criteria
are somewhat more liberally defined. Optional eligibility groups
include:

- *Poverty-related groups:* States may choose to cover certain higher-income pregnant women and children defined in terms of family income
  and resources. For example, States may choose to cover pregnant
  women and children under age one with family incomes up to 185%
  FPL.
- *The medically needy:* States may choose to cover individuals who do
  not meet the financial standards for program benefits but meet the
  categorical standards (i.e., pregnant women, children, elderly, and
  disabled) and have income and resources within special "medically
  needy" limits established by the States. Persons whose incomes or
  resources are above those standards may qualify by "spending down,"
  incurring medical bills that reduce their income and/or resources to the
  necessary levels. As of October 1996, 38 States covered at least some
  groups of the medically needy.
- *Recipients of State supplementary income payments:* Many States provide supplementary income payments to recipients of SSI. States have
  the option to provide Medicaid to this population.

Services

States have discretion to define what medically related services
their Medicaid program covers. There is much variation among
State Medicaid programs regarding not only which services are
covered but also the amount of care provided within specific service
categories (e.g., inpatient hospital services, physicians services, etc.).
The Medicaid "benefit package" is defined by each State based
on broad Federal guidelines. States are required to provide Medicaid coverage for certain medical services—referred to as "mandatory services"—to the mandatory eligible groups. Mandatory
services include: inpatient and outpatient services; nursing facility
services for individuals over 21 years of age; physicians' services;
laboratory and x-ray services; early periodic screening, diagnostic,
and treatment (EPSDT) services for individuals under age 21; home

health services for any individual entitled to nursing facility care; rural health clinic and Federally qualified health center services; nurse-midwife services, certified pediatric nurse practitioners, family planning services, and certified family nurse practitioners. Mandatory services are listed and defined in Title XIX and accompanying regulations.

States also may elect to cover other services as well. These are commonly referred to as "optional services." These services include prescription drugs, dental services, clinic services, optical services, and podiatric services. There are 34 approved optional medical services. The optional services States may choose to cover are listed in Title XIX, Federal regulations, and in the State Medicaid Manual.

While certain mandatory services tend to be the more expensive Medicaid services covered (e.g., inpatient hospital services), the bulk of State Medicaid spending is for optional services. In 1995, over 50% of total Medicaid expenditures were for optional services (U.S Department of Health and Human Services, 1995).

In addition to deciding which medical services are covered, States have the discretion to determine how much of each service is covered—the amount, duration, and scope of a service. The amount, duration, and scope of services are generally based on a State's determination of medical necessity for that service. States are permitted to limit coverage for services (e.g., restrict the number of hospital days, the number of covered physician visits, number of prescriptions, etc.). However, the level of coverage must be sufficient to meet the medical need of the beneficiary.

The broad Federal guideline States must follow is that coverage of a service must be sufficient reasonably to achieve its purpose. States cannot restrict coverage of services based solely on an illness or condition. Furthermore, States are not allowed to vary coverage of services among individuals within a given eligibility group (i.e., all categorically needy beneficiaries such as pregnant women must receive the same amount of coverage). States are allowed to have different benefit packages for the optional medically needy eligibility groups—but again, States are not allowed to vary the amount of coverage among beneficiaries within the medically needy populations.

Other Federal requirements States must comply with regarding Medicaid coverage of services are statewideness and freedom of choice. Statewideness means that coverage of Medicaid services must be the same for an eligibility group throughout the entire

State. In other words, States cannot discriminate based on geographic location. Freedom of choice means beneficiaries must be free to obtain Medicaid services from any Medicaid provider qualified to perform the medically necessary service. States can seek waivers from the Federal government for these requirements—which many have to implement managed care programs—see below.

Early and Periodic Screening, Diagnostic, and Treatment (EPSDT) Services

Although States have considerable discretion to define their Medicaid benefit package, there is one benefit States have very little discretion to vary—Early and Periodic Screening, Diagnostic, and Treatment services (EPSDT) for Medicaid children (i.e., individuals under age 21). Under this mandatory service benefit, Federal requirements are strict.

The mandatory Early and Periodic Screening, Diagnostic, and Treatment services (EPSDT) benefit provides preventive and comprehensive medical services for Medicaid children. Under this benefit requirement, States must provide screening, vision, hearing, and dental services at appropriate intervals that meet recognized medical and dental practice (e.g., the American Academy of Pediatrics, etc.). Furthermore, States are required to provide coverage for any service (mandatory or optional) it is permitted to cover under Medicaid that is necessary to treat any illness or condition identified during an "EPSDT screen" (i.e., physician's visit in which screening services are conducted) regardless of whether the State covers the service for Medicaid adults.

In other words, whereas States have authority to define benefits for Medicaid adult beneficiaries—covering the nine mandatory services and selecting among the 31 optional services—States have no authority to restrict Medicaid services for children under the EPSDT benefit. States must provide coverage for the full array of mandatory and optional benefits available under Medicaid to children under age 21.

Medicaid Program Reforms: Federal and State Efforts

Since the Medicaid program was enacted in 1965, there have been significant changes to the program—changes in eligibility, services provided, and administration of the program. Many of these changes were made with respect to eligibility and service requirements for low-income women and children. In general, changes in eligibility and service requirements were mandated by the Federal government while changes in program administration were initiated by the States.

Many of the changes to the Medicaid program have been in response to the growing number of low-income individuals in need of medical assistance, the need to improve access to care, and the need to contain the rising cost of providing medical assistance.

Federal Legislative Changes

Expansions in Eligibility

Throughout the late 1970s and early 1980s, Medicaid overall coverage, in general, declined. Early program growth due to liberal eligibility criteria for medically needy individuals was constrained by States during the 1970s in an effort to control growing costs. Domestic spending cuts in the Omnibus Reconciliation Act of 1981 included a cap on Medicaid expenditures, and States responded by cutting services and reimbursement or limiting eligibility. In 1978, almost all children from families with incomes below the poverty level received Medicaid; by 1983, only 7 out of 10 children received Medicaid (*Prenatal Care,* 1991).

During the 1980s, Congress passed a series of Medicaid expansions creating new mandates on States for covering low-income pregnant women and children. These mandates were a reaction to a decline in maternal and infant health. The slowing of downward trends in infant mortality and the declining use of prenatal care among low-income, poorly educated, unmarried mothers encouraged Congress to increase mandates on States and expand Medicaid coverage (Wolfe, 1996). Congress legislated changes to improve access to prenatal and child health services.

The expansions were done in a stepwise fashion with States being allowed to extend coverage voluntarily in one year's legislation and then being required to extend coverage in subsequent legislation. The legislative changes allowed higher-income individuals to qualify for Medicaid—they also began the severing of the link between

Medicaid and welfare by extending coverage to families that did not fit into traditional welfare categories.

Between 1986 and 1990, Congress enacted the following sequence of legislative options and mandates to expand Medicaid eligibility thresholds for pregnant women, infants, and children.

- The Omnibus Budget Reconciliation Act (OBRA) of 1986 permitted States to extend Medicaid eligibility to poor pregnant women and infants with family incomes above AFDC levels but below a State established level up to 100% of the Federal poverty level. OBRA 1986 also permitted pregnant women to be determined temporarily eligible at health care setting while full application processing is completed (i.e., presumptive eligibility).
- OBRA 1987 permitted States to extend Medicaid coverage to pregnant women and infants with household incomes up to 185% of the Federal poverty level. The 1987 Act also permitted immediate coverage for children up to age 5 with household incomes up to 100% of poverty.
- The Medicare Catastrophic Coverage Act of 1988 (MCCA) required States to cover pregnant women and infants with incomes below 100% of poverty.
- OBRA 1989 required States to provide Medicaid coverage to pregnant women and children to age 6 from households with incomes up to 133% of poverty.
- OBRA 1990 required States to phase in Medicaid coverage of children to age 19, born after September 30, 1983, in families with incomes under 100% of the Federal poverty level. OBRA 1990 also required States to provide continuous eligibility to newborns through the infant's first year of life provided the infant remains in the mother's household (CRS, 1993).

The goals of these expansions were to increase enrollment among pregnant women who otherwise could not afford appropriate care; increase the timeliness and adequacy of prenatal care; and improve birth outcomes. Many States used the opportunity of the legislative program expansions to implement revisions in application and eligibility procedures to overcome various barriers for enrolling potential beneficiaries in their programs. Outreach and public information campaigns were initiated in many States to inform potential beneficiaries about the program expansions (Wolfe, 1996).

As a result, the legislative and administrative changes implemented by Federal and State governments significantly increased Medicaid enrollment of low-income pregnant women. In 12 States between 1988 and 1990, Medicaid covered deliveries grew by 44%, Medicaid's share of total deliveries by 29%, and Medicaid payment for deliveries by over 400% ("Reform of State Medicaid Programs," 1996). Enrollment of the newly eligible populations is more difficult to determine. In 10 States from 1987 to 1990, a 10-percentage-point increase in the Medicaid-eligible population was associated with an increase of approximately 5% in Medicaid finance deliveries ("Reform of State Medicaid Programs," 1996).

It was intended that this improvement in the timeliness and comprehensiveness of health care result in improvements in health outcomes. Lack of early prenatal care has been directly linked to low birth weight. However, it is too early to tell whether these expansions have had an impact yet on low birth weight and infant mortality rates.

Balanced Budget Act of 1997

Although policy changes in the late 1980s helped increase the number of children enrolled in Medicaid, the overall number of children who were uninsured did not decline, because employer-based health care coverage for children and adults also declined during the same period. As a result, the Medicaid eligibility expansions of the late 1980s helped offset the impact of the decline in employer-based health care coverage. Without the Medicaid expansions, many more children would have been uninsured.

In 1997, Congress passed additional legislation to enhance health care coverage for children—Medicaid-eligible and otherwise. The Balanced Budget Act of 1997 contained several significant provisions related to children's health—including the creation of a new children's health insurance program to provide health insurance to low-income children with family incomes too high to qualify for Medicaid coverage (see below.)

Medicaid Provisions. The Medicaid provisions related to children's health were presumptive eligibility for children, 12-month continuous eligibility for children, and a new State option to expedite the coverage of children born after September 30, 1983 created under OBRA 1990. These provisions were designed to reach the estimated

3 million children who are eligible for Medicaid but not enrolled ("Heath Insurance for Children: Private Insurance," 1996).

The new presumptive eligibility authority allows States the option of establishing a presumptive Medicaid eligibility procedure to facilitate the enrollment of children. Certain qualified entities such as Head Start facilities, WIC centers, certain hospitals, and so on, may enroll children in Medicaid on a temporary basis and begin providing medical services immediately. Applicants must apply for Medicaid enrollment within a certain time period and are subject to the same eligibility criteria.

The new 12-month continuous eligibility provision allows States to guarantee 12 months of coverage to children enrolled in Medicaid regardless of whether changes in family income or other circumstances that would render them ineligible for Medicaid occur during the 12-month period. This provision ensures continuity of coverage for health care services, particularly in cases where fluctuations in family income result in temporary loss of Medicaid coverage.

The new State option to expedite the coverage of children born after September 30, 1983 allows States to accelerate the phasing in of coverage of all children under age 19 with family incomes below 100% FPL.

Title XXI: State Children's Health Insurance Program. The Medicaid expansions of the late 1980s provided many previously uninsured children access to health care coverage; however, the crisis of uninsured individuals—particularly children—continues to grow. The majority of uninsured children live in families in which one or both parents are working (Families USA, 1997a). Despite a strong economy, there has been a steady decline in employer-based coverage—particularly for dependents. Although the Medicaid expansions of the late 1980s helped offset the impact of the decline in employer-based coverage, it is estimated that there are approximately 10 million children without insurance for 12 months or longer in a 2-year period (Families USA, 1997a).

In 1997, Congress and the Administration responded to this crisis by creating a new program to expand health insurance coverage to millions of low-income children. The Balanced Budget Act of 1997 created a new children's health insurance program under Title XXI of the Social Security Act. This program is called the State Children's Health Insurance Program (SCHIP). SCHIP enables States to initiate and expand health insurance coverage for low-income children. Designed to assist with the provision of health insurance to children without private insurance who don't qualify for Medicaid, SCHIP provides States with a unique opportunity to design and implement innovative approaches to expanding health insurance coverage.

Many States had already implemented programs to provide health insurance coverage to these children. The SCHIP program was created to encourage other States to implement similar programs and to enhance and expand programs in operation at the time SCHIP was created.

Under SCHIP, Federal matching funds ($40 billion over 10 years) are provided to States that elect to provide health insurance coverage to uninsured children. States can cover uninsured children by expanding Medicaid, creating or expanding separate State insurance programs (e.g., purchase commercial insurance policies), or a combination of both options. The way States design their programs will affect how many children will be covered and the costs States incur (Kaiser, 1997).

For many States, an expansion of their Medicaid program to cover these children will be the easiest approach. For these States, a system is already in place for enrolling beneficiaries, paying providers, and monitoring and regulating quality of care. Administrative costs are lower under Medicaid than private insurance, and there is public administration and accountability. However, there are several disincentives to implement SCHIP through an expansion to Medicaid. States will have to adhere to all Medicaid rules under this approach. This means States must provide the complete Medicaid benefit package to this new population, including EPSDT services. States must also provide all beneficiary protections to this population. State discretion with respect to SCHIP cannot be more restrictive than Medicaid for States choosing to implement SCHIP through Medicaid.

States choosing to implement SCHIP by establishing a separate insurance program have much more discretion than they do under Medicaid. SCHIP can be more restrictive than Medicaid in terms of eligibility standards, the benefit package, coverage of preexisting conditions, managed care protections, due process, cost sharing, and other factors (Families USA, 1997a). States don't have to comply with Federal Medicaid mandates and may provide fewer protections than they would under Medicaid. SCHIP is not an entitlement program, so States can stop enrollment when funds are exhausted rather than have to allocate more funds to the program or reduce benefits to those already covered.

Expansion of Services

In addition to expansions in eligibility, Congress has also made changes in the services covered by Medicaid. These legislative changes to Medicaid services were mandated to improve health outcomes for beneficiaries. With respect to children, the two most substantial changes affecting Medicaid services are the treatment provision under the Early and Periodic Screening, Diagnostic, and Treatment program (EPSDT) and the creation of the Vaccines for Children program (VFC) in 1993.

EPSDT. In 1967, Congress added EPSDT services to the list of mandatory services States must cover under their Medicaid programs. EPSDT was designed to provide preventive and comprehensive services to children covered by Medicaid. The scope of services provided under the rubric of EPSDT has changed several times since EPSDT services were added to the list of mandatory services States must provide to their mandatory eligible groups.

Initially, EPSDT services were defined as "early and periodic screening and diagnosis of individuals who are under the age of 21, to ascertain their physical or mental defects, and such health care, treatment, and other measures to correct or ameliorate defects and chronic conditions discovered thereby, as may be provided in regulations of the Secretary."

OBRA 1989 defined in statute explicit services to be provided under EPSDT and removed the Secretary's authority to define EPSDT services. OBRA 1989 added distinct periodicity schedules for screening, dental, vision, and hearing services and required medically necessary interperiodic screening services. More significantly, however, OBRA 1989 added the following new service requirement: "other necessary health care, diagnostic services, treatment and other measures . . . to correct or ameliorate defects and physical and mental illnesses and conditions discovered by the screening services whether or not such services are covered under the State plan."

This last provision requires States to provide any Medicaid service necessary to correct an illness or condition in an individual under age 21 discovered by screening services—even if the State doesn't provide the service to its Medicaid population. This "treatment mandate" on States to provide whatever is necessary to correct an illness or condition is a contentious issue with States. Many States contend this treatment requirement under EPSDT is a significant factor affecting States' ability to keep Medicaid costs under control. In recent years, there have been several unsuccessful legislative proposals to redefine or eliminate the treatment requirement for EPSDT services.

VFC. In response to a variety of concerns regarding the timely vaccination of children, particularly preschool-aged children, Congress created a new entitlement program—the Vaccines for Children program (VFC) in 1993. One of the goals of the VFC program was to increase immunization rates among children by providing free pediatric vaccines. It was believed the provision of free pediatric vaccine would help eliminate a significant barrier to appropriate and timely vaccination—cost. VFC was created with the goal of ensuring that 90% of all children under the age of 2 were age-appropriately immunized.

Under this entitlement program, the Federal government purchases vaccines on behalf of "Federally Vaccine Eligible" children age 18 and under, including all Medicaid children, uninsured children, children receiving services at Federal health clinics whose insurance plans do not cover immunizations, and Native Americans/Native Alaskans. Vaccines are provided free to States for Federally Vaccine Eligible children. States can also purchase vaccine for other children at a discounted price. It is estimated by the U.S. Department of Health and Human Services that approximately 62% of the babies born each year are VFC eligible.

By Federalizing the purchase of childhood vaccine, the VFC program has allowed States and their Medicaid program to redirect certain public health dollars to other services.

State Changes

Eligibility

In addition to meeting the new Federal mandates on eligibility, States have used other mechanisms to expand eligibility and services beyond the Federal mandates. Taking advantage of coverage and waiver options provided in law, States have been successful in their efforts to expand Medicaid coverage to low-income individuals, improve access, and contain costs.

OBRA 1989 and OBRA 1990 allowed States to expand Medicaid coverage of pregnant women and children beyond the Federal mandates. As of August 1996, 34 States covered pregnant women and infants up to the optional maximum level of 185% FPL; 12 other States covered pregnant women and infants at levels above the minimum 133% but below the maximum income level allowed (National Governor's Association, 1996).

Some States have opted to broaden their eligibility coverage by using more liberal methods for calculating financial eligibility. Section 1902(r)(2) of the Medicaid statute—added by the Medicare Catastrophic Care Act of 1988—allows States to use more liberal income and resource methodologies than those used for the AFDC program to determine Medicaid financial eligibility. By disregarding additional amounts of income and resources, States can qualify certain populations for Medicaid that are not traditionally entitled to Medicaid benefits because they don't qualify for AFDC benefits. States have utilized this provision to expand Medicaid coverage broadly for pregnant women and children (National Governor's Association, 1996).

Numerous States have sought and been granted research and demonstration waivers from the Health Care Financing Administration that permit them more flexibility in designing their Medicaid programs. States have used these waivers to change their Medicaid program significantly—including expanding eligibility to cover nontraditional Medicaid populations (i.e., children in families with incomes above Medicaid levels). These broad-based demonstrations are commonly referred to as "Section 1115 demonstrations" (see below).

Managed Care

Like other health care purchasers, the Medicaid program is increasingly moving into a managed care environment. Managed care is of interest to States because it appears to offer a way to control Medicaid costs by changing beneficiary behaviors and provider incentives.

Since its inception, the Medicaid program has experienced rapid expenditure growth. In particular, Medicaid costs escalated sharply between 1985 and 1993. The reasons for the dramatic increase in costs were numerous. The Congressionally mandated eligibility expansions, medical price inflation, higher provider reimbursements, and utilization growth all contributed to the escalating costs. By 1995, 19% of state spending was attributed to Medicaid ("Health Insurance for Children: Many Remain Uninsured," 1995). To constrain rising Medicaid costs, States have increasingly turned to mandatory enrollment in managed care delivery systems.

States have been using various types of managed care almost since the program's inception. States have contracted with health maintenance organizations (HMOs) for voluntary enrollment to provide Medicaid services to beneficiaries since the early years of the Medicaid program. Since 1981, many States have mandated managed care enrollment for certain Medicaid beneficiaries—predominantly women and children—by using Federal waivers. Other States have opted to use primary care case managers, which are basically "gate keepers," in a fee-for-service setting. Some States use fully capitated systems with the providers being financially responsible for the services beneficiaries use; other States use "partial capitation systems" where the provider is not held at risk for the most expensive services such as inpatient hospital services.

In recent years, enrollment in Medicaid managed care plans has increased significantly. Since January 1, 1993, enrollment in Medicaid managed care plans has increased by more than 170%, including a 33% increase from 1995 to 1996. As of June 30, 1996, 13 million Medicaid beneficiaries were enrolled in managed care plans, representing 35% of all Medicaid beneficiaries. Currently, 48 States offer some form of managed care (U.S. Department of Health and Human Services, 1997).

Federal Waivers. The significant increase in Medicaid managed care enrollment is due to State utilization of Federal Medicaid waivers. The waivers allow States to increase enrollment in managed care and to develop other innovative changes to their Medicaid programs. Several States have used the resulting savings from managed care enrollment to expand the number of individuals covered by Medicaid and/or the number of services covered under their programs. The Federal government grants two kinds of Medicaid managed care waivers: Section 1915(b) waivers, known as "freedom of choice" waivers, and Section 1115 demonstrations.

"Freedom of Choice" Waivers. Section 1915(b) or freedom of choice waivers permit States to require beneficiaries to enroll in managed care plans. These waivers allow States to restrict the beneficiaries' choice of provider to those within a managed care organization. These waivers are approved for 2-year time increments and can be renewed. To receive such a waiver, States must prove that these plans have the capacity to serve Medicaid beneficiaries who will be enrolled in the plan. States often use Section 1915(b) waivers to establish primary care case management programs and other forms of managed care. Through January 1997, HCFA had approved 96 Section 1915(b) waivers.

In August 1997, Congress eliminated the 1915(b)(1) freedom of choice waiver and allowed States to mandatorily enroll beneficiaries into managed care without requiring a Federal waiver. Congress did this to eliminate the administrative requirements States must meet in order to initiate or renew managed care programs. Congress believed the elimination of the need for a Federal waiver would make it easier for States to move into managed care delivery systems for their Medicaid beneficiaries.

Section 1115 Demonstrations. Section 1115 demonstrations allow States to test new approaches to benefits, services, eligibility, program payments, and service delivery, often on a Statewide basis. These approaches are frequently aimed at saving money to allow States to extend Medicaid coverage to additional low-income and uninsured people. Generally, Section 1115 demonstrations have several common factors: the State wants to expand its use of managed care; savings are expected to be achieved as one of the outcomes of increased use of managed care; and the savings are used to finance coverage to individuals previously ineligible for Medicaid.

Section 1115 demonstration initiatives range from projects that test providing special services to special populations, to projects that test some major restructuring of the Medicaid program and facilitate the State's goal for health care reform, to expanding Medicaid coverage to previously uninsured individuals. Unlike the freedom of choice waivers, projects initiated under Section 1115 have to demonstrate something that has not been tried or proposed on a widespread basis.

Since January 1, 1993, the Secretary of Health and Human Services has approved 17 comprehensive Section 1115 health care demonstration waivers. Of the approved demonstrations, 15 have been implemented. According to the Health Care Financing Administration, these implemented demonstrations have permitted 2.2 million previously uninsured individuals to receive health coverage. The implemented demonstrations are in: Alabama, Arkansas, Delaware, Hawaii, Maryland, Massachusetts, Minnesota, New York, Ohio, Oklahoma, Rhode Island, Tennessee, and Vermont.

Welfare Reform

In addition to the direct changes made to the Medicaid program over the years, there have been some indirect influences on the program as well—namely through changes to the welfare program Aid for Families with Dependent Children (AFDC.)

During the 104th Congress there were direct efforts to drastically change the Medicaid program and other public assistance programs receiving Federal funding. The efforts to change the Medicaid program focused on creating a block grant of Federal funds with limited requirements on the States. This block grant proposal would have ended the entitlement status of Medicaid, eliminated certain Federal protections for beneficiaries, and left States with much more discretion for operating their State Medicaid programs.

The effort to block grant Medicaid did not succeed; however, Congress did succeed in changing the Aid for Families with Dependent Children (AFDC) program. Through the Personal Responsibility and Work Opportunity Act of 1996 (P.L. 104-193), Congress replaced the AFDC program with a welfare block grant to States. This new welfare block grant—Temporary Assistance for Needy Families (TANF)—provides States with extensive discretion for providing public assistance to low-income individuals. Although it did not directly address Medicaid, the elimination of AFDC and the creation of a new block grant significantly affected Medicaid eligibility.

Impact on Medicaid

The new welfare legislation changed Medicaid eligibility policy in four principal ways. First, the law decoupled welfare and Medicaid eligibility. Second, it narrowed the definition of childhood disability for receipt of Supplemental Security Income (SSI), thus reducing the number of children with disabilities or special needs qualifying for Medicaid. Third, the welfare law terminated SSI benefits for some legal immigrants—again eliminating their access to Medicaid. And finally, the welfare law barred most future legal immigrants from Medicaid (Coughlin & Ku, 1996). These changes resulted in a decrease in the number of individuals receiving Medicaid. Within a year of the welfare law passing, Congress started to take steps to reinstate Medicaid eligibility for some of these individuals.

However, it is believed that a decline in Medicaid coverage due to welfare reform will continue for a while due to a "chilling effect" caused by welfare reform. There are many concerns that the severing of welfare and Medicaid and new Federal restrictions on the receipt of welfare assistance has resulted in complex rules that will leave many people slipping through the system's cracks.

Prior to welfare reform, individuals who received AFDC cash assistance or who were deemed to have received AFDC were *automatically* eligible for Medicaid—in many cases they were enrolled in Medicaid and AFDC simultaneously. Families that lost AFDC cash assistance because of employment or receipt of child (or spousal) support payments were eligible for Medicaid for an additional period of time. Various rules of the AFDC program were used to establish Medicaid eligibility under other Medicaid-only eligibility groups (e.g., pregnant women and children whose eligibility is related to the poverty level, optional groups of children and caretaker relatives who do not receive AFDC, and the medically needy). Under the new welfare law, all of this has changed.

The new welfare law severed the link between welfare assistance and medical assistance (i.e., Medicaid). Receipt of assistance (e.g., cash payments) through the new welfare block grant does not automatically result in eligibility for Medicaid. The new Temporary Assistance to Needy Families (TANF) block grant is not an entitlement program, and eligibility for TANF is not linked to eligibility to any other Federally funded program.

Congress severed the connection between welfare and Medicaid because it was feared the tighter welfare eligibility criteria required by the new block grant would unintentionally cause many people to lose Medicaid coverage. Under the new welfare law, there are Federal "behavior" requirements that recipients of TANF benefits must adhere to or they will lose their benefits. For example, TANF recipients cannot receive TANF benefits for more than 5 years—they will automatically be cut off from benefits when they exceed 5 years. Another example is that unwed teenage mothers receiving TANF benefits must live at home with their parents or a guardian in order to maintain their benefits. These "behavioral require- ments" are the only Federal requirements imposed on recipients of TANF benefits. The authority for determining eligibility criteria and benefit levels is with the States.

States have the discretion to determine eligibility criteria and benefits provided under TANF. States are allowed to establish their own income, resource, and assets criteria for individuals applying for welfare assistance. States can establish their own income disre- gards for determining eligibility. Furthermore, States can determine what type of assistance an individual will receive. Cash assistance is no longer the sole form of public assistance. Under the welfare block grant, States can choose to provide vouchers for a variety of things including transportation, utility bills, day care, and more.

Because these tighter restrictions (Federal and State) will move individuals off of welfare—either by succeeding to move people into the workforce or through the termination of benefits due to the 5-year limit—Congress sought to maintain health insurance coverage for these individuals.

In order to maintain Medicaid coverage, Congress decided to "freeze" Medicaid rules. Congress imposed special provisions un- der which States are required, for purposes of Medicaid, to main- tain the AFDC eligibility rules that were in effect prior to enactment of welfare reform. In general, those who would have qualified for Medicaid under the old welfare rules—irrespective of whether they are eligible for TANF—will be eligible for Medicaid. For example, a family that loses TANF benefits due to the time limit will remain eligible for Medicaid as long as they meet the AFDC eligibility rules that were in effect as of July 16, 1996.

This means States have to do two eligibility determinations—one for TANF and a separate one for Medicaid. This may prove to be administratively difficult for States. If States establish TANF eligibility criteria that are substantially different from the AFDC criteria in place prior to enactment of the welfare law, the link between cash assistance and medical assistance is broken. States will have to find ways to ensure Medicaid-eligible individuals are identified and enrolled in the program. In general, it is in the States' financial interest to enroll all Medicaid-eligible individuals, and a link between eligibility for cash assistance and eligibility for medical assistance makes it easy for States to enroll the majority of their Medicaid population.

As a result, in the first few years since enactment of welfare reform, many States have chosen to administratively maintain a connection between welfare and Medicaid. Many States are retaining the welfare income and resource eligibility criteria that were in place for AFDC in 1996 for their new TANF programs (Koppelman, 1997). Two separate eligibility determinations still must take place; however, the common financial eligibility criteria makes it easier for States to identify and enroll Medicaid eligibles.

The complete impact, direct and indirect, of the welfare reform law on the Medicaid program won't be fully understood until State TANF programs are operating for a while and individuals start to leave the welfare system. One future challenge for States will be to identify former welfare recipients in the workforce still eligible for Medicaid and continue their participation in the program.

Conclusion

The Medicaid program has grown and evolved substantially since its inception in 1965. Future changes to the program are likely as Federal and State governments continue to balance the various social, economic, and political factors affecting the Medicaid program and other programs within the Federal safety net.

Congress and States will likely continue their efforts to provide access to health care to uninsured children. A part of this effort will be a continued push to enroll all Medicaid-eligible children in the program. The success of this effort will be tied to the operation of the new State welfare block grant, Temporary Assistance to Needy Families, and the new State Child Health Insurance Program.

The impact of the new welfare program on Medicaid participation rates will determine if cash assistance and medical assistance remain separate in terms of eligibility criteria. If the number of Medicaid-eligible children not enrolled in the program increases, Federal and State changes to the program are likely to occur. Congress may choose to "re-link" the eligibility criteria of the two programs, and States may pursue new options to enhance outreach efforts and to streamline their Medicaid eligibility process to better facilitate enrollment.

The operation and success of the SCHIP program will also affect decisions for any future changes to the Medicaid program. Designed to provide health care coverage to children with family incomes too high to qualify for Medicaid, the success of the program to cover these children will directly affect the need for any future eligibility expansions under Medicaid. States implementing SCHIP programs must determine how the program is to interact and/or build off of the State Medicaid program. Coordination between the two programs is essential to ensure seamless access to health care coverage for all low-income children.

Note

1. Prior to welfare reform in 1996, Medicaid eligibility was directly linked to receipt of AFDC. The new welfare law now requires States to provide Medicaid to individuals who meet the AFDC financial criteria the State had in place on July 16, 1996.

References

Congressional Research Services. (1993). *Medicaid source book: Background data and analysis: A 1993 update.* Washington, DC: Government Printing Office.

Coughlin, T., & Ku, L. (1996). *How the new welfare reform law affects Medicaid.* Washington, DC: Urban Institute Press.

Families USA. (1997a). *A preliminary guide to expansion of children's health coverage* [Issue brief posted on the World Wide Web]. Washington, D.C. Retrieved December 1997 from the World Wide Web: http.//www.epn.org/tcf/mdcdrght.html

Families USA. (1997b). *What's right with Medicaid?* [Issue brief posted on the World Wide Web]. Washington, D.C. Retrieved December 1997 from the World Wide Web: http.//www.epn.org/tcf/mdcdrght.html

Health insurance for children: Many remain uninsured despite Medicaid expansion. (GAO/HEHS-95-175 July, 1995). Washington, DC: Government Printing Office.

Health insurance for children: Private insurance coverage continues to deteriorate. (GAO/HEHS-96-129). Washington, DC: Government Printing Office.

The Henry Kaiser Family Foundation, The Kaiser Commission on the Future of Medicaid. (1997, November). *Child health facts* (Available from Henry Kaiser Family Foundation, 1450 G St., NW, Suite 250, Washington, D.C. 20005)

Holahan J., & Liska, D. (1997, January). Variations in Medicaid spending among states. *The Urban Institute—New Federalism Issues and Options for States*, Series A, No. A-3.

Koppelman, J. (1997). *Impact of the new welfare law on Medicaid* (Issue Brief No. 697). Washington, DC: National Health Policy Forum.

Medicaid: Restructuring approaches leave many questions. (GAO/HEHS-95-103, April 1995). Washington, DC: Government Printing Office.

Medicaid Section 1115 waivers: Flexible approach to approving demonstrations could increase federal costs (GAO/HEHS-96-44, November 1995). Washington, DC: Government Printing Office.

Medicaid—States turn to managed care to improve access and control costs (GAO/HRD-93-46, March 1993). Washington, DC: Government Printing Office.

National Governor's Association, Center for Policy Research. (1996, September). *MCH update—State coverage of pregnant women and children—Summer 1996.* Washington, DC: Author.

Prenatal care: Early success in enrolling women made eligible by Medicaid expansions (GAO/PEMD-91-10, February 1991). Washington, DC: Government Printing Office.

Reform of state Medicaid programs. (1996). *Focus, 17*(3), 24-29.

U.S. Department of Health and Human Services, Health Care Financing Administration. (1997). *Brief summaries of Medicaid and Medicare* [Summaries posted on World Wide Web]. Washington, D.C. Retrieved January 1997, http//www.HCFA.gov.

U.S. Department of Health and Human Services, Health Care Financing Administration. (1995). *Medicaid statistics 1995.* Baltimore, MD: Author.

U.S. House of Representatives, Democratic Policy Committee. (1997, January). *A democrat's briefing book on Medicaid issues for the 105th Congress.* January 1997. Washington, DC: U.S. House Democratic Policy Committee.

Wolfe, B. (1996). A Medicaid primer. *Focus, 17*(3), 1-6.

CHAPTER 3

Mental Health Care Coverage for Children and Families

MICHAEL M. FAENZA

ELIZABETH STEEL

Many of us believe that when it comes to mental health services, children get the short end of a short stick. As many as 41 million people in the United States do not have adequate access to primary health care. Access to mental health care is even more limited, and children have less access than adults to those few services that do exist. Not only does stigma make people with psychiatric symptoms an easy target for discriminatory health insurance practices, but attempts to avoid stigma make us reluctant to admit that children can suffer from mental illness. That makes it easier for policymakers to decide to target resources only toward people, primarily adults, who carry certain catastrophic diagnoses. Children who have emotional disturbances may receive little or nothing in the way of service, although integrated systems of care and flexible wraparound services for these children can save both lives and money.

The extent of need is clear:

- One in five American children between birth and 17 years of age has a diagnosable mental disorder (Brandenberg, Friedman, & Silver, 1990).
- Almost 7 million youngsters between 9 and 17 years of age have serious emotional disturbances accompanied by substantial or extreme functional impairments ("Estimation Methodology," 1997).

117

- Suicide is the sixth leading cause of death for 5- to 14-year-olds in the United States (Chidley, 1998).
- Sixty-one percent of youth entering the Georgia juvenile justice system have psychiatric disorders (Emory University, 1996).

The inadequacy of present coverage has also been demonstrated:

- The children's mental health system is seriously underfunded and in most states is serving only about 25% of children in need (Pritchard, 1997).
- By law, children covered by Medicaid must receive Early and Periodic Screening, Diagnostic, and Treatment (EPSDT) services, but 6 in 10 children enrolled in Medicaid managed care plans did not get these services ("Tennessee Officials Reach Settlement," 1998).
- In Tennessee, the Medicaid mental health carve-out program sets criteria that make it difficult for a child to be considered to have a serious emotional disorder (SED). Children with mental health problems but without the SED designation can qualify only for inpatient and outpatient care. Day treatment services have been reduced by 75% (NMHA State Healthcare Reform training summary, 1997).

But there are reasons to hope:

- Advances in research and theory have led to a better understanding of how to meet the mental health needs of children. The concept, philosophy, and structure of *system of care* were developed and promoted (Stroul & Friedman, 1994) when parents banded together as advocates and joined in partnership with mental health professionals on behalf of their children. At the same time, scientists began to prove the effectiveness of pharmacologic treatments for disorders such as childhood depression.
- Federal parity legislation requires large employers to provide the same aggregate annual and lifetime benefit limits in health insurance plans for mental and physical health care (the Domenici-Wellstone, Mental Health Parity Act of 1996; see U.S. Congress, 1996) Unfortunately, children's needs weren't met by this legislation despite the best advocacy efforts of the National Mental Health Association (NMHA) and other advocacy organizations (Faenza, 1996).
- Many states are passing or considering more comprehensive parity laws that can make a full range of appropriate, community-based mental health services available to children and their families.

- A new $24 billion federal block grant program can make health insurance coverage (including at least minimal mental health benefits) available to as many as 2.5 million currently uninsured children.

Thus, having worked in a variety of roles as mental health practitioners and public policy advocates, the authors view the past two decades as years that produced both progress and missed opportunities in the United States for children and adolescents with mental disorders. Tragically, in 1998, millions of our most vulnerable children and families still lack access to the decent medical and social services that are crucial to their future well-being and productivity. There has been only limited political will to improve the plight of young people with mental disorders or to set a high priority on children's mental health.

Perhaps some of this neglect stems from the complexity of the task and, indeed, of the population involved. Those who are concerned about children's health understand that complexity is a hallmark of childhood. Each child changes throughout an extended period of development and growth. A child's health must be evaluated in terms of both the context and the flow of his or her life. At any particular point in time, the child's mental health is inseparable from his physical condition, the environment in which he functions, and the people with whom he interacts. Therefore, services for a child with mental health treatment needs must flow from a multifaceted *system of care,* rather than from one or a group of identified mental health provider(s).

Vulnerability is another hallmark of childhood. A child must depend heavily on others for physical care and for the nurture and guidance that lead to successful development. Adults must serve as caregivers for children, calibrating the amount of care given to the amount of care needed, which is a fluctuating measure. In addition, children cannot be expected to ensure that adequate support is available to meet their needs, so adults must also serve as advocates for children. Therefore, parents or parent surrogates must be completely involved in any treatment decisions related to their child's mental health.

This is the framework within which we at the National Mental Health Association view our role in children's mental health. We believe there is a great, unmet need for adequate and appropriate mental health services for children and their families. We are concerned about children who suffer from biologically based brain disorders and about their families. We are also advocates for children and families who are dealing with emotional disorders that cannot necessarily be traced to physiologic phenomena. More generally, we seek ways to promote mental health and prevent mental and behavioral disorders in all children and adolescents and in their families.

Historical Perspective

Early History

Children's mental health is a relatively recent addition to the public policy agenda. In 1969, a study issued by the Joint Commission on the Mental Health of Children (1969) addressed the needs of children with serious emotional, behavioral, or mental disturbance. It concluded that most such children were either underserved or served within overly restrictive institutional settings. Other studies and reports agreed with the Commission's findings that the children and their families would best be served by community-based, family-centered, coordinated systems of care.

The service problems identified by the Commission had not changed significantly by 1982, when Jane Knitzer's classic work, *Unclaimed Children* was published by the Children's Defense Fund. "Preventive or intensive community-based services are in scarce supply," she wrote in the preface. "Overreliance on costly institutional and residential care is the norm" (Knitzer, 1982, p. vii).

Fortunately, Knitzer's report made a difference. Largely in response to her findings, the National Institute of Mental Health began its highly regarded Child and Adolescent Service System Program (CASSP). CASSP and its successor, the Planning and System Development Program (PSDP), will be addressed in greater detail later in this chapter. First, however, we will briefly address mental health services that predate these formal federal efforts.

Medical historian Gerald Grob (1994) has pointed out the cyclical nature of the history of services for the mentally ill in America. Although he addresses services for adults, there is much in his work that is applicable to children. For more than four centuries, he says, we have vacillated between "enthusiastic optimism and fatalistic pessimism," between a belief that we can "cure" all mental illnesses and a hopeless surrender to "chronicity" (p. 543). Grob writes of times when the responsibility for a community's vulnerable people remained with the family and the community. He contrasts these with other times when the costs and responsibilities were shifted to broader governmental levels ("the transformation of insanity into a *social* problem requiring state intervention"). He discusses the effect of diagnostic changes on service needs, such as the redefinition of senility in psychiatric terms, and he notes therapeutic advances that have helped many people with severe and persistent mental illnesses to live successfully in community settings.

Most important, Grob reminds us that people with mental illnesses may have need of both therapy and management. *Even in the absence of cure, a good quality of life may be achieved through appropriate use of a range of social and environmental supports.* The children we are talking about usually can be served in their home communities. These services may even cost less than the treatment we now often provide in distant and impersonal institutions. Many children in our systems of care will graduate to participation in adult society. Others will need help in making the transition into the adult mental health system, and they may need ongoing medication management, therapies, and supportive services so they can take part in community life. These, too, are our children and they, too, deserve the best we can provide according to the best scientific knowledge of our day.

The early history of services for children with emotional and behavioral disorders is a bit difficult to track. Early American laws and policies were addressed toward poverty rather than illness. The English Poor Laws, for example, were adapted for use in the Colonies. They offered some support for people with disabilities, but they were far more emphatic about deterring indolence among those who were able to work. Families that were not financially independent were considered morally unfit to care for their children. The children were often removed from the home and bound out as apprentices, thus protected from the contagion of their parents' inadequacies (Axinn & Levin, 1992, chap. 2). We suppose that, with a stretch of the imagination, this might be characterized as a mental health prevention program!

The history of children's mental health services tends to travel along lines related to specific systems, that is, the schools and the juvenile courts. The concept of comprehensive systems of care, involving multiple child-serving systems, is relatively new, as we have already stated.

Sedlak (1997) provides an overview of the history of school-based mental health services, tracing their origins to a period surrounding the start of the 20th century (1890-1917). A high school education, once a luxury for the elite, became available to the masses. At the same time, educators came to believe that the schools could and should address all social problems. "Visiting teachers," who often came out of the settlement house movement and later evolved into professional school social workers, helped the mostly immigrant families to find work and obtain material goods so their children could remain in school. A few programs were set up to diagnose and treat emotional and mental problems among schoolchildren, and guidance counselors began to help adolescents plan and initiate their careers. Perhaps the first psychological clinics were set up in the late 1890s in Philadelphia and other urban centers by universities and medical institutions. Their purpose was to help the schools take care of children with "mental and moral retardation."

After World War I, interest rose in treating the middle and privileged classes, rather than attacking the problems of the working class and the poor. Professionalization led to helpers who preferred to focus on individual psychology rather than on broad social and economic problems. Basically, mental health professionals were expanding their client base to include all children with or at risk for maladjustment and behavioral problems.

At around the same time that schools were discovering mental health services, so were juvenile courts beginning to codify a reform-based approach for children who were not yet hardened offenders (Axinn & Levin, 1992, p. 141). The first juvenile court law, titled *An Act to Regulate the Treatment and Control of Dependent, Neglected, and Delinquent Children,* was enacted in 1899 in Illinois. However, rehabilitation had been addressed earlier in the century by, for example, providing separate prison facilities for children and adults to avoid contamination of the potentially "redeemable" children. In an article reviewing the early history of juvenile courts, Fox (1996) notes that houses of refuge, which developed in the first half of the 19th century, shared basic operating principles: (a) segregating youngsters from adult offenders, (b) setting a goal of rehabilitation, and (c) restricting treatment to children who were deemed amenable to treatment. Unfortunately, the houses of refuge and later institutions often failed in attempts to separate children who had committed criminal acts from children who were victims of abuse, neglect, or emotional disturbance. There were continued tensions, as well, between a focus on rehabilitation and a focus on punishment.

Around the beginning of the 20th century, some juvenile judges took on the role of advocate (and perhaps therapist) for the individual children who came before them. Judge Ben B. Lindsey of Denver, for example, is cited by Fox (1996) as someone whose "juvenile court was a vigorous machine for social engineering, reaching out to reform everything that adversely affected children, from the corruption of the police to the need for playgrounds. But reaching out to foster a close relationship with each individual child was the quintessence of [his] . . . court" (p. 34). The influence of activist juvenile judges was extended through the use of probation staff, who soon evolved into professionally trained social workers and other mental health professionals. Child guidance clinics became affiliated with some juvenile courts, but an outcome study in Boston in 1934 that showed an almost 90% recidivism rate led to a loss of confidence in the utility of psychological treatment (Fox, 1996, p. 37).

Juvenile court systems continue to generate controversy, particularly in regard to issues related to the legal rights of the children versus the broad authority of the court to make decisions about placement and care. Concerns about the availability of mental health services for adjudicated or incarcerated children with serious emotional disturbances also continue into the present day.

Recent History and Current Trends

Children with mental health disorders generally have been treated far from their homes and families in institutional inpatient settings. Perhaps the most important change in public policy relating to the mental health of children has been a move toward trying to marshal the resources of a variety of systems to meet the needs of individual children and families in their home communities. Bringing the children home has been a great cost-saver as well as a welcome step toward normalization. However, setting up and maintaining true systems of care is a challenge for all child-serving systems (e.g., child welfare, education, primary health care, and juvenile justice, as well as mental health).

There is a fair consensus that integrated systems of care are best for the children. Lourie, Howe, and Roebuck (1996, p. 99) date this "modern era of system building" to the work of the Joint Commission on the Mental Health of Children. In its final report in 1969, the Commission recommended that a national child advocacy system should be set in place to operate simultaneously at all levels of government. It also cited the need for an array of services, a trained cadre of personnel, and a research agenda.

Implementation efforts moved in the right direction but were less than noteworthy until after Knitzer's report was issued. Congress responded with a $1.5 million dollar appropriation to the National Institute of Mental Health and instructed it through report language to spend the money on a program for children and adolescents that would be similar to the Community Support Program for adults. As a result, the Child and Adolescent Service System Program (CASSP) was initiated in 1984. Renamed the Planning and Systems Development Program (PSDP), the program is currently housed within the federal Center for Mental Health Services (CMHS) of the Substance Abuse and Mental Health Administration.

CASSP funds supported the identification of core principles and values for systems of care, as well as planning initiatives by states and localities that wanted to demonstrate and test system models. A later program, Comprehensive Community Mental Health Services for Children with Serious Emotional Disturbances, was authorized and funded beginning in 1993 and presently supports 31 demonstrations. Technical assistance has been an important part of both programs.

Other service planning and demonstration money has come from the Robert Wood Johnson Foundation, the Annie E. Casey Foundation, and from federal Mental Health Block Grant legislation. Funds for service delivery primarily came from state appropriations until the 1980s. Since then, additional sources of funds have been identified, including Medicaid, child welfare entitlements, and flexible funding streams developed by integrating both services and resources across child-serving agencies (Behar, 1996).

Medicaid has been and remains a particularly important source of funds for children with serious emotional disorders and their families. Authorized under Title XIX of the Social Security Act of 1935, Medicaid provides money for health care for low-income people. It is a state and federal partnership under which states pay for part of the cost of serving their targeted populations. The federal government provides matching funds according to a formula that takes state poverty levels into account. States develop individual Medicaid plans within certain parameters, and many state mental health agencies have used Medicaid funds for wraparound services to meet the needs of individual children and their families. Medicaid is an *entitlement* program, which means that all the children who meet the criteria established by a state are entitled to receive Medicaid-funded services.

Recently, there has been a trend to enroll Medicaid-eligible clients in managed care systems, a profound social experiment (Faenza, 1997; Faenza & Rubenstein, 1996). Children and adolescents with special needs traditionally received health and mental health services under a fee-for-service payment system. Under federal law (the Balanced Budget Act of 1997, or BBA), states may not enroll these children in managed care plans involuntarily. However, states may apply for a federal waiver for that purpose, and many states that have received waivers are choosing to enroll children with mental health needs into managed mental health carve-out programs. These managed care entities may or may not link adequately with other child-serving systems. Brach and Scallet (1996) point out that managed care is not just a force in the health arena, but it is also spilling over into in the education system and other child-serving systems, partly because systems of care initiatives have been built successfully in some communities: "Such systems rely on a patchwork of revenue streams, and often depend heavily on Medicaid. . . . Ironically, the success in blending funds and maximizing federal revenue . . . now means that these systems face disruption . . . unless they become partners in managed care" (p. 5). The question of whether they will do this remains open. Stroul and her colleagues (1996) suggest that systems of care will become more targeted in focus "in order to achieve significant outcomes within ever-increasing resource constraints" (p. 609). They posit that systems of care will make major contributions through planning, community development, system reform activities, early intervention efforts, and advocacy, perhaps focusing less on direct service functions.

Block grants are another major trend in public health care financing. The major provision of the BBA as it affects children is the creation of the State Children's Health Insurance Program (SCHIP). SCHIP was created as new Title XXI of the Social Security Act. It is a block grant program that authorizes the transfer of $24 billion dollars from federal to state governments over a period of 5 years to expand children's access to health care, including mental health and substance abuse services. Two-and-a-half million currently uninsured, low-income children are expected to benefit from SCHIP.

States are required to match the federal funds according to a formula based on their ability to pay. It is conceivable, but we hope unlikely, that some shortsighted state would reject the federal funds rather than provide the match.

Those states that decide to draw down SCHIP money can use it in one of three ways. They can expand Medicaid to cover additional children, create a new child health insurance program, or purchase health care services directly. NMHA has concluded that the best of these options—indeed, the only one that would provide adequate coverage for children with mental and emotional disorders—is an expansion of Medicaid. Medicaid expansion has the following advantages:

- Through the Early and Periodic Screening, Diagnostic, and Treatment program (EPSDT), states must provide all services included in the Medicaid law to treat or ameliorate any condition identified in a child by a comprehensive screening process. Ideally, this provides for broad coverage of child mental health services and it is likely to increase access to a full array of effective services. It increases the chance that comprehensive interagency systems will be implemented.

- It gives states more federal money by providing for an enhanced federal match for state Medicaid funds.

- It creates an entitlement. SCHIP itself is a block grant program, not an entitlement program. States may stop providing services under SCHIP when their SCHIP funds for that year have been expended. Needy children then can be turned away *unless they have been enrolled in Medicaid,* in which case they have become *entitled* to services.

- It gives consumers and families access to the established Medicaid appeals process.

States that choose to create a new program must follow certain federal guidelines, but they are allowed a great deal of flexibility in designing their plans and in determining eligibility. In some cases, they may provide very limited mental health services or even none at all. To the extent that mental health is addressed, states have the option of covering a full array of community-based services, but they need not choose to do so. Therefore, NMHA recommends that advocates encourage their states to expand Medicaid rather than take one of the other optional courses of action.

Overview of Children's Mental Health Issues: The Current Plight of America's Troubled Families

Nature and Extent of the Problem

As many as one in five American children, or 13.7 million youngsters, have been estimated to have a diagnosable emotional disorder (Brandenburg et al., 1990). Approximately half of them (up to 7 million who are between the ages of 9 and 17) suffer from a serious emotional disturbance with substantial or extreme functional impairment ("Estimation Methodology," 1997, table 1). Prevalence rates have not been determined for children between birth and 8 years of age, so this may be taken as a low estimate of children who have are likely to need mental health services.

Earlier, the Center for Mental Health Services had presented the following definition of children with serious emotional disturbance (U.S. Government, 1993, p. 29425):

Persons:

- From birth up to age 18
- Who currently or at any time during the past year
- Have had a diagnosable mental, behavioral, or emotional disorder of sufficient duration to meet diagnostic criteria specified within *DSM-III-R*

- That resulted in functional impairment, which substantially interferes with or limits the child's role or functioning in family, school, or community activities

Children are subject to a wide range of disorders, including depression, anxiety, attention-deficit/hyperactivity disorder, and conduct and eating disorders. Any of these disorders can result in *functional impairment,* which has been defined as "difficulties that substantially interfere with or limit a child or adolescent from achieving or maintaining one or more developmentally-appropriate social, behavior, cognitive, communicative, or adaptive skills" ("Center for Mental Health Services," 1993, p. 29425).

The startlingly high prevalence figures are based on the work of a group of technical experts convened by the federal government to develop an estimation methodology to "operationalize the key concepts" in the definition of children with a serious emotional disturbance. In the absence of national epidemiological data, the group reviewed a series of smaller studies in drawing its conclusions. The federal definitions are intended to guide the provision of services funded under the Federal Community Mental Health Services Block Grant, but other funding sources may use different parameters.

Despite the extent of childhood mental illness that was identified, only about one third of children with serious emotional disturbances receive treatment from a mental health professional in any given year. The episodic nature of psychiatric disorders contributes to this treatment deficit. Also, children with mental health needs often come to the attention of society first through the education, child welfare, or juvenile justice systems. Although these children may receive services, they may not receive services aimed at treating their psychiatric disorders.

Integrated Community-Based Services
for Children and Families

The holistic approach to preventing and treating illness is certainly not new. Hippocrates suggested that physicians address a patient's illness in the context of social, behavioral, and environmental factors. The idea of coordinating services flows naturally from this, but it is not easily translated into action. A few of the barriers to coordinated efforts include differential levels of power and financing among service systems and varying attitudes about the population(s) to be served, provider credentials, and family involvement. A recent report on Medicine and Public Health, for example, devotes considerable effort to illustrating the potential for improving community health, individual access to care, and the quality and cost-effectiveness of health care through collaboration among medical, public health, and other service systems (Lasker, 1997). At the same time, the report acknowledges that collaborative efforts have been hampered by the absence of "a compelling need to work together, and . . . supportive incentives and organizational structures" (Lasker, 1997, p. 44).

A system of care for children with serious emotional disorders and their families is a concept that goes well beyond the already ambitious goal of service coordination. CASSP was an effort to redirect thought from how the child fits into the system to how a system can be organized to fit the child. As Stroul and Friedman (1994) decided early on, a system of care is far more than a network of service components. Rather, a system of care is a philosophy—a conceptual model that communities can use to meet their own needs within their own boundaries. The core values of a system of care were outlined as follows:

- The system is child-centered and family focused, with the type and mix of services determined by the needs of child and family.
- The system is community based. Decision making and service management reside at the community level.
- The system is culturally competent; that is, responsive to the cultural, ethnic, and racial differences of the population(s) served.

Ten guiding principles for a system of care have also been delineated:

- Children with emotional disturbances should have access to a comprehensive array of services that address their physical, emotional, social, and educational needs.
- They should receive individualized services based on their unique needs and potentials and guided by individualized service plans.
- They should receive services within the least restrictive, most normative environment that is clinically appropriate.

- Their families and surrogate families should participate fully in all aspects of planning and delivering services.
- The children should receive integrated services, with linkages between child-serving agencies and programs and mechanisms for planning, developing, and coordinating the services.
- Case management services or similar mechanisms should ensure coordination of services and facilitate movement through the system of services in accordance with the child's individual needs.
- The system of care should promote early identification and intervention for children with emotional disturbances to enhance the likelihood of positive outcomes.
- A smooth transition to adult services should be assured as children reach maturity.
- Children's rights should be protected and advocacy on behalf of children and adolescents should be promoted.
- Children should receive services that are responsive to their cultural differences and special needs.

Obviously, this is a view of an ideal system of care. It has been widely accepted, partially implemented in many communities, and in the presence of the aforementioned "compelling need to work together, and . . . supportive incentives and organizational structures," it has proven to be a worthwhile approach.

Children's Mental Health Services in an Era of Managed Care

Both public and private health and mental health insurers are using managed care techniques to meet their stated goals of controlling costs while improving access to an expanded array of services. In theory, this is a sensible way to proceed. In practice, however, "cost control" too often translates as "reduction in expenditures," a highly problematic course of action in a society that already spends far too little on children's mental health. Even without reduced funding, cost-containment efforts may well conflict with the principles of the CASSP system.

Still, the NMHA believes managed care is more than a transient phenomenon and will continue to have an impact on mental health systems and services. Consequently, we have gathered information about children's managed care initiatives, as summarized by Pritchard (1997) using NMHA experience and information from the Healthcare Reform Tracking Project (Pires et al., 1995).

- Evidence from the states indicates that problems that existed before managed care was implemented are continuing to exist afterwards.
- Initial administrative cost increases have been very high.
- Under the pressure of massive change, mistakes are being made during planning, procurement, and implementation.
- Shifting to managed care requires the blending of two cultures, business and human services, that are historically very different.

Some of the specific risks that were identified for children under managed care are as follows:

- *Lack of family involvement.* Families of children with serious emotional disorders are consistently underrepresented at every level of managed care planning and implementation. Even when their views are solicited, they do not believe their concerns are heard and accepted.
- *Restricted range and level of service.* Families may not be able to continue to use providers who are not in the managed care organization's network. Types of services needed may not be in place.
- *Closing of nontraditional services and loss of unlicensed providers.* Providers and services that do not meet state credentialing and licensing requirements may be forced out of business. Such services may not be deemed "medically necessary," even though vital to the communities they serve.
- *Decreased attention to cultural diversity.* Cultural competence was added to the initial version of the systems of care philosophy as a core value, reflecting the recognition of its importance. To date, there is no evidence that managed care has had either a negative or a positive impact on the availability of culturally appropriate providers.

Studies conducted for SAMHSA by Rosenbaum and her colleagues (Rosenbaum, Silver, & Wehr, 1997) at George Washington University noted many weaknesses in contracts involving managed care organizations (MCOs). This is a serious problem, in that an MCO cannot be compelled to do anything that isn't specifically written into its contract. For example, if an expansive definition of medical necessity is to be used, medical necessity must be defined expansively in the contract. "With the advent of healthcare reform as it is shaping up in most states," writes Gabriele (1997), "th[e] social contract between government and citizens is in danger of being superseded by an explicit, written contract between the state/public authority and the MCO/service provider" (pp. 31-35). Families and advocates must pay close attention to the language that goes into the explicit, written contract. Primary stakeholders must be educated about the technical aspects of contracting as well as the basics of managed care, and they must be included at all stages of planning, development, implementation, and evaluation of managed care contracts. Coalitions of families and advocates can engage stakeholder groups and educate them about how to "get to the table" and how to make sure that their specific concerns are addressed.

Hopes for America's Future: A Response to the Behavioral Health Needs of America's Families

Every New Year's Eve as the clock strikes midnight, Americans wish happiness and good health to their relatives and friends. Many of us will live on well into the 21st century, having been convinced to give up smoking and encouraged to eat wisely and exercise regularly. If these preventive measures fail, our health insurance will give us access to the best known treatments. And if, God forbid, science should have nothing more to offer us, our loving and supportive children will see us through our final days. What's missing in this scenario?

As we write this, too many children lack access to adequate behavioral health care or, indeed, to any behavioral health care at all. Too many prevention programs lack sufficient funding. Too much energy goes into punishment rather than treatment. Too much attention is given to controlling costs rather than saving lives. We have runaway children and throwaway children. We have children who can't get treatment for their mental disorders until their parents relinquish them into state custody. We have advocates vying for a very small piece of a very small pie, so that no one gets enough to serve the children and families in need.

We are not now providing enough to help many of our most troubled youngsters to achieve a healthy adulthood. The first author recently visited a juvenile correctional facility in Georgia.

In February 1998, that state and the U.S. Department of Justice settled a federal lawsuit that had cited the state for violating the constitutional rights of young people caught in the state's juvenile justice system. A major cause of concern was the systematic neglect of the mental health needs of the large proportion of incarcerated youngsters who had mental health problems. In the Georgia system, as elsewhere, the needs are known but the resources are lacking.

The bottom line is that researchers, clinicians, parent advocates, and public officials have learned a great deal about how to treat children and families that have mental health needs. We have done a poor and incomplete job, however, of implementing programs that are known to help troubled youngsters. Similarly, much is known about how to prevent emotional and behavioral disorders in children, but our society has failed to act on this knowledge. There is a substantial relationship between access to high-quality mental health services and reduction in the onset, severity, and duration of emotional and behavioral disorders.

Our hope is that we are on the verge of an era when

- A child with an emotional disorder receives appropriate treatment within a family-centered, community-based system of care
- The knowledge gained from research and experience can be adequately disseminated and applied, so that all children and families can have the benefit of a "best practices" approach to mental health services
- All children have sufficient insurance coverage for all their health and behavioral health needs, whether preventive or interventive
- Public policymakers affirm and act upon the premise that each child is precious, that each child must be supported in achieving his or her highest potential, and that the future of our nation depends on the health and strength of its children

This would truly signify the beginning of a happy new year.

References

Axinn, J., & Levin, H. (1992). *Social welfare: A history of the American response to need* (3rd ed.). White Plains, NY: Longman.

Behar, L. B. (1996). Financing systems of care. In *Children's mental health: Creating systems of care in a changing society* (pp. 299-311). Baltimore, MD: Brooks.

Brach, C., & Scallet, L. (1996). Trends. In L. Scallet, C. Brach, & E. Steel (Eds.), *Managed care: Challenges for children and family services* (pp. 3-9). Baltimore, MD: Annie E. Casey Foundation.

Brandenburg, N. A., Friedman, R. M., & Silver, S. E. (1990). The epidemiology of childhood psychiatric disorders: Prevalence findings from recent studies. *Journal of the American Academy of Child and Adolescent Psychiatry, 29*(1), 76-83.

Chidley, E. (1998). Depression in childhood & adolescence: Are you overlooking it? *PA Today,* 19-22.

Estimation methodology for children with a serious emotional disturbance (SED). (1997, October 6). *Federal Register, 62*(193), 52139-52145. Washington, DC: Government Printing Office.

Faenza, M. M. (1996). Ending discrimination in health insurance through federal law: A children's mental health perspective. *Focal Point, 10*(2), 19-22.

Faenza, M. M. (1997). Foreword. In *Mental health policy and practice today.* Thousand Oaks, CA: Sage.

Faenza, M. M., & Rubenstein, L. S. (1996). An advocacy perspective on the AMBHA/NASHMPD white paper. *Behavioral Healthcare Tomorrow, 5*(2), 25-29.

Fox, S. J. (1996). The early history of the court. *Future Child, 6*(3), 29-39.

Gabriele, R. J. (1997). Key contracting issues for consumers, families, and advocates. In R. J. Gabriele (Ed.), *Healthcare reform: A consumer, family and advocate perspective* (pp. 31-35). Alexandria, VA: National Mental Health Association.

Grob, G. N. (1994). Mad, homeless, and unwanted: A history of the care of the chronic mentally ill in America. *Psychiatric Clinics of North America, 17*(3), 541-558.

Joint Commission on the Mental Health of Children. (1969). *Crisis in child mental health: Challenge for the 1970's.* New York: Harper & Row.

Knitzer, J. (1982). *Unclaimed children: The failure of public responsibility to children and adolescents in need of mental health services.* Washington, DC: Children's Defense Fund.

Lasker, R. D. (1997). *Committee on Medicine and Public Health. Medicine and Public Health: The power of collaboration* (Report). New York: New York Academy of Medicine.

Lourie, I. S., Howe, S. W., & Roebuck, L. L. (1996). *Systematic approaches to mental health care in the private sector for children, adolescents, and their families: Managed care organizations and service providers.* Washington, DC: Georgetown University Child Development Center, National Technical Assistance Center for Child Mental Health.

Pires, S. A., Stroul, B. A., Roebuck, L. A., Friedman, R. M., McDonald, N., Barrett, B., & Chambers, K. L. (1995). Tracking state health care reforms as they affect children and adolescents with emotional disorders and their families. *Health Care Reform Tracking Project: The 1995 state survey.* Tampa: University of South Florida.

Pritchard, L. (1997). Children and managed care: Lessons from the states. In *Healthcare reform: A consumer, family and advocate perspective.* Alexandria, VA: National Mental Health Association.

Rosenbaum, S., Silver, K., & Wehr, E. (1997). *An evaluation of contracts between managed care organizations and community mental health and substance abuse treatment and prevention agencies* (SAMHSA Managed Care Technical Assistance Series). Washington, DC: U.S. Department of Health and Human Services.

Sedlak, M. W. (1997). The uneasy alliance of mental health services and the schools: An historical perspective. *American Journal of Orthopsychiatry, 67*(3), 349-362.

Stroul, B. A., & Friedman, R. M. (1994). *A system of care for children and youth with severe emotional disturbances* (Rev. ed.). Washington, DC: Georgetown University Child Development Center, CASSP Technical Assistance Center.

Stroul, B. A., Friedman, R. M., Hernandez, M., Roebuck, L., Lourie, I. S., & Koyanagi, C. (1996). Systems of care in the future. *Children's mental health: Creating systems of care in a changing society* (pp. 591-612). Baltimore, MD: Brooks.

Tennessee officials reach settlement on EPSDT class-action lawsuit. (1998). *Mental Health Weekly, 8*(9), 1-2.

U.S. Congress, House of Representatives. (1996). *Mental Health Parity Act of 1996.* 104th Cong., H.R. 3666. *Congressional Record.* Vol. 104, No. 204, daily ed. (26 September 1996), H.R. 3666.

U.S. Government. (1993, May 20). Center for Mental Health Services, SAMHSA. *Federal Register, 58*(96), 29422-29425.

• CHAPTER 4 •

School-Based Health and Social Service Centers

JOY G. DRYFOOS

School-based health and social service centers (SBCs) in many different forms are rapidly proliferating in all parts of this country (Institute of Medicine, 1997). In this chapter, I present evidence that school sites have the potential to become the preferred places for offering needed services to children and families. First, I describe various models and then explain what is driving this movement toward providing health and social services in schools. I then review the research on the impacts of these types of programs. A number of current issues are discussed related to organization, staffing, and funding, and finally I speculate about the future of the SBC model in the 21st century.

Models of School-Based Centers

School-based programs vary considerably depending on the professional domain from which they emerge and the funding mechanisms that support them. If the founding practitioner is in health services, then the model is frequently a school-based primary health clinic (Institute of Medicine, 1997; Juszczak & Fisher, 1997). Mental health workers create school-based centers providing individual and group counseling, family counseling, and even treatment (Dryfoos, 1997; Taylor & Adelman, 1996). Educators are more likely to start with school reorganization in the classroom, but they also rely on partnerships to bring in outside support services. This collaboration can generate a community school organized in conjunction with a settlement house or a university (Dryfoos, 1998). Community-based youth advocates, through models that have been called Beacons, bring services to light up schoolhouses after hours (Cahill, Perry, Wright, & Rice, 1993). Foundations and state governments have influenced the design of these different models.

Each version of school-based services packages the components in different ways, moving along a continuum from simple to complex administrative arrangements. Relocation of a contract service from one site (a public health, mental health, or social service agency) to another (a school building) is much less complicated than the creation of a new type of community-school where the educational system and the support interventions are completely integrated and operated collaboratively by several agencies. In this chapter, and other work, I have used the phrase *Full Service School* to define a broad framework that encompasses both school reform and sufficient support services to ensure that the school reform is effective (Dryfoos, 1994).

In addition to school-based services, another form of increasing access is school-linked services, referral locations to which school personnel send students or families for the services they need. One example would be an Adolescent Health Center located near a school where students could go for reproductive health care along with primary health care and counseling. Almost any community agency such as the local health department, community mental health center, or drug treatment program could be designated as "school linked" if school personnel ever referred students or families to that source. Here, I focus primarily on services provided directly at school sites, reflecting my own preference for colocation "one-stop" programs.

School-Based Primary Health Care Clinics

The simplest model is the school-based clinic (SBC), a designated center within a school building that delivers comprehensive health, mental health, and social services to the student body (Guernsey & Pastore, 1996; Rickett, Lear, & Schlitt, 1995). The provider is typically a local health department, community health center, medical facility, or a youth-serving agency. Staff may include nurse practitioners, social workers, clinic aides, health educators, and part-time physicians, with after-hours medical backup assured by the provider agency. In a few school systems, the Board of Education (local education authority) directly operates the medical services, but this is rarely feasible because of insurance, personnel, and backup emergency care requirements.

SBCs, after a slow start, are growing rapidly, increasing over the past decade from 10 locations to nearly 1,200 (personal communication, Kate Fothergill, director of Support Center for School Based Services, Advocates for Youth, Washington, D.C., 1998). The earliest programs were located in urban high schools. Today about 42% are in high schools, 17% in middle schools, 32% in elementary schools, and the rest (9%) in other configurations (Making the Grade, n.d.). The growing recognition of the importance of early intervention has generated many programs in elementary schools, some encompassing preschool children.

School districts along with community agency partners are responding eagerly to Requests for Proposals (RFPs) promulgated by state health departments, foundations (especially Robert Wood Johnson [RWJ]), and most recently, by the federal Bureau of Primary Health Care. Although the total appropriation for the Maternal and Child Health (MCH) Block Grant is substantial ($678 million), only about $13 million is passed by states to school-community partnerships for school clinics. In addition, states spend about $28 million of their own revenues on school-based health centers. Healthy Schools, Health Communities is the initiative of the Bureau of Primary Health Care and the MCH bureau that produced direct federal grants for the first time for school-based clinics. Only $3 million was made available for direct health services at 27 school sites, $1 million for health education in school health centers, and $1.5 million for staff training grants. The Bureau of Primary Health Care has also stimulated the involvement of more than 200 of its community health centers in the provision of primary health care services in schools, using state, city, or foundation grants.

As these school centers open, students crowd in with a profusion of complaints ranging from respiratory diseases and menstrual cramps, accidents and injuries, to personal crises and family problems (McKinney & Peak, 1994). The school-based clinic protocol generally includes a medical history and routine lab tests of hematocrit, hemoglobin, and urinalysis. Enrolled students may be asked to complete a psychosocial assessment, which reveals risk levels for substance abuse, violence, suicide, pregnancy, sexually transmitted diseases (STDs), accidents, and family conflict. Depending on indications from the health history and assessment tool, the student is scheduled for a visit with the nurse practitioner and/or counselor. Most clinics are open from 8:00 a.m. to 5:00 p.m. for scheduled appointments and walk-in visits for emergency care and crisis intervention.

At the clinic, students receive physical examinations, immunizations, pregnancy and STD tests, and individual counseling. More than half of the clinics dispense medications, diagnose and treat sexually transmitted diseases, and perform gynecological exams. Most provide reproductive health counseling and exams, about one third give out condoms, and 15% distribute oral contraceptives on site. States, school districts, and sponsoring agencies set policies regarding the provision of contraceptives and other medical practices. SBC staff run group counseling workshops in the school on relevant subjects such as living with asthma, substance use, bereavement, sexual abuse, weight control, pregnancy prevention, and family relationships. SBC staff may also offer health education and health promotion curricula in the classroom. Parental consent is required for enrollment in these programs, and families are involved when appropriate.

The literature on how to implement school-based clinics includes a detailed curriculum (National Association of Community Health Centers, 1997), material available from the University of Colorado school health program (School Health Resource Services, 1995), and the recent volume *Health Care in Schools* (Juszczak & Fisher, 1996). The National Assembly on School-Based Health Care has a growing membership and acts as coordinator of national meetings, regional workshops, and advocacy. Advocates for Youth (AFY) operates a support center to provide technical assistance to the field.

School-Based Mental Health Centers

When school-based clinic providers are asked what the largest unmet need is among their clients, they most frequently mention mental health counseling (Dryfoos, 1997). Students come in to the medical clinics with a litany of stress and depression, their typical adolescent problems exacerbated seriously by the deteriorating and unsafe social environment in which they live. As one provider described it, "As soon as we opened our doors, kids walked past the counselor's office, past the school nurse, past the principal, and come into our clinic to tell us that they are being sexually abused or that their parents are drug users." The fact that the clinic staff are outsiders and provide confidential services probably explains why students will bring their problems to the clinic rather than disclosing to school staff. The demand for mental health counseling has led to the development of school clinics that have a primary function of screening and treating for psychosocial problems. A mental health center in a school transfers the functions of a community mental health center to a school building. In this model, a room or group of rooms in a school building is designated as a services center. This center is not usually labeled as a "mental health" facility but rather presented as a place where students can go for all kinds of support and remediation. Staff typically include psychologists and social workers. Depending on the range of additional services, other staff might be youth workers, tutors, and mentors. The goals of school-based mental health centers are to improve the social adjustment of students and help them deal with personal and family crises.

But mental health interventions in schools take many forms. In some communities, a mental health worker, such as a psychologist or a social worker, is outstationed by a community mental health agency in a school, usually under a contractual relationship. Communities-in-Schools has been using this approach to bring case managers into schools. A number of universities have collaborative arrangements with schools for internship experiences in mental health counseling. Within a broader framework of training young people to enhance their social skills, many university-based psychologists have been busy designing and implementing school-based curricula. Health educators, social workers, and psychologists are placed in schools to focus on specific categorical issues such as substance abuse, teen pregnancy, and even school failure. These efforts generally augment pupil personnel services in school systems that want/need additional staff resources for dealing with psychosocial problems.

The School Development Program is a school-based mental health approach to school reorganization, by making the school a more productive environment for poor minority children. In this case, outsiders come into the school to conduct training in a "process" developed by James Comer from the Yale University Child Study Center (Millsap et al., 1995). The program attempts to transfer mental health skills to schools where "change agents" must be created by strengthening and redefining the relationships among principals, teachers, parents, and students.

The Bureau of Maternal and Child Care has funded two centers to promote mental health services in schools, one at the University of Maryland and the other at the University of California in Los Angeles.

School-Based Youth Service Centers

Some school-based centers focus more on coordination and referral than colocation of services in schools. Kentucky's significant school reform initiative in 1988 called for the development of youth service centers in high schools with more than 20% of the students eligible for free school meals (an indicator of economic disadvantage). In this case, small grants were given to school systems to set up a designated room in the school with a full-time coordinator to oversee referrals to community agencies for health and social services and to provide on-site counseling related to employment, substance abuse, and mental health (Dryfoos, 1994).

In New York City, the Beacons program, created by the city youth agency, supports community-based agencies to develop "lighted school houses," open from early morning until late at night, as well as weekends and summers (Annie E. Casey Foundation, 1993). These Beacons offer a wide range of activities, depending on the neighborhood needs, including after-school recreation, educational remediation, community events, and health services as well as health workshops and health fairs. One impressive program attracts 400 participants to meetings of Narcotics Anonymous several evenings each week in the school. Another has organized students to clean up the neighborhood, plant trees, and run their own news stand at the corner. Beacons were used as the prototype for the 21st Century Community Learning Centers, a new $1 billion over 5 years initiative of the Department of Education, to start up school-community collaborations for before- and after-school programs for school-age children.

Family Service/Resource Centers

The Kentucky legislation also called for family resource centers in elementary schools, which would offer parent education and refer parents to infant and child care, health services, and other community agencies. In other states such as Connecticut and Colorado, family resource centers are being supported through state initiatives and federal grants that deliver comprehensive services on school sites, including parent education, child care, counseling, health services, home visiting, and career training.

Community Schools

In the past, the phrase *community-school* has been applied mainly to opening up school buildings after hours for adult education classes and local events. The new generation of community-schools begins to follow the broader construct of full service schools, the integration of quality education with support services. Several schools have been identified as potential models (Children's Aid Society schools in New York City; Robertson and Hanshaw in Modesto, California; Fanning Middle School in St. Louis; Marshalltown, Iowa, Caring Connection schools; Farrell School System in Pennsylvania; Turner School in Philadelphia), and many more exist in all parts of the country. In these community-schools, the following components are generally present: restructured academic programs integrated with comprehensive support systems; substantive parent involvement and services for parents; health centers and family resource rooms; after-school activities; cultural and community activities; and open all hours and days. Mental health services are provided through contracted services with community mental health agencies and interns from social work schools. Each of these community schools is striving (in different ways) to become a village hub, with joint efforts from school and community agencies to create as rich an environment as possible for the children and their families.

A national movement to promote federal support for full-service community-schools has been initiated by leading practitioners, facilitated by the Institute for Educational Leadership in Washington, D.C., along with the National Center for School and Commu-

nity at Fordham University and the Mott Foundation National
Center for Community Education.

Common Attributes of School-Based Centers

What do these models have in common? They are all located in
schools but are rarely operated by school systems. Most SBCs result
from a lengthy planning process that involves school and community representatives in arduous fact finding and drawn-out negotiations about space, confidentiality, and other policy issues. The SBC
staff is most frequently supplied by a local health, mental health,
or social service agency, or by university faculty and graduate
students, or by a "think tank." Almost all of the SBCs are supported
by non-educational resources, mostly state-generated funds, state-
operated federal block grants, or foundation grants. SBCs are
"backed up" by provider agencies or have links to hospitals or
mental health agencies for emergency care and crisis intervention.
They typically operate longer than traditional school hours—afternoons, weekends, and during the summer.

Impetus for School-Based Services

What is motivating state governments and foundations to create
these new kinds of institutional arrangements that put together
schools and community agencies? First, we see a rising concern
about the vulnerabilities of youth, resulting from early sexual
"acting out," drugs, violence, and other behavioral and health
problems that may stand in the way of future success. Families are
increasingly vulnerable, as well, facing daunting economic and
social barriers to fulfilling their roles as parents. So-called welfare
reform is exacerbating the tensions, with mothers forced to try to
get jobs without assurance of adequate child care. Schools cannot
deal with these youth and, at the same time, retool to compete in
a new technological world that requires more rigor and discipline.
And while many social and educational programs have been promulgated to deal with these needs, they are fragmented and not
successfully achieving the goals of helping young people become
responsible adults. Finally, the nagging question of access to primary health services has led to the search for new sites and new
fiscal arrangements.

Adolescents who have access to health care generally go to pediatricians or family doctors who are reticent about discussing drugs or sex or feelings of depression, and rarely raise such issues in the course of annual examinations. Traditional health professionals have not been trained to deal with these kinds of social and behavioral problems. In any case, many high-risk adolescents do not have access to private medical care, and few other resources are available to them. As a result, if a crisis occurs, or even an illness, teenagers are likely to present at hospital emergency rooms. This is not only costly, it does not allow for health education, health promotion, or continuity—the components most essential to efficient and effective health care for young people.

Julia Lear, director of the Robert Wood Johnson Foundation's Making the Grade program that supports 10 states to provide school-based services, observed that the "emergence of managed care as a way of organizing and paying for health services, the movement of Medicaid beneficiaries into managed care plans, and proposed government health care reforms" are all leading toward expansion of school health programs (Lear, 1996).

Connecting these movements together—prevention of the new morbidities, improvement of educational outcomes, integration of services for children and families, and access to primary health care—provides the argument for school-based services. Schools are where most of the young people can be found. Schools are where most of the families can establish contact with the people who educate their children and where they can obtain the help they need to be effective parents. If we could produce quality education at one site along with access to requisite health, mental health, social, and cultural services for children and families, both educational and psychosocial outcomes should be better. Of course, to accomplish this will require major changes in the educational, health, and human services establishments in the way they relate to each other and conduct their business.

Do School-Based Centers Make a Difference?

Research on the utilization of school-based health clinics has advanced well, with substantial accountability for the large numbers of students who use services. Documentation of the impact and outcomes has been more challenging. Methodological problems abound, limiting the possibilities for identifying control groups or tracking student populations over time (Dryfoos, Brindis, & Kaplan, 1996). Turnover rates are extremely high in schools likely to provide health services–often more than half of the students leave during a school year. Despite these obstacles, over the past decade several significant studies of school-based clinics have been published and more are currently under way.

Utilization Studies

Enrollment. SBCs generally start out with low enrollments and gradually build over the years, when a high proportion of the students sign up. Advocates for Youth (AFY) has conducted frequent surveys of providers and reports that about two thirds of the students in respondent schools are enrolled in their SBCs, and 75% of enrollees utilize the program over a year (Hauser-McKinney & Peak, 1995).

Client Characteristics. Among the respondents to the AFY survey, clinics reported that about 60% of enrolled students were female. One third of the enrollees were African American, one third non-Hispanic white, 20% Hispanic, and the rest Asian, Native American, and other (Hauser-McKinney & Peak, 1995). Most reports show that while clinic users tend to mirror the student population in regard to race/ethnicity, females are more likely to use clinics (especially if reproductive health care is offered). However, when services are conveniently located, young men will also use them, especially for sports and work physical exams.

A study of a sample of students from nine Baltimore school-based clinics compared enrollees with non-enrollees and found the those who enrolled were significantly more likely to have had health problems, were in families with Medicaid, in special education, and African American. Those who did not enroll in the clinic reported a variety of reasons, primarily being satisfied with their current provider (Santelli, Kouzis, & Newcomer, 1996).

Enrollees show very different patterns of use. In one year in a Los Angeles SBC, 5% of enrollees had made no visits, 41% visited once, 39% made between 2 and 5 visits, 8% made between 6 and 10 visits, and 6% used the clinic more than 10 times (Adelman,

Barker, & Nelson, 1993). Clinic users reported ease of access as the most important reason for using the facility in the school, and perceived the care provided as helpful and confidential. Nonusers stated that they did not use the clinic because they did not need it, or they were concerned about lack of confidentiality. In this sample, frequent clinic users were more likely to score high on indices of psychological stress. Adelman et al. concluded that "an on-campus clinic can attract a significant number of students who otherwise would not have sought out or received such help."

Students in Oregon and Delaware who reported higher rates of problem behaviors such as substance abuse, early initiation of sexual intercourse, and suicidal ideation, were more likely to use school-based clinics than other students (National Adolescent Health Resource Center, 1993; Stout, 1991). While users of Denver's three high school clinics made an average of 3 visits per year, a small number of students (11%) made 15 or more visits per year, accounting for 40% of all patient visits (Wolk & Kaplan, 1993). Some 23% of the frequent visitors were diagnosed with mental health problems at the time of their initial visit, compared to 4% of the average users. By the end of the school year, 61% of all visits by frequent users were for mental health-related issues, compared to 10% of all visits by the average users. High-risk behaviors were significantly more prevalent among frequent users, particularly unprotected sexual activity and use of alcohol and drugs (but not tobacco use). Most of the frequent users initially came into the clinic for acute medical problems, at which time they were identified as students in need of mental health counseling. Many practitioners believe that the provision of comprehensive services offers a means for troubled students to enter into counseling and treatment for psychosocial problems without being stigmatized. Student surveys in Florida schools with school-based services showed that students who engaged in high-risk behaviors were more likely to visit the health room than the other students. Students reported high levels of satisfaction with the program, as did school administrators and parents. "Principals seemed very accommodating (of school based health services staff) because their presence relieved other staff from dealing with students with various health needs: calling parents for pick up, delivering first aid, and at least in one site, delivering a baby in the school parking lot" (Emihovich & Herrington, 1993).

An evaluation of 19 clinics supported by the Robert Wood Johnson Foundation reported on the characteristics of the total population of students in the schools with SBCs (rather than of students who used the clinics) (Kisker, Brown, & Hill, 1994). One in five families were on welfare, and one third received free or reduced-price school lunches. Some 30% of the health center school students reported that their families had no health insurance, 20% were covered by Medicaid, 31% had private insurance or belonged to an HMO, and the remaining 19% didn't know what type of coverage they had. As would be expected, health insurance coverage varied widely by school, ranging from 1% to 48% for families that had no coverage at all.

Outcome Data

In the early 1980s, the potential of school-based clinics as a strategy for pregnancy prevention was stimulated by the publication of data from St. Paul showing a decline in pregnancy rates in schools with clinics (Edwards, Steinman, Arnold, & Hakanson, 1980). But a later examination of birthrates showed large year-to-year fluctuations and no impact of the clinics. In fact, a review of the earlier studies showed mixed results for an array of behavioral impact measures (Kirby, 1994). Those studies that found positive effects on high-risk behaviors were offset by those that found negative effects or, more likely, no effects. Recent studies also contain a mix of results.

Pregnancy Related. Outcomes of interest include delaying the onset of intercourse, consistent use of contraception if sexually active, lower birthrates, and lower pregnancy rates. In general, studies have confirmed that the presence of a clinic in a school has no effect on the rates of sexual intercourse (e.g., the rates do not go up) and little effect on contraceptive use unless the clinic offers a visible pregnancy prevention program. A study of two schools with clinics that dispensed contraceptives on site compared to two schools where contraceptives were prescribed and not dispensed found few differences in contraceptive use. The only significant variable related to use was the higher number of contacts the students had with the clinic staff (Brindis, Starbuck-Morales, Wolfe, & McCarter, 1994).

A unique pregnancy prevention program in a middle school clinic in Washington Heights, New York City, showed that an intensive risk-identification and case management approach was effective among young students (Tiezzi, Lipshutz, Wrobleski, Vaughan, & McCarthy, 1997). This *In Your Face Program* uses group counseling to bring students who are at high risk of early unprotected inter-course together with specially trained Hispanic health educators who work closely with students. These workers escort the students from the school to a hospital-based family planning clinic if they are sexually active and want contraception. Method use among sexually active participants improved dramatically and pregnancy rates dropped 34% over 4 years in the program schools.

An intensive case-management program including follow-up phone calls was offered by the school-linked Daly City Youth Health Center in California. Evaluation showed that participants compared to a control group were much more likely to use effective contraception and improved their communication with partners (Brindis, Mamo, & McCarter, 1996).

When Florida created a Supplemental School Health Services Program, the legislation mandated evaluation to study the effective-ness of the program in meeting its objectives (pregnancy prevention and the promotion of student health; Emihovich & Herrington, 1993). The first-year report revealed that all of the grantees in the 12-county study area had a designated health room in the school with heavy utilization rates, primarily for physical complaints, physical examinations, and minor injuries. The evaluation also found that school-reported pregnancy rates had declined in some of the schools, but the data presented appeared to be estimates and were not validated. However, the following comment from the report is interesting: "The most dramatic shift occurred at Glades Central High School in Palm Beach where the pregnancy rate dropped almost 73%. This project is also the only one where students can obtain prescriptions for contraceptives at the school and where there is a family practice physician available three days a week" (p. 11).

The first evaluation of the California Healthy Start initiative presented data on 40 different grantees, including eight youth service programs, five of which were school-based clinics. The report showed that adolescent clients of programs with the explicit goal of reducing teen pregnancy had significant reductions in the rate of initiation of sexually activity and an increase in the rate of reliable contraceptive use (Wagner, Golan, Shaver, Wechsler, & Kelley, 1994). Among teenagers in pregnancy prevention programs, about 45% were sexually active at the end of the first 6-month follow-up period, a significant 23% decrease from the proportion at intake (77%). Youth service programs showed large gains in linking clients to sources of health care.

Other High-Risk Behaviors. At Lincoln High School in Denver, students who commit drug offenses can enter into a treatment contract for seven sessions at the school-based clinic rather than receive suspension. This component has resulted in an 80% reduction in suspensions (Bureau of Primary Health Care, 1993).

The Healthy Start data from California showed that in school-based youth programs with a goal of reducing violence, a significant reduction in gang activity was reported at the 6-month follow-up (from 7% to 2%; Wagner et al., 1994).

Mental Health. The evaluation of California's Healthy Start clients included families as well as students. Six months after the initiation of the program, the proportion of core clients who reported some level of depression dropped from 28% to 22%, and when depression did occur, it was significantly less likely to be reported as a major problem at follow-up (32% vs. 23% of those who were depressed; Wagner et al., 1994).

Health System Related. Students attending the nine school-based clinics in Baltimore were compared with students in four matched schools in regard to their access to medical and social services and their hospitalizations and use of emergency rooms (Santelli et al., 1996). Students in schools with health clinics were more likely to report seeing a social worker (11%) than those in schools without clinics (8%). Those in schools with clinics were more likely to have received specific health services (physicals, acute health care, family planning, counseling) and reported significantly lower rates of hospitalization. In regard to use of emergency rooms, rates were reduced only for those students who had been enrolled in the schools with clinics for more than a year.

Decreases in the use of emergency rooms by students in schools with clinics were reported in San Francisco (from 12% to 4% over

2 years) and San Jose (from 9% to 4%). At the same time, significant increases were shown in the percentage of students who said they were able to access health services when needed, presumably through the school-based clinics (Center for Reproductive Health, 1993). The school-based clinic in San Fernando, California, specifically targets students with little or no access to health care—93% of its clinic enrollees report no other source of medical care and no health insurance (Bureau of Primary Health Care, 1993). A unique finding was the high level of use of mental health services in school-based clinics among students with HMO and private insurance. According to the report, the extensive use of the school clinic by students with other health care options

> implies that the clinic is able to provide mental health services in a manner that is more acceptable to the adolescents, and that the integration of this service with a comprehensive array of health services may help diminish the stigma often associated with this kind of service . . . [it] may also reflect the relative unavailability . . . of these services as provided through HMO or private insurance coverage. (Center for Reproductive Health, 1993)

In a survey of 500 users of school-linked Teen Health Centers in Michigan, 21% of the respondents indicated they would not have received health care if the Center did not exist (Anthony, 1991). The main reasons given were lack of transportation and no family physician. Some 38% reported learning of new health problems during the visit, including cancer symptoms, penicillin allergy, ear trouble, and high cholesterol, and 65% indicated their behavior had changed as a result of their contact with the Teen Health Centers.

The RWJ evaluation found that students in schools with health centers received significantly more health care and were more likely to have a usual place of health care than they would have if their health care use had followed the same pattern as that of urban youths nationally (Kisker, 1994). SBC schools' students reported greater increases in treatment for illnesses and injuries. Students who used the Healthy Start youth service programs reported significant gains in access to medical care and a marked improvement in having a regular source of care.

School-based health centers have been shown to identify students with serious physical or mental health problems. The survey of students in Delaware showed that during a year, center users were more likely than nonusers to have had physical exams (72% vs. 55%) gynecological exams (24% vs. 19%), psychological counseling (21% vs. 14%), and eye exams (73% vs. 60%; National Adolescent Health Resource Center, 1993). Students who used the services cited convenience in scheduling and transportation, and confidentiality as their main reasons.

When the California Healthy Start evaluation looked at all clients (including adults), it found an increase from 19% to 26% of the number of core families who had children participating in the California Health and Disability Program within 6 months of enrolling in a Healthy Start intervention (Wagner et al., 1994). A reduction in health care due to illness or injury (from 36% to 29%) was also reported.

Parents at the Walbridge Caring Community school reported fewer problems with health care access and were more likely than parents in a comparison school to report that it was easy for students to get help with health problems (96% vs. 59%) and that the school helped a lot with their own health care needs (47% vs. 25%) (Philliber, 1994).

School Related. Advocates of SBCs assert that achievement and graduation rates should increase when health services are made accessible. Washington Senator Brock Adams claimed at a Senate hearing that a school clinic in Seattle's Rainier Beach High School "prevented 40 students from dropping out of school and significantly reduced the number of youth sent home from school" (*Helping America's Youth in Crisis,* 1992). In the San Fernando (California) high school, school-based clinic users were half (9%) as likely to drop out of school as nonusers (18%; Bureau of Primary Health Care, 1993). A study of a clinic located in an alternative school and run by a health department is a unique example of an evaluation that focuses entirely on school performance (McCord, Klein, Foy, & Fothergill, 1993). Students who used the clinic were twice as likely to stay in school and nearly twice as likely to graduate or be promoted than nonregistered students. The more visits that the student made to the clinic, the higher the graduation or promotion rates. The researchers found this relationship "particularly striking" among black males, and attributed these successful outcomes to the trust and support provided by the clinic staff to help students bond with and function better in the school.

Results from California's Healthy Start program showed that children who received intensive services in school-based programs made a significant improvement in grade point average, particularly for younger students and those who were performing least well before participating in Healthy Start (Wagner et al., 1994). Teacher ratings of student behavior also improved significantly for those who received intensive services.

Evaluation of the Walbridge Caring Community program showed that students who received intensive services had a 27% increase in teacher ratings of their work habits, a 16% improvement in their social-emotional growth, and a 23% improvement in grade point average (Philliber, 1994).

The Children's Aid Society reported "overwhelmingly positive results" after the first 2 years that IS 218 Community School had been open: "student scores are up 15 points in both math and reading, attendance is the highest in the district; there has been no incidence of violence . . . no destruction of property or even graffiti" (Children's Aid Society, 1994). At least 1,000 parents have been involved, and the schools (included PS5) have become a central meeting place in the community.

The study of school-based health programs in Florida showed a high percentage of students who were returned to class after being seen in the health room (Emihovich & Herrington, 1993). Only 10% of elementary students and 18% of high school students were unable to return, much lower rates than in routine school nursing practices. In the Baltimore study, absenteeism because of illness was not significantly different between SBC schools and other schools where 51% of the sample of students reported having been absent in the past 30 days (Santelli et al., 1996).

Organizational Research

A few studies have been conducted to document the design and implementation of SBCs. A unique survey of 90 clinics focused on planning strategies and barriers to implementation (Rienzo & Button, 1993). Key variables that influenced the SBCs' capacity to offer comprehensive services (number of clinical and outreach services provided) included the presence of a strong coordinator; using information such as needs assessments for gaining support in the community; and obtaining funding from national sources, particularly foundations. The ideal coordinator was described as a "workaholic" with ability to acquire funding and expertise in adolescent care. The more successful programs carefully organized planning committees and community advisory boards, and relied on committed school administrators to facilitate "navigation" through the approval process. Barriers to implementation were attributed to insufficient funding (66%) and, related to that, problems with staff training and turnover (33%). Many programs initially confronted organized opposition, dealt with controversy through public hearings, and as a result, several changed their policies in regard to birth control and abortion counseling. Birth control was limited in 28% of the cases and abortion counseling proscribed in 9%.

One study documented the importance of providing services on school property (school-based) rather than near-by (school-linked). A health center was moved from school grounds to the other side of the street in Quincy, Florida, during the tenure of a conservative governor who refused to allow public funds to be used for school-based clinics (Center for Human Services, 1990). The level of service activity declined immediately, with a drop of 30% during the year, particularly among males and younger students, and particularly for those who needed first aid. Almost the first act of a new governor (Lawton Chiles) in 1990 was to return the center to the school grounds. A new building was dedicated in early 1991 on the campus and utilization immediately climbed back to its previous level.

Testimony

One could generate reams of anecdotal data about school-based services programs from the mountains of reports. Here's just one example from a mother of two students who used the Sheridan School-Based Health Center in Colorado:

> I have taken both my children to the clinic; it was the best physical they ever had. The clinic staff asked a lot of questions, they don't overlook anything. Both of my children have been seen for rapid strep tests for sore throats. It saved me from taking a lot of time off from work. My son has also been seen for an upper respiratory infection

and a possible ear infection. I felt I received excellent counseling on how to care for him. ("The Carter/Bumpers campaign for early immunization," 1995, p. 4)

Key Factors in Success

Although the emerging school-based models—centers, community-schools, clinics—have many differences, research has yielded a number of common components of successful programs as measured by utilization (Godin, Woodhouse, Livingwood, & Jacobs, 1993). Key factors include:

- School and community people join together to develop a shared vision of new institutional arrangements. Open communication is essential at every stage. The planning process starts off with a needs assessment to ensure that the design is responsive to the requirements of the students and their families. An Advisory Board includes school and agency personnel, parents, and community leaders (and, in some places, students). Parental consent is required for receipt of services.

- The building principal is instrumental in the implementation and smooth operation of school-based programs. Schools provide space, maintenance, and security. School doors are open before and after school, weekends, and over the summer. Classrooms, gyms, playgrounds, music rooms, and computer facilities are open for community use.

- A special space is designated within the school as a center for individual and group counseling, parent education, career information, offices for case managers, kitchen, play space, clothes/food distribution, and arrangements for referrals. If primary health care is provided, adequate space is designated in or near a school building for a medical clinic with examining rooms, a lab, an area for confidential counseling, and arrangements for record keeping and referrals.

- The configuration of services brought in by community agencies from the outside is dependent on what already exists in the school. School personnel have to participate in the process from the beginning.

- A full-time coordinator or program director runs the support services in conjunction with school and community agencies. Personnel are trained to be sensitive to issues related to youth development, cultural diversity, and community empowerment.

- Staff recruitment requires time and attention. It is difficult to locate certified youth workers with appropriate language skills (Spanish, Asian, etc.) in many areas.
- Parents are involved at many program levels, as users of services, volunteer aides, paid program workers, Advisory committee members.
- A data system is in place, preferably a computerized management information system that can process records, update needs assessments, and be used for evaluation.
- The process of program development is greatly enhanced by the availability of technical assistance. State and foundation staffs have played a major role in extending these models, especially in rural areas.
- A designated space such as a center in a school acts as an anchor for bringing in other services from the community.

Issues in Development of Centers

School-based services appear to have great potential for serving needy children, adolescents, and families. Does this mean that every school should have a clinic? Even in disadvantaged communities, are schools the best place to locate health programs? In addition to those general questions, specific barriers to the development of school-based services that must be addressed include turf problems in the schools, finding adequate trained staff, confidentiality, transportation, and, of course, funding.

Resources Needed

At least $100,000 a year is necessary to create the infrastructure for operating a school-based clinic. The total cost would be higher than that (about $250,000 in a medium-sized school), but drawing on Medicaid, health insurance, local funds like United Way, and relocating existing resources could make up the gap. In any case, if you multiply that minimum amount by 85,000 public schools, the total bill would be about $8.5 billion per year. In my view, this would be a sound public investment, ensuring immunizations and complete health screening in elementary schools, identification and counseling of high-risk students in middle schools, and treatment of problem behaviors in high schools for all children. Currently, however, this large amount of money is not in the offing.

It is hard to predict exactly how much of the new $24 billion children's health insurance can be accessed by SBCs. The amount is expected to cover about half of the 10 million children who are currently uninsured. Under the law, states can either expand Medicaid or set up new state programs that provide private health insurance plans to children, or both. John Schlitt, executive director of the National Assembly on School-Based Health Care is optimistic:

> It is a new era for SBCs. Federal and state policy makers have declared war on uninsurance among low-income children. Managed care has been embraced by state Medicaid programs as a primary care solution for poorly served enrollees. The need for these special access programs like SBCs can be best described as "value added" . . . as unique models rewarded not just for cost containment and utilization control, but for increasing access to comprehensive preventive services in a setting that values caring and confidentiality. (Schlitt, personal communication, March 1, 1998)

As Schlitt points out, however, the allotment of from $6 to $12 monthly provided in most health plans will not be enough, and other funders such as states and foundations will always be required to expand "our vision of what health care for school age youth can and should be."

According to estimates made for the distribution of Title 1 (funds for disadvantaged students), about 16,000 public schools—one in five in the country—have student bodies in which more than half of the children are in poverty-level families (Dryfoos, 1998). A major effort to create SBCs in these neediest schools would cost a minimum of $1.6 billion. That would finance at least a coordinator who could work with community agencies to bring in services that are covered by existing sources. But some of this funding already exists in other pots.

Funding

The expression "shaking the tree" of categorical funding sources has been used to describe the action needed by providers to capture some of the existing funds for their programs. Drug Free Schools, Title 1, maternal and child health, community health, teen pregnancy, suicide, AIDS, and violence prevention are all federal cate-gorical streams that can be tapped for different program compo-nents that fit into school-based services (National Association of Community Health Centers, 1997; Shearer & Holscheider, 1995). However, the acquisition and continued use of these funds requires knowledge of regulations and eligibility and the capacity to account for dollars to a variety of funding sources. Early on, program developers believed that much of the support for school-based health and counseling services would come through Medicaid. Although many students were believed to be in families that were eligible, some were not enrolled and others did not want to jeop-ardize their privacy by having their families notified that they had used this mechanism for reimbursement. The latest twist in funding is managed care; Medicaid families in most states are required to be served in a designated medical facility. School-based clinics have to contract with HMOs or other managed care providers to serve the students. Practitioners report great difficulty in making these arrangements with providers who are not eager to give up any of the reimbursement monies.

With the rise in recognition of the potential of school-based services and community schools, the Clinton administration is making an effort to ensure the coverage of eligible students through managed care agencies. Several meetings and publications have attempted to point the way toward contractual arrangements. States are also heavily involved in adjusting eligibility requirements and policy changes that will give local providers more funding flexibility.

Governance

Much of the rhetoric in support of school-based services has been presented in the language of "systems change," calling for radical reform of the way educational, health, and welfare agencies provide services. Consensus has formed around the goals of "one-stop," "seamless" service provision whether in a school or in a commu-nity-based agency, along with empowerment of the "target popula-tion." My review of current models reveals that little systems change has taken effect. Most of the programs reviewed have moved services from one place to another; for example, a medical unit from a hospital or health department relocates into a school through a contractual arrangement, or staff of a community mental health center are reassigned to a school, or a grant to a school creates a coordinator in a center. As the program expands, the center staff work with the school to draw in additional services, fostering more contracts between the schools and community agencies. As a result, few of the school systems or the agencies have changed their governance. The "outside" agency is not involved in school restructuring or school policy, nor is the school system involved in the governance of the provider agency. Partners— schools and community agencies—have agreed on goals and signed contracts or memoranda of understanding that leave the status quo of the organizations entirely intact. The agreement may specify policies regarding fiscal responsibility, client-student data collection, confidentiality, and other administrative issues.

In fact, most school-based health clinics are funded by grants from state health departments directly to local health agencies that then contract with school systems to provide services. This is a matter of policy for some state health departments and foundations that believe that the school system should not be burdened with the responsibility for providing primary health and social services to the students. At the same time, the local education agencies are the grant recipients for the largest state programs (California, Florida, and Kentucky), and these systems may either provide services themselves or, more typically, contract out.

That few full-service school models have been able to overcome the barriers to the formation of new kinds of governance should not be perceived as a deterrent to further service integration efforts. Past attempts at systems reform have shown that it is much more difficult to alter the way that entrenched administrators operate across agencies than to make incremental changes in the existing systems they run. The movement toward service integration as exemplified in full-service schools has clearly had an effect on cutting red tape in some programs, but practitioners are still confronted with the conflicting eligibility criteria and restrictions that go along with categorical programs (Melaville, Blank, & Asayesh, 1993).

Turf

Bringing outside health or social services into a school building under the auspices of an outside agency is an invitation to turf wars.

Two or more different staffs operate under separate jurisdictions in terms of unions, policies, pay schedules, hours of work, and direction. Without careful planning and negotiation, the school staff can be very threatened by the appearance of a new group of workers in the school ("It's like having your mother-in-law move into your house"). School nurses have been particularly vulnerable because they feel replaced by a differently trained nurse, a nurse practitioner who is allowed to conduct complete physical examinations, prescribe and administer medication, suture wounds, and other "hands-on" activities. But school social workers, psychologists, and guidance counselors often have similar initial negative responses. Who is responsible for the children and their families? Some teachers oppose school-based services if students leave their classes for clinic appointments. Custodians resent keeping buildings open so families can use them. A significant area for potential conflict is discipline. The school has its own practices such as suspension and other forms of punishment that may be antithetic to the ethos of the newcomers.

One key to overcoming these situations successfully appears to be a sensitive principal who, right from the planning stage, involves his school personnel along with the outside personnel to create a team approach. Serious and ongoing inservice training must take place with both the existing staff and the outside agency staff to negotiate areas of tension and to learn to understand where each side is "coming from." Experience shows that within a short period of time most schools find more than enough crises to go around. School personnel become major supporters of school-based services when attendance improves and behavioral problems are addressed by practitioners. Practitioners recognize how difficult it is to maintain order in today's schools.

Quality of Care

A review of SBC research, conducted by the Johns Hopkins Child and Adolescent Health Policy Center, highlighted many of the positive findings cited above (*Improving Access to Primary Care for Adolescents,* n.d.) The review also pointed out significant potential weaknesses with the emerging models. Some centers restrict their hours of operation, only half are open all summer, and very few are open weekends. The turnover in clinic personnel is quite high, especially in those places that use rotating physicians. Working with disadvantaged children and families is labor intensive and can lead to burnout if personnel issues are not addressed with care and sensitivity. It is often difficult to recruit trained personnel, particularly those who can speak languages other than English. Some clinics are not truly comprehensive, and their procedures for referring students to other health services are not always efficient. While many of the centers are in communities where the whole family could use access to the SBC, funding and policies restrict the services to only enrolled students.

Demands for health services by increasingly destitute populations may also exacerbate the operational problems for SBCs. Tuberculosis is reaching epidemic proportions in some poor communities. *Joining Hands,* the newsletter of the National Assembly on School-Based Health Care, describes an SBC in Brooklyn that provides Isoniazid (INH) therapy for tuberculosis to students with nonactive TB. Other conditions such as elevated lead levels, sickle cell disease, and HIV positivity are presented at SBCs. Children with asthma and their parents are being taught self-management techniques.

According to Kate Fothergill (personal communication, 1997), director of the Support Center for School Based Health Services (AFY), SBCs have acquired much greater sophistication about operations and coordination: "Over the last five years, states have taken on much of the oversight of SBC operations, funding, and monitoring, helping the movement to track and evaluate progress in the field, setting guidelines and standards." Technical assistance is available to programs to help them establish essential medical protocols and administrative policies and procedures (Guernsey & Pastore, 1996).

Transportation

Program reviews in both Florida and Kentucky cited transportation as a major issue for people who used their centers. Those who relied on school-linked services found that referrals to community agencies were not carried out because the students and families were not able to get to those places. School-based models that were open after school hours, or that wanted to bring parents into school during school hours, also had transportation problems. School buses are usually run by contractors with inflexible schedules. Few programs have the necessary resources to offer van service to families, particularly those that live in outlying rural areas.

Issues such as transportation can be dealt with through the planning process (Terwilliger, 1994). School systems may be willing to alter contracts with bus companies or negotiate with their own bus driver unions to schedule bus runs for the convenience of the families rather than the convenience of the system. Buses can be scheduled for late afternoons, evenings, and weekends. In many places the precedent exists if the destination involves a competitive athletic event.

Staffing and Training

If programs are already experiencing difficulty hiring nurse practitioners and social workers, where will the staff for 16,000 school-based centers come from? If the concept catches on, and schools are seen as the locus for new kinds of institutional arrangements that cut across categorical lines, almost every category of professional worker will need to be retrained and new professionals will need to be cross-trained. Educators will have to better understand youth and family development issues, become more culturally sensitive, and further master their own specialties. Human service workers will have to learn how to function in schools and understand the culture of educational institutions. New types of coordinator/directors for school-based services will have to be able to interrelate with both schools and community agencies and help everyone bridge the gap. In addition, they will need strong management skills to handle the fiscal complexities that go along with multiple funding sources and accountability.

The need for appropriately trained personnel stands as a major barrier to replication. It is already being addressed on a small scale in a few university settings with efforts to change curricular offerings and coordinate master's level requirements. The major professional organizations for pupil personnel services (school nurses, school psychologists, school social workers, guidance counselors) are already working together to define the roles of their constituencies in new program models.

Controversy

The phrase *school-based clinic* is like a red flag for those waiting for an excuse to raise community tensions over sexuality issues. The most highly publicized school-based health programs in the early 1980s were heralded as pregnancy prevention programs, leading to attacks from the opposition that schools were opening "sex clinics" and "abortion mills." When later replications of these models were shown to have little effect on pregnancy rates because they did not include family planning services, the attack shifted and the opposition organized against bringing any kind of services into school buildings, even into elementary schools. At the time the Kentucky Youth and Family Centers were first proposed, the Eagle Forum put out brochures referring to the program proponents as "child snatchers."

In reality, few programs have been stopped in their tracks because of organized opposition. Accounts of these events are elucidating. Parents invariably surface as the most articulate and credible advocates for school-based services. National and local polls have documented the high level of support for these concepts. The 1997 Gallup Poll reported that 61% of respondents thought that providing health care services in schools would improve the achievement of children "a great deal or quite a lot" (Rose, Gallup, & Elam, 1997). A 1993 sample survey of North Carolina registered voters showed that 73% believe that health care centers offering prevention services should be located at high schools—with the strongest support from African Americans, 18- to 34-year-olds—and no differences by gender, religion, or parental status. More than 60% favored providing birth control at the centers (North Carolina Coalition, 1993).

Many of the state programs were authorized by legislation that prohibited the distribution of contraceptives and referral for abortions on school premises. Even now, "comprehensive" programs emerge from the school-community planning process without including the distribution of birth control methods, suggesting that the expectation of controversy has a cooling effect on service provision. States without restrictions leave the decision about how to provide family planning up to the local school and community. In recent years, school systems have been more willing than in the past to allow the distribution of condoms in schools, as long as parents do not object (Kirby, 1997).

Experience across the nation has shown that the response to SBC funding initiatives supported by state governments and foundations has been overwhelming. Fear of controversy appears to be secondary to the need for support for innovative services in schools. The media could play a more positive role in emphasizing the comprehensive scope of full-service schools and their potential for creating better institutions for children and families.

Future of School-Based Services

The School of the Future

Everyone has his own vision of what a school might look like in the future. My own vision is of a new kind of institution that is designed to meet the many-faceted needs of the community. I call these buildings Safe Passage Schools (Dryfoos, 1998). They are modeled after the emerging full-service community-schools that put together the best in reorganization for quality education with the highest quality health and social supports for children and their families. No two buildings will look alike because each one must be shaped by the people who work in it and use it, the providers and the consumers.

The design of Safe Passage Schools is predicated on a very important hypothesis: *School reform cannot succeed without attention to child and family health and social support services, and the provision of support services without attention to reformation of schools will have little long-term impact.*

Experience has shown that health, mental health, and social service practitioners are ready and willing to move into schools. Whether the educational establishment is committed to the ideas implicit in Safe Passage Schools is not quite so clear. Part of the problem is that most school people have not made the link between school success and support services. They still believe that changing the climate in the classroom and adapting new teaching methods will boost those ubiquitous test scores. In some communities that may work, but for those students who are stressed out from trying to cope with family and community problems, teachers cannot do it alone. We are all in this battle together, to create social environments that will ensure that children grow into responsible adults.

Challenging goals are driving the proliferation of school-based services—reduction of poverty, lessening of high-risk behaviors, movement toward comprehensive services, restructuring of health care, and the restructuring of education. It is in the hands of youth workers and practitioners, health advocates and educational authorities, to join together to shape the forces that will determine our society in the future.

References

Adelman, H., Barker, L., & Nelson, P. (1993). A study of a school-based clinic: Who uses it and who doesn't? *Journal of Clinical Child Psychology, 22*(1), 52-59.

Annie E. Casey Foundation. (1993). The Beacons: A school-based approach to neighborhood revitalization. *AEC Focus.* Greenwich, CT: Author.

Anthony, D. (1991). Remarks to Support Center for School Based Clinics Annual Meeting, Michigan Department of Public Health, Dearborn, October 1991.

Brindis, C., Mamo, L., & McCarter, V. (1996). *Daly City Youth Health Center: Reproductive Health Case Management Program: Final evaluation report.* San Francisco: University of California, Center for Reproductive Health Policy Research.

Brindis, C., Starbuck-Morales, S., Wolfe, A., & McCarter, V. (1994). Characteristics associated with contraceptive use among adolescent females in school-based family planning programs. *Family Planning Perspectives, 26,* 160-164.

Bureau of Primary Health Care. (1993). *School-based clinics that work.* Washington DC: DHHS Public Health Services, Health Resources and Services Administration.

Cahill, M., Perry, J., Wright, M., & Rice, A. (1993). *A documentation report on the New York City Beacons Initiative.* New York: Fund for the City of New York.

Center for Reproductive Health and Policy Research. (1993). *Annual report to the Carnegie Corporation of New York and the Stuart Foundations July 1, 1991-June 3, 1992.* San Francisco: University of California, Institute for Health Policy Studies.

Center for Human Services Policy and Administration. (1990). *Shanks Health Center evaluation. Final report: Third year of program operation.* Tallahassee: Florida State University.

Children's Aid Society. (1994). [Handout, prepared for Invitational Conference sponsored by the Office of Educational Research and Improvement of the U.S. Department of Education, September 28-October 2.]

Dryfoos, J. (1994). *Full service schools: A revolution in health and social services for children, youth, and families.* San Francisco: Jossey-Bass.

Dryfoos, J. (1997). School-based youth programs. Exemplary models and emerging opportunities. In R. Illback, C. Cobb, & H. Joseph (Eds.), *Integrated services for children and families: Opportunities for psychological practice* (pp. 23-52). Washington, DC: American Psychological Association.

Dryfoos, J. (1998). *Safe passage: Making it through adolescence in a risky society.* New York: Oxford University Press.

Dryfoos, J., Brindis, C., & Kaplan, D. (1996). Research and evaluation in school-based health care. In L. Juszczak & M. Fisher (Eds.), *Adolescent medicine: State of the art. Health care in schools* (pp. 207-220). Philadelphia: Hanley & Belfus.

Edwards, L., Steinman, M., Arnold, K., & Hakanson, E. (1980). Adolescent pregnancy prevention services in high school clinics. *Family Planning Perspectives, 12*(1), 7.

Emihovich, C., & Herrington, C. (1993). *Florida's Supplemental School Health Services Projects: An evaluation.* Tallahassee: Florida State University.

The Carter/Bumpers campaign for early immunization. (1995, Winter). *Every Child by Two,* p. 4.

Godin, S., Woodhouse, L., Livingwood, W., & Jacobs, H. (1993). Key factors in successful school-based clinics. *NMHA Prevention Update, 4*(1), 3.

Guernsey, B., & Pastore, D. (1996). Comprehensive school-based health centers: Implementing the model. In L. Juszczak & M. Fisher (Eds.), *Health care in schools* [Special issue]. *Adolescent Medicine: State of the Art Reviews, 7,* 181-196.

Hauser-McKinney, D., & Peak, G. (1995). *Update 1994.* Washington, DC: Advocates for Youth, Support Center for School-based and School-linked Health Care.

Helping America's youth in crisis. Committee on Labor and Human Resources, U.S. Senate, 102nd Cong., 1st Sess. (1990, July 28) (testimony of Sen. Brock Adams).

Improving access to primary care for adolescents: School health centers as a service delivery strategy (MCH policy research brief). (no date). John Hopkins University Child and Adolescent Health Policy Center, Baltimore, MD.

Institute of Medicine. (1997). *Schools and health: Our nation's investment.* Washington DC: National Academy Press.

Juszczak, L., & Fisher, M. (Eds.). (1996). Health care in schools [Special issue]. *Adolescent Medicine: State of the Art Reviews, 7.*

Kirby, D. (1994, September 23). *Findings from other studies of school-based clinics.* Presentation at meeting on evaluation sponsored by the Robert Wood Johnson Foundation, Washington, D.C.

Kirby, D. (1997). *No easy answers.* Washington, DC: National Campaign to Prevent Teen Pregnancy.

Kisker, E., Brown, R., & Hill, J. (1994). *Healthy caring: Outcomes of the Robert Wood Johnson Foundation's school-based adolescent health care program.* Princeton, NJ: Mathematica Policy Research.

Lear, J. (1996). School-based services and adolescent health: Past, present and future. In L. Juszczak & M. Fisher (Eds.), Health care in schools [Special issue]. *Adolescent Medicine: State of the Art Reviews, 7,* 163-180.

Making the Grade. (no date). *The picture of health: State and community leaders on school-based health care.* Washington, DC: George Washington University.

McCord, M., Klein, J., Foy, M, & Fothergill, K. (1993). School-based clinic use and school performance. *Journal of Adolescent Health, 14,* 91-98.

McKinney, D., & Peak, G. (1994). *School-based and school-linked health centers: Update 1993.* Washington, DC: Center for Population Options.

Melaville, A., Blank, M., & Asayesh, G. (1993). *Together we can: A guide for crafting a profamily system of education and human services.* Washington, DC: Government Printing Office.

Millsap, M., Gamse, B., Beckford, I., Johnston, K., Chase, A., Hailey, L., Brigham, N., & Goodson, B. (1995). *The school development program and implementation: Preliminary evaluation evidence.* Paper presented at American Educational Research Association, San Francisco.

National Adolescent Health Resource Center. (1993). *Evaluative review: Findings from a study of selected high school wellness centers in Delaware.* University of Minnesota, Division of General Pediatrics and Adolescent Health.

National Association of Community Health Centers, Inc. (1997). *How to establish & implement successful school-based health centers.* Washington, DC: Author.

North Carolina Coalition on Adolescent Pregnancy. (1993). *We the people.* Charlotte: Author.

Philliber Research Associates. (1994). *An evaluation of the Caring Communities Program at Walbridge Elementary School.* Accord, NY: Author.

Rickett, K., Lear, J., & Schlitt, J. (1995). Select school-based health center publications. *Journal of School Health, 17,* 77-82.

Rienzo, B., & Button, J. (1993). The politics of school-based clinics: A community-level analysis. *Journal of School Health, 63*(6), 266-272.

Rose, L., Gallup, A., & Elam, S. (1997, September). The 29th annual Phi Delta Kappa/Gallup poll of the public's attitudes toward the public schools. *Phi Delta Kappan,* pp. 41-56.

Santelli, J., Kouzis, A., & Newcomer, S. (1996). School-based health centers and adolescent use of primary care and hospital care. *Journal of Adolescent Health, 19,* 267-275.

School Health Resources Services. (1995). *Focus on school-based health centers* (Resource Packet Series). Denver: University of Colorado Health Sciences Center, Office of School Health.

Shearer, C., & Holscheider, S. (1995). *Starting young: School-based health centers at the elementary level.* Washington, DC: National Health and Education Consortium.

Stout, J. (1991). *School-based health clinics: Are they addressing the needs of the students?* Unpublished master's thesis, Department of Public Health, University of Washington.

Taylor, L., & Adelman, H. (1996). Mental health in the schools: Promising directions for practice. In L. Juszczak & M. Fisher (Eds.), Health care in schools [Special issue]. *Adolescent Medicine: State of the Art Reviews, 7,* 303-318.

Tiezzi, L., Lipshutz, J., Wrobleski, N., Vaughan, R., & McCarthy, J. (1997). Pregnancy prevention among urban adolescents younger than 15: Results of the "In Your Face" program. *Family Planning Perspectives, 29*(4), 173-176.

Terwilliger, S. (1994). Early access to health care services through a rural school-based health center. *Journal of School Health, 64*(7), 284-289.

Wagner, M., Golan, S., Shaver, L., Wechsler, M., & Kelley, F. (1994). *A healthy start for California's children and families: Early findings from a statewide evaluation of school-linked services.* Menlo Park, CA: SRI International.

Wolk, L., & Kaplan, D. (1993). Frequent school-based clinic utilization: A comparative profile of problems and service needs. *Journal of Adolescent Health, 14,* 458-463.

CHAPTER 5

From Individual to Social Change: Current and Future Directions of Health Interventions

WILLIAM D. MARELICH

MARY JANE ROTHERAM-BORUS

As the new millennium approaches, intervention strategies that focus on improving health have been aggressively pursued by medical and social/behavioral practitioners. The emergence and application of the biopsychosocial model has led to the realization that health-related behaviors are interdependent with psychological and social factors (e.g., diabetes and schizophrenia are driven by both medical and psychological factors; see Engel, 1977). Hence, solutions for changing health behaviors encompass social-environmental factors as well as psychological issues.

Shaping or changing health behaviors can be a monumental task. Whether the behavior is simple (e.g., brushing one's teeth every day) or complex (e.g., adhering to a 6-month tuberculosis drug regimen), individuals must make an effort to maintain healthy behaviors and avoid unhealthy behaviors. Often, barriers in complying with the new behavior or lack of confidence with adherence leads to failure (Janz & Becker, 1984). In particular, the early stages of behavior change are the most crucial because habituation of the replacement behaviors has not occurred; hence, constant reinforcement is required for the new behaviors to persist. However, behavior change can and does take place given time, the individual's willingness to comply, and the acceptability of the new behavior within cultural norms (Rogers, 1962).

Health behavior interventions focus on both individual behavior change (e.g., changing an individual's attitudes, behavioral intentions, and actions) and social change (e.g., changing population attitudes and behaviors). Together, these interventions address different parts of the epidemiologic spectrum of disease and infection gradient, yet are interdependent. *Individual-level* intervention strategies (e.g., case-level interventions or small group interventions) have been very successful in changing behaviors (for broad reviews, see McGuire, 1985, and Oskamp, 1991; for applications to health issues, see Taylor, 1995). Since health intervention research may be viewed as applied or action oriented, these intervention strategies typically are applied to individuals manifesting a disease (i.e., at risk for spreading the disease) or those at risk for infection.

However, this emphasis on high-profile cases is analogous to treating the "tip of the iceberg" of a disease (Lilienfeld & Lilienfeld, 1980), whereby cases that manifest the disease receive individual treatment, but those with unapparent infections (i.e., infected cases that show no symptoms) remain untreated. The AIDS epidemic in the United States is a good example of the "iceberg" phenomenon and individual behavior change interventions. HIV/AIDS health interventions focus on those individuals practicing high-risk behaviors such as unprotected intercourse with multiple partners or unsterile needle sharing, and include changing the attitudes, intentions, and actions of those at high risk for HIV. However, regardless of these interventions, incidence rates continued to increase through the 1980s and have remained at high levels through the 1990s. Although the people at highest risk are being addressed, many infected individuals continue to bridge into the uninfected population and perpetuate the epidemic.

Other health change interventions focus on broader *social change* strategies, where normative social behaviors and attitudes of the population are altered through mass appeals, social activism, and public policy (Stokols, 1992; Susser, 1995). These interventions are intended to influence the entire population, including those at high risk for disease spread or infection and those at low risk. One key to societal adoption of healthy behaviors (e.g., daily exercise or quitting smoking) may lie in discovering the "tipping point" for mass acceptance of the behavior. Gladwell (1996) has illustrated this principle with the metaphor, "Tomato ketchup in a bottle—none will come and then the lot'll" (p. 36). In other words, social change may appear slow or even stagnant at first, yet over time momentum builds and change "spills" into the normative behaviors of the population. Recent examples of populationwide changes in health-related behaviors include declines in smoking and increases in the use of vehicle restraints.

Together, individual and social change strategies are important tools for influencing health-enhancing behaviors and deterring unhealthy or risky health behaviors. The current chapter provides an overview of successful health behavior interventions addressing individual and societal change. The first part presents theory-driven intervention strategies applied at the level of the individual. The second part reviews health interventions from a social influence perspective, focusing on changes in behavioral norms of communities and the larger U.S. population. These interventions can have wide-ranging social impact, yet have received little attention. The final section of the chapter elaborates on the future of health interventions, including how the individual and social influence approaches need to be expanded to address providers, managed care settings, and legislative changes.

Behavioral Interventions at the Individual Level

Over the past 30 years, health researchers have undertaken the task of making sense of an individual's health behaviors and his or her interconnectivity to surrounding systems. Using a biopsychosocial model, the physical, mental, and social factors that affect health have been investigated. Health behavior change research and interventions have focused on a wide range of issues, including heart disease (Farquhar et al., 1990; Miller, Smith, Turner, Guijarro, & Hallet, 1996), HIV/AIDS sexual behaviors (Kalichman, Carey, & Johnson, 1996), smoking (Bruvold, 1993), weight loss (Black, Gleser, & Kooyers, 1990) and eating disorders (Mann, Nolen-Hoeksema, Huang, & Burgard, 1997), cancer (Meyer & Mark, 1995), obesity (Kirsch, Montgomery, & Sapirstein, 1995), exercise behavior (Hausenblas, Carron, & Mack, 1997), and health/work issues (Donaldson, Gooler, & Weiss, 1998).

This section will focus on individual-based models of behavior and behavior change that have been shown to be effective. To date, there have been a number of excellent reviews that have addressed many of these models and their application to health issues (e.g., Glanz, Lewis, & Rimer, 1990; Rodin & Salovey, 1989; Taylor, 1995). Hence, this section provides a brief sample of various theories and models. In addition, models based on social/behavioral theory are given preference for coverage because they illustrate or explain the "black box" (i.e., causal mechanisms) of behavioral intervention strategies (Lipsey, 1993; Scott & Sechrest, 1989), thereby providing powerful, replicable explanations for health behaviors and health behavior change (Van Ryn & Heaney, 1992).

For example, in their review of HIV/AIDS behavior change studies, Fisher and Fisher (1992) found that a majority of studies utilized informal conceptual approaches to behavioral intervention as opposed to formal theory-driven approaches. They concluded that "AIDS-risk-reduction interventions that are conceptually based and group specific and that focus on providing AIDS-risk-reduction information, motivation, and behavioral skills are the most impactful and sound bases for intervention" (p. 463). Similar findings have been shown for theory-driven drug adherence interventions (Haynes, McKibbon, & Kanani, 1996) and theory-driven behavioral outcomes and HIV-risk reduction (Kalichman et al., 1996).

Some of the most successful theories of individual health behavior change include the *health belief model* (Janz & Becker, 1984), the *theory of reasoned action* (Fishbein & Ajzen, 1975; Fishbein et al., 1993), and the *theory of planned behavior* (Ajzen & Madden, 1986). In general, these models may be considered attitudinal models of behavior change (Taylor, 1995). If an individual's attitude (emotive or affective response) toward the faulty behavior can be changed, then the individual should strive to change the behavior and replace it with a healthy response. Other theories of behavior change include *social cognitive theory* (Bandura, 1986) and the *transtheoretical model of stages and processes of change* (Prochaska, DiClemente, & Norcross, 1992). These theories tend to be broader in scope than the attitudinal models, often encompassing attitudinal and cognitive-behavioral components and decision-making processes.

All the models noted above have received considerable empirical support. As such, the task of overviewing each of these models may seem inhibitive. However, there is considerable overlap across these competing models, especially when examining factors that may impede health behavior change, future goals, and health outcome expectations (Bandura, 1997). The most successful components from these and other models (see Fishbein et al., 1991; see also Bandura, 1997) include the following:

- intentions
- environmental constraints (i.e., barriers)
- outcome expectations
- social norms
- emotion
- self-efficacy

Intentions. An intention is the cognitive antecedent to a behavior, and may be seen as the mediating factor between attitudes (i.e., affective association toward an object or a person) and behavioral actions (which historically have shown only weak causal links; see Wicker, 1969). Behavioral change comes from altering the individual's intention of performing the behavior. Intentions are altered by influencing attitudes and beliefs. The models most associated with behavioral intentions are the theories of reasoned action (Fishbein & Ajzen, 1975), planned behavior (Ajzen & Madden, 1986), and stages/processes of change (Prochaska et al., 1992).

Environmental Constraints (Barriers). Environmental constraints are those mental or physical barriers that hinder performance or adoption of healthy behaviors. Behavioral change comes from removal of the barriers or by showing the individual how to work around the offered constraints. Barriers are a major factor in the health belief model (Janz & Becker, 1984) and social cognitive theory (Bandura, 1997), and have been shown to play an important role in health interventions (Janz & Becker, 1984).

Outcome Expectations. Outcome expectations are the beliefs "that a particular course of action will produce certain outcomes" (Bandura, 1977, p. 193). In other words, if the benefits to behavior change outweigh the costs, then the probability of behavior change is increased. Therefore, behavior change comes from bolstering perception of benefits and downplaying costs. Most models of behavior change focus on at least one facet of outcomes, either physical/health improvements, improvements in social relations, or self-evaluation (Bandura, 1997).

Social Norms. Social norms are the individual's perceptions of the normative behavioral pressures surrounding the individual (e.g., from peers or family members). Behavior change is instigated either by changing the individual's perception of normative influences, or by restructuring the individual's social environment (e.g., changing peer groups). All the models noted above contain a social-norm component.

Emotion. The emotional reaction (positive or negative) of the individual when confronted with making a behavior change can also determine whether the change is successful or unsuccessful. Behavior intervention is thus undertaken by promoting positive emotional reactions (e.g., coping strategies; see Lazarus & Folkman, 1984). Since attitudes are, by nature, affective (Oskamp, 1991), all the attitudinal models of behavior change contain this component. In addition, social cognitive theory and the stages/processes of change model also incorporate emotion.

Self-Efficacy. Self-efficacy is a cognitive component and may be defined as the individual's self-perception of his or her capability to perform the required behavior change. Therefore, self-efficacy is antecedent to behavioral intention and action. However, self-efficacy has also been shown directly to influence behavior above and beyond behavioral intentions (Ajzen & Madden, 1986). Behavioral change comes from training individuals that they are capable of making the requested behavior change. Models of behavioral change associated with self-efficacy include social cognitive theory, the theory of planned behavior, and the stages/processes of change model.

Although we have presented components from various models, it is important to note that the use of these components without their respective theories, known as *eclecticism,* may suffer from inherent philosophical problems (Slife & Williams, 1995). For example, by measuring the effects of barriers, applied researchers are forced to accept the underlying assumptions associated with the health belief model even though none of the other components of the model may be addressed. Theories such as the health belief model are intended to *explain* health behavior and behavior change by themselves, and are often derived from different theoretical frameworks and assumptions. Indeed, "every part [of a theory component] brings with it the whole of the host of hidden ideas that any theory always has" (Slife & Williams, 1995, p. 48).

It has been argued that transtheoretical models bridge theoretical accounts of behavior and the goal of helping individuals alter or solve their behavioral problems (Slife & Williams, 1995). For example, Prochaska and DiClemente (1992) have provided excellent evidence for the utility of their transtheoretical model of stages/processes of change in "describing, predicting, and explaining changes in a broad range of behavior problems" (p. 204). However, as noted earlier, behavior change interventions that are theory based produce more reliable and valid results than those that are not (e.g., Fisher & Fisher, 1992; Haynes et al., 1996). Indeed, as Bandura (1997) has concisely stressed, "scientific progress is better achieved by encompassing more fully the determinants within an integrated theory than by creating conglomerate models with constructs picked from divergent theories with the attendant problems of redundancy, fractionation, and theoretical disconnectedness" (p. 286).

Interventions at the Group Level: Effecting Social Change

There must be no let to social action against . . . known health hazards. (Susser, 1995, p. 158)

Although interventions aimed at affecting the individual's attitudes and behaviors have produced the bulk of empirical findings, those aimed at influencing social change have an important place in changing health behaviors and in maintaining behavior change across time. Broad social change in regard to health behaviors and promotion have been noted for smoking, diet, and exercise in recent years, with changes in social normative behaviors suggested for these changes (McGinnis, Richmond, Brandt, Windom, & Mason, 1992; Stokols, 1992; Taylor, 1995).

How are social norms changed? One suggestion is that normative behaviors are changed in small, incremental steps, also known as "small wins" (Weick, 1984). Applied to health behavior change and interventions, the small wins approach functions to ease individuals into changing their health behaviors through small, controllable actions. This approach is analogous to the "foot-in-the-door" phenomenon (Freedman & Fraser, 1966). The foot-in-the-door approach suggests that if an individual commits to a lesser request, then he or she is likely to perform a more costly act in order to remain in consonance with his or her earlier action (Oskamp, 1991). For example, Freedman and Fraser (1966) found that individuals who acquiesced to having a small, driver safety sign placed in their window were more likely to allow a large "drive carefully" sign placed on their lawn compared to a control group that were asked only to display the large sign.

Weick (1984) has cited a number of non-health-related examples to support the small wins approach to societal change. For example, the Task Force on Gay Liberation succeeded in having the Library of Congress reclassify works on the gay liberation movement from "abnormal sexual relations" to "sexual life," thus winning a small battle that raised public consciousness about the acceptability of being gay. In another example, Weick (1984) suggests that although feminists have suffered setbacks in big win situations (e.g., equal rights legislation), they have been successful with small wins in degendering the English language. These small wins, in turn, will affect public consciousness and, subsequently, future legislation.

In regard to health promotion and societal change, Stokols (1992) notes that "incremental health promotion . . . can exert a positive, albeit gradual, influence on the quality and healthfulness" (p. 6) of individuals. For example, Corea (1992) illustrated how social activism and empirical research culminated in changing the AIDS diagnostic definition to include clinical symptoms specifically related to women. McGinnis et al. (1992) cited gradual changes in social norms as the reason why smoking has declined since 1980 and for increases in seat belt use (e.g., from 1975 to 1995, seat belt use has seen an almost 10-fold increase; National Highway Traffic Safety Administration, 1996). In another study, Berger and Marelich (1997) also suggested incremental changes in societal norms as the salient factor behind steep declines in alcohol-impaired driving attitudes, beliefs, and behaviors, comparing two cross-sectional samples of California drivers from 1983 to 1994.

What types of intervention strategies best effect social change? From social-learning theory, we know that individuals acquire new behaviors and change old ones through direct experience and positive feedback offered by others, through self-reinforcement, or through indirect or vicarious experiences of *others* being reinforced (or not punished) for particular behaviors (Bandura, 1986). Further, individuals exist as part of larger social webs of interdependencies. These "loose couplings" (Weick, 1979) allow for some individual differences, yet underscore the importance of social networks that surround and influence behavior. Hence, intervention strategies that focus on altering individuals' perceptions of social-normative behaviors may have the greatest effect.

Social change may best be shaped by exposing individuals to health prevention or health change messages over time using communication channels such as the mass media (e.g., television and radio). Media communication influences how individuals perceive the world, and can be viewed as a "belief" cultivation process (Roberts & Maccoby, 1985). Further, the media can forge cohesiveness of individuals by generating shared experiences and social comparison (Meyrowitz, 1985).

Once a core group of individuals has been exposed, the new information filters or diffuses its way into society and social acceptance (Rogers, 1962). For example, say a town is exposed to a series of health-promotion messages over a one-month period. The messages will filter their way around the community due to simple communication processes. Those who comprehended the message will pass the information along to those who did not attend to the message and to those who attended but did not comprehend. Finally, message adherence will slowly occur as more and more individuals begin to conform.

Community-based health interventions using mass media often show positive results. For example, in a well-documented study by Farquhar et al. (1990), reductions in cardiovascular disease were noted in a communitywide intervention. The intervention focused on educational strategies, including mass media campaigns that included television, radio, newspaper, and other print media, and interpersonal training programs. Two California cities served as treatments and two as controls. Results also indicated modest significant decreases in cholesterol level and blood pressure. It was also noted that the media intervention accelerated smoking declines in the treatment cities. Other community health interventions using mass media have also shown positive results (see Lando et al., 1995; Multiple Risk Factor Intervention Trial Research Group, 1982; Owen, Bauman, Booth, Oldenburg, & Magnus, 1995).

However, community-based interventions can also fail to have an impact (Susser, 1995). For example, COMMIT (Community Intervention Trial for Smoking Cessation; COMMIT Research Group, 1995a, 1995b) focused on smoking cessation in 11 matched community pairs, with cessation of smoking for heavy smokers as one of the target outcomes. The intervention consisted of educational messages presented through different mediums (e.g., mass media, community events, work sites, and health care providers). Results indicated that quit rates for heavy smokers (the main target group) were not affected by the intervention.

The successes and failures of these and other mass media interventions may be attributed to a number of factors. One reason for null results is because the society may not be prepared to take such large steps, with individuals taking big countermeasures against change (Weick, 1984). Indeed, an individual's behavior is bound by attitudes and behaviors of his or her social group (Mead, 1934), and instability or dissonance is experienced when there is a "lack of correspondence" between the normative expectations of society and the individual's behavior (Schneiderman, 1988, p. 71). Hence, behaviors that are embedded and accepted in society, albeit unhealthy or risky, are by nature hard to alter due to the initial dissonance individuals experience in making the changes.

For example, Rotello (1997, p. 56) has suggested that the AIDS epidemic in U.S. gay males could be attenuated if gay men adopted a more monogamous lifestyle, thereby limiting "bridging" or sexual mixing of high HIV-risk core group members with those outside the core. He notes further, however, that modern gay culture tolerates multiple sexual partners as part of its ideology. Moving the culture toward a monogamous lifestyle would encounter resistance from many group members because of violation of cultural norms.

Another reason for the null results is the complex nature of information communication. According to McGuire (1985), there are five key factors that affect attention and communication of information: source, message, channel, receiver, and target. *Source* focuses on who the source of the message is. *Message* indicates the type of message, for example fear-related or informational. *Channel* refers to the route by which the message is delivered, such as radio, television, and so on. *Receiver* indicates who is going to receive the information, for example, children or adults. Finally, *target* indicates the target behavior that takes place. These five factors must be met for messages to be attended to. Further, individuals need to process the received information, understand it, and retain the information in order for the message to have an effect.

Social marketers of health promotion messages note similar concerns with communication. In their overview of the social marketing of AIDS education, Rabin and Porter (1996) suggested a number of factors that must be present for social marketing to work. First, the consumer should want what is being marketed. If the goal is increasing condom use, social marketers must provide a message that indicates the benefits of condom use and creates a need for the condoms. Second, consideration should be given to consumer acceptance of the particular product. This may include increasing the comfortableness of condom wear or providing alternative products (e.g., the female condom).

Third, price or investment should be considered. This includes not only actual cost of the product, but also access issues and emotional barriers. Fourth, message delivery must be considered. In other words, effort should be placed on the particular communication channels that are used for the health messages. Fifth, the target audience should be considered. If the purpose of the intervention is to influence condom use in gay men, then communication channels and products should be marketed with this in mind. Sixth, the socially marketed message needs to be constantly promoted and redesigned. Single or short-term interventions, although cost-effective, generally produce weaker effects than longer interventions. In addition, constant exposure (i.e., mere exposure) to the same message can lead to message disregard (Zajonc, 1968). Therefore, new messages must continue to be generated that pique the consumer's interest.

By integrating the small wins approach, communication factors, and social marketing, we may attribute the *success* of large scale interventions to successful diffusion of new information, ideas, or innovations into society. Rogers (1962) has summarized a strong body of empirical research in this area, labeling this approach the *diffusion of innovations* framework. An *innovation* is simply an idea "perceived" as new to those exposed to the idea, while *diffusion* is the spread of the innovation (i.e., new idea) across individuals. For diffusion to take place, the innovation must be *adopted* by individuals. This adoption process occurs in steps, which include awareness of the innovation, interest, evaluation of the innovation before adoption, a trial-run period (i.e., "dry run"), and finally adoption of the innovation by the individual. Hence, the diffusion process consists of interdependent components, including the innovation or idea, communication of the innovation from person to person, a social system that encourages communication across individuals, and time for the idea to filter through the society or community (Smith, 1976).

In a demonstration of the diffusion of innovations framework, Kelly et al. (1992) used a multiple-baseline health-related intervention to change social norms and HIV-risk behaviors. In their study, community opinion leaders (called "trendsetters") in three cities were trained to disseminate risk-reduction information in informal social settings (e.g., nightclubs or bars). Findings showed that HIV-risk behaviors declined over a 2-month period. In addition, changes in perceived social norms were noted, with greater peer acceptance of safer sex and precautionary measures noted over a 2-month period in all three cities. Other direct applications of diffusion of HIV-prevention messages have also shown positive results (see Kelly et al., 1997; also see Rotheram-Borus et al., 1998).

The Future of Health Behavior Interventions

The vast majority of interventions for the health behaviors described in the first part of this chapter were typically targeted at individuals at high risk and typically used a group delivery format. In general, these interventions have focused on Phase 3 research (i.e., demonstrating that a program can be efficacious with the target population). However, Phase 4 research trials (i.e., those that evaluate whether the implementation of an intervention program in real-world settings is effective) have been few and have often had equivocal results. As noted in the second part of the chapter, programs such as The Stanford Heart Trial (Maccoby, Farquhar, & Fortmann, 1985), the Community Intervention Trial for Smoking Cessation (COMMIT; Commit Research Group, 1995a, 1995b), and the Medical Outcome Study (MOS; Wells, Hayes, et al., 1989; Wells, Stewart, et al., 1989) are examples of large scale intervention projects that emphasized individuals' behaviors over time when multifaceted, multilevel interventions are mounted. A primary issue in each of these trials has been the fidelity of the intervention that is being implemented when the intervention is diffused to community settings.

These individual- and group-level interventions have offered many theories and behavioral tools to affect health outcomes. However, what will the future of health interventions bring? What should be the focus of future interventions, and what kinds of changes need to be made? This final section will address important, yet underemphasized facets related to health behavior interventions: intervention providers, managed care, and legislative changes.

Intervention Providers and the Managed Care System

Intervention providers (i.e., those actually implementing the intervention) are often ignored by social scientists in the planning of successful intervention programs. Many good intervention programs have failed to be replicated and disseminated by failing to address providers' needs (Weisz & Weiss, 1993). Children's mental health service delivery is one example. A number of effective programs have been shown to improve children's behavioral outcomes (Hibbs & Jensen, 1996b). These include adolescent suicide attempters (Rotheram-Borus, Piacentini, Cantwell, Belin, & Song, in press; Rotheram-Borus, Piacentini, Van Rossem, et al., in press), children with attention deficit disorder (Anastopoulous, Barkley, & Sheldon, 1996; Barkley, Guevremont, Anastopoulous, & Fletcher, 1992), children with depressive disorders (Brent, Holder, Kolko, Birmaher, et al., 1997; Silverman & Kurtines, 1996), conduct disordered children (Patterson, Dishion, & Chamberlain, 1993), anxious children (Barrett, Dadds, & Rapee, 1996; Kendall, 1994; Kendall & Southam-Gerow, 1996), and those with obsessive compulsive disorder (March, Mulle, & Herbel, 1994). Each of the successful programs is cognitive-behavioral in orientation, lasts between 12 and 20 sessions, includes the involvement of adults in the children's environments, and has clearly targeted outcomes. However, practice in community-based clinics does not follow these general guidelines that have demonstrated positive outcomes (Weisz & Weiss, 1993).

One challenge for implementation of effective programs comes from the provider community, whose training, experience, and expertise is inconsistent with the emerging consensus in the research literature on how to deliver effective programs. For example, many providers of care (e.g., those psychodynamically oriented) are not trained in brief treatment techniques and do not set goals that can be defined as achieved or not achieved (Weisz & Weiss, 1993). Although each of the successful programs noted above were guided by a manual, very few providers are actually trained to implement interventions by following such a guide. Providers are typically socialized to believe that the quality and conditions of the interpersonal relationship established between the client and themselves is the key element influencing behavior change (Strupp, 1977). This expectation is not supported by the empirical literature, and perpetuates a failure to implement effective programs (Beckman & Fischer, 1997).

A second challenge for implementation of effective programs comes from managed care. In contrast to the small wins approach that has characterized the implementation of interventions for individuals, there are major changes currently occurring in the organization and financing of physical and mental health care in the United States (*Remarks on the Advisory Commission,* 1997). These changes in the organization of the health care system result in substantial revisions in the process of delivering care. The primary concerns driving these changes are improved cost efficiency with a desire simultaneously to improve quality of care.

There has been far less attention to methods of guiding the behavior of the health care providers in the specific process of delivering their interventions. The failure to have a strong empirical basis for the providers' behavior creates the opportunity for health care companies and management concerns to alter the process of care without anticipating or being constrained by information that would force the organization and delivery of care to be addressed in a very different fashion. Therefore, it is important to determine standards of care in key disease areas. Then managed care organizations must provide that standard of care.

One area in which potential standards could be developed is the area of children's mental health services. Recently, effective programs were reviewed and identified by Hibbs and Jensen (1996b). Each of the effective programs was 12 to 20 sessions in length (Hibbs & Jensen, 1996a). In no case was a program identified that could be successfully implemented in under 10 sessions (Giles & Marafiote, 1998). However, Miller (1996) reports that managed care administrators are pressuring providers to complete treatment in 3 to 4 sessions.

One example where standards of care need further development is in the treatment of depression in children, which is typically addressed in primary health care within managed care settings (Starfield, 1992). Similar to adults (Wells, Sturm, Sherbourne, & Meredith, 1996), the existing research documenting positive outcomes for children with depressive disorders has been conducted primarily in mental health clinics (Weiss & Weisz, 1993). There are at least three different manual-based interventions for the treatment of depressed adolescents (Brent, Holder, Kolko, Birmaher, et al., 1997; Moreau & Mufson, 1997; Rotheram-Borus, Piacentini, Miller, Graae, & Castro-Blanco, 1994), but none of these programs could be effectively implemented within a primary health care setting. Most youth have mental health symptoms that remit relatively quickly (Rotheram-Borus, Piacentini, Cantwell, et al., in press); therefore, treatment of the depression is not likely to differ significantly from a brief intervention delivered in primary health care settings. However, the interrelatedness of symptoms among adolescents is rarely examined, particularly when evaluating depressed youth in medical settings. Adolescent problem behaviors cluster (Ensminger, 1987). Therefore, youth who are depressed are also likely to be attempting suicide, using drugs, having problems in school, and are at higher risk for teenage pregnancy and sexually transmitted diseases.

These problems will not be noticed within a medical setting that focuses solely on remitting symptoms of depression. The long-term negative outcomes for depressed youth are a key issue that needs some way of being assessed and monitored within managed care settings. The status of treatment research in the area of adolescent depression is similar to the status of research in most areas for preventive interventions with children. There are very few domains where the standards for quality care have been identified and evaluations have been conducted and replicated for positive outcomes of preventive interventions (Institute of Medicine, 1992).

When no standards of care exist that are well documented, managed care organizations have a huge opportunity to restructure the service delivery system in a manner consistent with high-quality care. The existing literature on preventive and clinical interventions for children point us to delivering preventive services in short-term interventions (12-20 sessions) by highly trained paraprofessionals using a structured and specific manual to guide the delivery of the intervention. In contrast, care is being delivered by Ph.D. and M.D. practitioners over a much briefer period (3-6 sessions) in an open-ended format that lacks clear guidelines (Weiss & Weisz, 1993).

Neither the current practice of preventive interventions in field settings nor the practices of mental health and psychosocial aspects of care being delivered (or being proposed to be delivered) in managed care settings follows these practice guidelines. Managed care settings are generally providing preventive care for both physical and mental health problems in primary health care settings by nurses and family practitioners. When mental health care is authorized, there are seldom manual-based interventions that are being systematically implemented. Instead, the dose of the interventions is being decreased with little attention to the content or the quality of the care. The level of professional, typically a licensed person with a professional degree, and the associated costs of care are reduced by providing large numbers of patients at reduced reimbursement rates to providers. Thus, costs are being constrained, but the primary area of cost containment is duration, or number of sessions of care. The quality of services is rarely addressed, especially at the level of provider specialization and training.

An alternative strategy for the field of psychosocial- or mental health-focused preventive interventions is to consider a major revision in the certification and licensing of providers. Two fields offer excellent prototypes for these types of changes over the past 20 years: mental retardation (Szymanski, 1987) and psychiatric rehabilitation (Fairweather & Fergus, 1993; Risley & Reid, 1996). In regard to *mental retardation,* retarded children as recently as the 1950s were sent to mental hospitals that were staffed by nurses and doctors where they would remain in inpatient settings throughout their lifetime. Today, there are interdisciplinary teams of talented paraprofessionals who provide the great majority of care. Training is provided to these paraprofessionals through specialized training programs. Hospitalizations are time limited and behavior focused; for example, to receive toilet training or eating skills, or learn eye contact and smiling behaviors. Once skills are acquired, daily life is managed in community settings (Jacobson, Burchard, & Carling, 1992). Many who previously would have been maintained for life in a hospital setting now hold jobs and assist in providing for themselves with support from the community support companion (Wolfe, Kregel, & Wehman, 1996). The training of almost all professionals in this field is behaviorally based. This is a very different, nonmedical approach to the organization of care for a subgroup covered by the public safety net.

Similar shifts have occurred in the field of *psychiatric rehabilitation* (Liberman & Yager, 1994). Persons with behaviorally based psychotic disorders who typically would have been maintained in hospital settings often can exist in assisted living programs (Drake et al., 1998; Rosenheck & Neale, 1998; Salyers, Masterton, Fekete, Picone, & Bond, 1998). Disordered individuals can share jobs and compensate for each other when symptoms impair daily functioning in a way that demands withdrawal from the job for a period of time.

These two fields present potential models for the field of prevention. It is possible that higher quality of care can be provided by persons with lower levels of degrees, but delivered by persons with higher levels of specialized training within a specific area. The costs of care would drop not because professional skills were being discounted, as is currently happening in Independent Physicians Associations (IPAs) and Preferred Provider Organizations (PPOs), but because the level of training has been reduced. The quality of care would more closely resemble the standards that are implemented and demonstrated to be appropriate within the research literature. Over time, it would be expected that general competence of the field consistently to manage persons with mental health problems in a more effective fashion would increase.

The fields of mental retardation and psychiatric rehabilitation provide alternative models for organizing care that do not typify the current organization of care in preventive, psychosocial, or mental health care (Pulcini & Howard, 1997). These fields also present us with a model of the problems that society must avoid if imitating the organization of care. Both the mentally retarded and the psychiatrically disturbed need a continuum of levels of support services for different points in their illness that has the potential for being comprehensive. While these needs are clearly recognized for severely impaired populations, the funding levels are so low in appropriations for persons with these problems that it is impossible to provide the continuum of care (Austad, Hunter, & Morgan, 1998). If preventive services were to adapt models similar to these subspecialties, the policies would have to include sufficient funds to implement the programs in the manner that is designed (Minihan, Dean, & Lyons, 1993).

For example, in California, services for the mentally retarded are typically subcontracted to behavioral health care organizations that receive a capitated payment for each of the disabled served by the program. The greatest amount of the care is provided by community support companions who attempt to teach clients skills in coping with stressful hassles that accompany everyday life: scheduling doctor appointments, changing the water in a fish bowl, fixing a meal, going to a movie. These companions accompany the clients to doctor's appointments, taking public transportation on a bus, and resolve interpersonal conflicts and clarify understanding between the provider and clients. The funds allocated for these programs are so low, however, that only those willing to accept the lowest paid jobs accept the position, although considerably greater skills are needed. The low rates of compensation, high levels of overtime work required, high turnover rates of employees, and low status of the field lead to poor services often being delivered to the persons in community settings. It is not clear whether the care received is of lower quality overall to persons in community settings versus in inpatient settings. However, the failure to operationalize and fund the services at a viable level is leading to much poorer care than would be anticipated given the research literature that has demonstrated interventions to be efficacious when funded at appropriate levels. Thus, if these models are to be emulated, the problems that have plagued these systems of care (Gardner, 1992;

Johnston & Shook, 1993) need to be anticipated and addressed in the planning stage.

Legislation and Health Behavior Change

There are many possibilities in the ongoing reorganization of delivery and financing of care for providers dramatically to shift their roles, responsibilities, and the content of the care provided. For such a revolution to occur within preventive services, major shifts will need to occur. Legislation is one area that may result in significant benefits to reorganization of the systems for the delivery of care and result in major societal changes regarding healthy behaviors and disease prevention. Indeed, legislative changes and related sanctions have been shown to have strong effects on health issues, including alcohol consumption, smoking, vehicle accidents, and child safety issues (Stokols, 1992; Susser, 1995). In addition, broader legislation has had an indirect impact on health through public safety concerns such as air quality, toxic waste cleanup, and clean water.

Legislation change, however, may have only short-term effects. For example, Ross (1994) found that increased sanctions had at most a limited effect on deterrence of alcohol-impaired driving. In addition, Rogers and Schoenig (1994) found that legislative changes alone could not account for reductions in drinking and driving witnessed in the early 1980s in California. Indeed, factors such as personal morality (i.e., a sense of an internalized obligation of what is right and wrong) and socialization of preventative habits may be the strongest operatives on behavior even in the absence of punishment threat (Andenaes, 1977; Gibbs, 1975).

Further, legislative changes and levied sanctions can be implemented only when issues of public safety or concern are raised. For example, public safety issues surrounding alcohol-impaired driving (for both the driver and passenger) have been a priority of state legislators due to high death and injury rates (17,274 alcohol-related fatalities in 1995; National Highway Traffic Safety Administration, 1996). This is evidenced by a constant retooling of state legislation toward stricter sanctions (e.g., from 1981 to 1985, over 450 new alcohol-impaired driving laws were passed by state legislation; National Commission Against Drunk Driving, 1985).

For legislation to be accepted, arguments must be made for the public safety. Although progress has been made for sanction intervention for issues such as smoking in public places and bicycle helmet use for children (Stokols, 1992), other areas will probably never be addressed. For example, how would the public react to forced physical exercise programs? Even when these programs are offered in the workplace, few employees participate in such programs (Donaldson et al., 1998). Could sanctions be levied against those who consume high levels of dietary fat? Even when an individual's disease leads to a public health threat (e.g., an active tuberculosis patient refuses to adhere to his or her drug regimen and continues to expose others to infection, or an HIV-positive individual continues to have unprotected sexual relations), prosecution is difficult and rare.

Susser (1995) has suggested an approach that integrates social action and legislative changes. Health prevention and protection must start at the nongovernmental level. As the social movement gains strength, legislation can be introduced. For example, Rogers and Schoenig (1994) concluded that reductions in alcohol-impaired driving witnessed in the 1980s could be attributed to the initiation and popularity of MADD (Mothers Against Drunk Driving), a volunteer organization intent on reducing alcohol-impaired driving. Further, MADD increased public awareness of drinking and driving, no doubt leading to changes in legislation over the past 20 years.

In addition, community interventions should be continued, with constant refinements made to interventions that have shown null or marginal results (Susser, 1995). Even null results may, over time, filter through the population, given that diffusion of an idea or message often takes years (Rogers, 1962). This constant "poking" at the society resembles the aforementioned small wins approach, with small unassuming wins eventually leading to larger societal changes.

Summary

This chapter has been an attempt to understand the current state of health intervention strategies and to suggest future paths. The exploration of past and current interventions has revealed that health behavior change may be successfully effected through individual and societal change strategies. As for the future of health-related interventions, we have suggested an emphasis on the intervention provider and changes in the current managed care system, and we have underscored the importance of legislative changes that can have strong effects on health behavior. Although often overlooked, these areas can play a pivotal role in the success of an intervention and may be expected to offer the best hope for efficient and effective health interventions in the future.

As has been noted, there are many theories that address health behavior change. Whether through attitudinal pressures on the individual or diffusion of societal norms, people *will* and *do* change their behavior. With this in mind, it appears the tools are available to help "tip" our society toward healthy behaviors, and to reach those with unapparent infections to keep them from "bridging" (see Rotello, 1997) into uninfected populations. Further, these tools may be used to perpetuate the societal acceptance of healthy behaviors (e.g., exercise, limiting dietary fat consumption), and to avoid risky health behaviors (e.g., needle sharing). The emphasis now lies on (a) how to integrate successfully the existing health-related research and knowledge developed, (b) the providers who will use these theoretical and behavioral tools in applied settings, (c) the managed care system in which the providers operate, and (d) future legislation that can impact individuals directly, their providers, and the existing care system.

Although there are no simple solutions to changing health behaviors, the past 50 years have offered much in the areas of social theory and program evaluation. The emergence of the biopsychosocial model, and the fields of health psychology and program evaluation (Shadish, Cook, & Leviton, 1991) together have provided successful paradigms for investigating and evaluating health-related behaviors and their psychosocial components. The next millennium no doubt will have much to offer—and much to consider.

References

Ajzen, I., & Madden, T. J. (1986). Prediction of goal-directed behavior: Attitudes, intentions, and perceived behavioral control. *Journal of Experimental Social Psychology, 22,* 453-474.

Anastopoulous, A. S., Barkley, R. A., & Sheldon, T. L. (1996). Attention deficit disorder. In E. D. Hibbs & P. S. Jensen (Eds.), *Psychosocial treatments for child and adolescent disorders: Empirically based strategies for clinical practice* (pp. 267-284). New York: American Psychological Association.

Andenaes, J. (1977). The moral or educative influence of criminal law. In J. L. Tapp & F. J. Levine (Eds.), *Law, justice, and the individual in society: Psychological and legal issues* (pp. 50-59). New York: Holt, Rinehart & Winston.

Austad, C. S., Hunter, R. D. A., & Morgan, T. C. (1998). Managed health care, ethics, and psychotherapy. *Clinical Psychology, 5,* 67-76.

Bandura, A. (1977). Self-efficacy: Toward a unifying theory of behavioral change. *Psychological Review, 84*(2), 191-215.

Bandura, A. (1986). *Social foundations of thought and action: A social cognitive theory.* Englewood Cliffs, NJ: Prentice Hall.

Bandura, A. (1997). *Self-efficacy: The exercise of control.* New York: Freeman.

Barkley, R. A., Guevremont, D. C., Anastopoulos, A. D., & Fletcher, K. E. (1992). A comparison of three family therapy programs for treating family conflicts in adolescents with attention-deficit hyperactivity disorder. *Journal of Consulting & Clinical Psychology, 60,* 450-462.

Barrett, P. M., Dadds, M. R., & Rapee, R. M. (1996). Family treatment of childhood anxiety: A controlled trial. *Journal of Consulting and Clinical Psychology, 64,* 333-342.

Beckman, P. A., & Fischer, T. J. (1997). Negotiating managed care contracts. *Comprehensive Therapy, 23,* 554-559.

Berger, D. E., & Marelich, W. D. (1997). Legal and social control of alcohol-impaired driving in California: 1983-1994. *Journal of Studies on Alcohol, 58*(5), 518-523.

Black, D. R., Gleser, L. J., & Kooyers, K. (1990). A meta-analysis of couples weight-loss programs. *Health Psychology, 9,* 330-347.

Brent, D. A., Holder, D., Kolko, D., Birmaher, B., et al. (1997). A clinical psychotherapy trial for adolescent depression comparing cognitive, family, and supportive therapy. *Archives of General Psychiatry, 54*(9), 877-885.

Bruvold, W. H. (1993). A meta-analysis of adolescent smoking prevention programs. *American Journal of Public Health, 83,* 872-880.

COMMIT Research Group. (1995a). Community intervention trial for smoking cessation (COMMIT): I. Cohort results from a four-year community intervention. *American Journal of Public Health, 85,* 183-192.

COMMIT Research Group. (1995b). Community intervention trial for smoking cessation (COMMIT): II. Changes in adult cigarette smoking prevalence. *American Journal of Public Health, 85,* 193-200.

Corea, G. (1992). *The invisible epidemic: The story of women and AIDS.* New York: HarperCollins.

Donaldson, S. I., Gooler, L. E., & Weiss, R. (1998). Promoting health and well-being through work: Science and practice. In X. B. Arriaga & S. Oskamp (Eds.), *Addressing community problems: Research and intervention* (pp. 160-194). Thousand Oaks, CA: Sage.

Drake, R. F., McHugo, G. J., Clark, R. E., Teague, G. B., Xie, H., Miles, K., & Ackerman, T. H. (1998). Assertive community treatment for patients with co-occurring severe mental illness and substance use disorder: A clinical trial. *American Journal of Orthopsychiatry, 68,* 201-215.

Ensminger, M. E. (1987). Adolescent sexual behavior as it relates to other transition behaviors in youth. In S. L. Hofferth & C. D. Hayes (Eds.), *Risking the future: Adolescent sexuality, pregnancy, and childbearing* (pp. 36-55). Washington DC: National Academy of Sciences.

Engel, G. L. (1977). The need for a new medical model: A challenge for biomedicine. *Science, 196,* 129-136.

Fairweather, G. W., & Fergus, E. O. (1993). *Empowering the mentally ill.* Austin, TX: Fairweather Publishing.

Farquhar, J. W., Fortmann, S. P., Flora, J. A., Taylor, B., Haskell, W. L., Williams, P. T., Maccoby, N., & Wood, P. D. (1990). Effects of communitywide education on cardiovascular disease risk factors: The Stanford Five-City Project. *Journal of the American Medical Association, 264*(3), 359-365.

Fishbein, M., & Ajzen, I. (1975). *Belief, attitude, intention, and behavior: An introduction to theory and research.* Reading, MA: Addison-Wesley.

Fishbein, M., Bandura, A., Triandis, H. C., Kanfer, F. H., Becker, M. H., Middlestadt, S. E., & Eicher, A. (1992). *Factors influencing behavior and behavior change: Final report—Theorist's Workshop.* Rockville, MD: NIMH

Fishbein, M., Chan, D. K.-S., O'Reilly, K., Schnell, D., Wood, R., Beeker, C., & Cohn, D. (1993). Factors influencing gay men's attitudes, subjective norms, and intentions with respect to performing sexual behaviors. *Journal of Applied Social Psychology, 23*(6), 417-438.

Fisher, J. D., & Fisher, W. A. (1992). Changing AIDS-risk behavior. *Psychological Bulletin, 111*(3), 455-474.

Freedman, J. L., & Fraser, S. C. (1966). Compliance without pressure: The foot-in-the-door technique. *Journal of Personality and Social Psychology, 4,* 195-202.

Gardner, J. F. (1992). Quality, organization design, and standards. *Mental Retardation, 30*(3), 173-177.

Gibbs, J. P. (1975). *Crime, punishment, and deterrence.* New York: Elsevier.

Giles, T. R., & Marafiote, R. A. (1998). Managed care and the practitioner: A call for unity. *Clinical Psychology, 5*(1), 41-50.

Gladwell, M. (1996, June 3). The tipping point: Why is the city suddenly so much safer—Could it be that crime really is an epidemic? *The New Yorker,* pp. 32-38.

Glanz, K., Lewis, F. M., & Rimer, B. K. (Eds.). (1990). *Health behavior and health education: Theory, research, and practice* (2nd ed.). San Francisco: Jossey-Bass.

Haynes, R. B., McKibbon, K. A., & Kanani, R. (1996). Systematic review of randomised trials of interventions to assist patients to follow prescriptions for medications. *Lancet, 348,* 383-387.

Hausenblas, H. A., Carron, A. V., & Mack, D. E. (1997). Application of the theories of reasoned action and planned behavior to exercise behavior: A meta-analysis. *Journal of Sport and Exercise Psychology, 19,* 36-51.

Hibbs, E. D., & Jensen, P. S. (1996a). Analyzing the research: What this book is about. In E. D. Hibbs & P. S. Jensen (Eds.), *Psychosocial treatments for child and adolescent disorders: Empirically based strategies for clinical practice* (pp. 3-8). New York: American Psychological Association.

Hibbs, E. D., & Jensen, P. S. (Eds.). (1996b). *Psychosocial treatments for child and adolescent disorders: Empirically based strategies for clinical practice.* New York: American Psychological Association.

Institute of Medicine. (1992). *Toward a national health care survey: A data system for the 21st century.* Washington, DC: National Academy Press.

Jacobson, J. W., Burchard, S. N., & Carling, P. J. (Eds.). (1992). *Community living for people with developmental and psychiatric disabilities.* Baltimore, MD: Johns Hopkins University Press.

Janz, N. K., & Becker, M. H. (1984). Health belief model: A decade later. *Health Education Quarterly, 11*(1), 1-47.

Johnston, J. M., & Shook, G. L. (1993). Model for the statewide delivery of programming services. *Mental Retardation, 31*(3), 127-139.

Kalichman, S. C., Carey, M. P., & Johnson, B. T. (1996). Prevention of sexually transmitted HIV infection: A meta-analytic review of the behavioral outcome literature. *Annals of Behavioral Medicine, 18*(1), 6-15.

Kelly, J. A., Murphy, D. A., Sikkema, K. J., McAuliffe, T. L., Roffman, R. A., Solomon, L. J., Winett, R. A., & Kalichman, R. A. (1997). Outcomes of a randomized controlled community-level HIV prevention intervention: Effects on behavior among at-risk gay men in small U.S. cities. *Lancet, 350,* 1500-1504.

Kelly, J. A., St. Lawrence, J. S., Stevenson, L. Y., Hauth, A. C., Kalichman, S. C., Diaz, Y. E., Brasfield, T. L., Koob, J. J., & Morgan, M. G. (1992). Community AIDS/HIV risk reduction: The effects of endorsements by popular people in three cities. *American Journal of Public Health, 82*(11), 1483-1489.

Kendall, P. C. (1994). Treating anxiety disorders in children: Results of a randomized clinical trial. *Journal of Consulting and Clinical Psychology, 62,* 100-110.

Kendall, P. C., & Southam-Gerow, M. A. (1996). Long-term follow-up of a cognitive-behavioral therapy for anxiety-disordered youth. *Journal of Consulting and Clinical Psychology, 64,* 724-730.

Kirsch, I., Montgomery, G., & Sapirstein, G. (1995). Hypnosis as an adjunct to cognitive-behavioral psychotherapy: A meta-analysis. *Journal of Consulting and Clinical Psychology, 63*(2), 214-220.

Lando, H. A., Pechacek, T. F., Pirie, P. L., Murray, D. M., Mittlemark, M. B., Lichtenstein, E., Nothwehr, F., & Gray, C. (1995). Changes in adult cigarette smoking in the Minnesota Heart Health Program. *American Journal of Public Health, 85*(2), 201-208.

Lazarus, R. S., & Folkman, S. (1984). *Stress, appraisal, and coping.* New York: Springer.

Liberman, R. P., & Yager, J. (Eds.). (1994). *Stress in psychiatric disorders.* New York: Springer.

Lilienfeld, A. M., & Lilienfeld, D. E. (1980). *Foundations of epidemiology* (2nd ed.). New York: Oxford University Press.

Lipsey, M. W. (1993). Theory as method: Small theories of treatments. *New Directions for Program Evaluation, 57,* 5-38.

Maccoby, N., Farquhar, J. W., & Fortmann, S. P. (1985). *The community studies of the Stanford Heart Disease Prevention Program.* In R. M. Kaplan & M. H. Criqui (Eds.), *Behavioral epidemiology and disease prevention* (NATO ASI Series A: Life Sciences, Vol. 84, pp. 385-400). New York: Plenum.

Mann, T., Nolen-Hoeksema, S., Huang, K., & Burgard, D. (1997). Are two interventions worse than none? Joint preliminary and secondary prevention of eating
  disorders in college females. *Health Psychology, 16*(3), 215-225.

March, J. S., Mulle, K., & Herbel, B. (1994). Behavioral psychotherapy for children
  and adolescents with obsessive-compulsive disorder: An open trial of new
  protocol-driven treatment package. *Journal of the American Academy of Child
  and Adolescent Psychiatry, 33,* 333-341.

McGinnis, J. M., Richmond, J. B., Brandt, E. N., Jr., Windom, R. E., & Mason, J.
  O. (1992). Health progress in the United States: Results of the 1990 objectives
  for the nation. *Journal of the American Medical Association, 268*(18), 2545-2552.

McGuire, W. J. (1985). Attitudes and attitude change. In G. Lindzey & E. Aronson
  (Eds.), *The handbook of social psychology* (3rd ed., Vol. 2, pp. 233-346). New
  York: Random House.

Mead, G. H. (1934). *Mind, self, and society.* Chicago: University of Chicago Press.

Meyer, T. J., & Mark, M. M. (1995). Effects of psychosocial interventions with adult
  cancer patients: A meta-analysis of randomized experiments. *Health Psychology,
  14*(2), 101-108.

Meyrowitz, J. (1985). *No sense of place: The impact of electronic media on social
  behavior.* New York: Oxford University Press.

Miller, I. J. (1996). Managed care is harmful to outpatient mental health services:
  A call for accountability. *Professional Psychology: Research and Practice, 27,*
  349-363.

Miller, T. Q., Smith, T. W., Turner, C. W., Guijarro, M. L., & Hallet, A. J. (1996).
  A meta-analytic review of research on hostility and physical health. *Psychological
  Bulletin, 119*(2), 322-348.

Minihan, P. M., Dean, D. H., & Lyons, C. M. (1993). Managing the care of patients
  with mental retardation: A survey of physicians. *Mental Retardation, 31,* 239-
  246.

Moreau, D., & Mufson, L. (1997). Interpersonal psychotherapy for depressed
  adolescents. *Child and Adolescent Psychiatric Clinics of North America, 6,*
  97-110.

Multiple Risk Factor Intervention Trial Research Group. (1982). Multiple Risk
  Factor Intervention Trial: Risk factor changes and mortality results. *Journal of
  the American Medical Association, 248,* 1465-1477.

National Commission Against Drunk Driving. (1985). *A progress report on the
  implementation of recommendations by the Presidential Commission on Drunk
  Driving* (DOT HS-806-885). Washington, DC: National Highway Traffic Safety
  Administration.

National Highway Traffic Safety Administration. (1996). *Traffic safety facts 1995:
  A compilation of motor vehicle crash data from the fatal accident reporting system
  and the general estimates system* (DOT HS-808-471). Washington, DC: Government Printing Office.

Oskamp, S. (1991). *Attitudes and opinions* (2nd ed.). Englewood Cliffs, NJ: Prentice
  Hall.

Owen, N., Bauman, A., Booth, M., Oldenburg, B., & Magnus, P. (1995). Serial
  mass-media campaigns to promote physical activity: Reinforcing or redundant?
  American Journal of Public Health, 85(2), 244-248.

Patterson, G., Dishion, T., & Chamberlain, P. (1993). Outcomes and methodological issues relating to treatment of antisocial children. In T. Giles (Ed.), *Handbook of effective psychotherapy* (pp. 43-88). New York: Plenum.

Prochaska, J. O., & DiClemente, C. C. (1992). States of change in the modification of problem behaviors. *Progress in Behavior Modification, 28,* 183-218.

Prochaska, J. O., DiClemente, C. C., & Norcross, J. C. (1992). In search of how people change: Applications to addictive behaviors. *American Psychologist, 47*(9), 1102-1114.

Pulcini, J., & Howard, A. M. (1997). Framework for analyzing health care models serving adults with mental retardation and other developmental disabilities. *Mental Retardation, 35,* 209-217.

Rabin, S. A., & Porter, R. W. (1996). Application of social marketing principles to AIDS education. In M. Gluck, E. Rosenthal, H. Gelband, R. Colindres, L. Esslinger, C. J. Behney, & S. R. Tunis (Eds.), *The effectiveness of AIDS prevention efforts* (pp. 277-308). Washington, DC: Office of Technology Assessment, American Psychological Association Office of AIDS.

Remarks on the Advisory Commission on Consumer Protection and Quality in the Health Care Industry. (1997, March 31). Weekly compilation of presidential documents: 1997 Presidential Documents Online via GPO Access. [Available: http://frwebgate3.access.gpo.gov/cgi-bin/waisgate.cgi?WAISdocID=446292 2964+0+0+0&WAISaction=retrieve]. Washington, DC: Government Printing Office.

Risley, T. R., & Reid, D. R. (1996). Management and organizational issues in the delivery of psychological services for people with mental retardation. In J. W. Jacobson & J. A. Mulick (Eds.), *Manual of diagnosis and professional practice in mental retardation* (pp. 383-391). Washington, DC: American Psychological Association.

Roberts, D. F., & Maccoby, N. (1985). Effects of mass communication. In G. Lindzey & E. Aronson (Eds.), *The handbook of social psychology: Vol. 2. Special fields and applications* (pp. 539-598). Reading, MA: Addison-Wesley.

Rodin, J., & Salovey, P. (1989). Health psychology. *Annual Review of Psychology, 40,* 533-579.

Rogers, E. M. (1962). *Diffusion of innovations.* New York: Free Press.

Rogers, P. N., & Schoenig, S. E. (1994). A time series evaluation of California's 1982 driving-under-the-influence legislative reforms. *Accident Analysis and Prevention, 26,* 63-78.

Rosenheck, R., & Neale, M. (1998). Intersite variation in the impact of intensive psychiatric community care on hospital use. *American Journal of Orthopsychiatry, 68,* 191-200.

Ross, H. L. (1994). *Confronting drunk driving.* New Haven, CT: Yale University Press.

Rotello, G. (1997). *Sexual ecology: AIDS and the destiny of gay men.* New York: E. P. Dutton.

Rotheram-Borus, M. J., Piacentini, J., Cantwell, C., Belin, T. R., & Song, J. (In press). The long-term impact of an emergency room intervention for adolescent suicide attempters. *Journal of the American Academy of Child and Adolescent Psychiatry.*

Rotheram-Borus, M. J., Piacentini, J., Miller, S., Graae, F., & Castro-Blanco, D. (1994). Brief cognitive-behavioral treatment for adolescent suicide attempters and their families. *Journal of the American Academy of Child & Adolescent Psychiatry, 33*(4), 508-517.

Rotheram-Borus, M. J., Piacentini, J., Van Rossem, R., Graae, F., Cantwell, C., Castro-Blanco, D., & Feldman, J. (In press). Treatment adherence among Latina female adolescent suicide attempters. *Suicide and Life-Threatening Behavior.*

Rotheram-Borus, M. J., Towns, B., Lightfoot, M., Cline, T. R., Webber, D., & Murphy, D. A. (1998). *Diffusing HIV prevention messages through religious groups.* Manuscript submitted for publication.

Salyers, M. P., Masterton, T. W., Fekete, D. M., Picone, J. J., & Bond, G. R. (1998). Transferring clients from intensive case management: Impact on client functioning. *American Journal of Orthopsychiatry, 68,* 233-245.

Schneiderman, L. (1988). *The psychology of social change.* New York: Human Sciences Press.

Scott, A. G., & Sechrest, L. (1989). Strength of theory and theory of strength. *Evaluation and Program Planning, 12,* 329-336.

Shadish, W. R., Cook, T. D., & Leviton, L. C. (1991). *Foundations of program evaluation: Theories of practice.* Newbury Park, CA: Sage.

Silverman, W. K., & Kurtines, W. (1996). Transfer of control: A psychosocial intervention model for internalizing disorders in youth. In E. D. Hibbs & P. S. Jensen (Eds.), *Psychosocial treatments for child and adolescent disorders: Empirically based strategies for clinical practice* (pp. 267-284). New York: American Psychological Association.

Slife, B. D., & Williams, R. N. (1995). *What's behind the research? Discovering hidden assumptions in the behavioral sciences.* Thousand Oaks, CA: Sage.

Smith, A. D. (1976). *Social change: Social theory and historical processes.* New York: Longman.

Starfield, B. (1992). *Primary care: Concept, evaluation, and policy.* New York: Oxford University Press.

Stokols, D. (1992). Establishing and maintaining healthy environments: Toward a social ecology of health promotion. *American Psychologist, 47*(1), 6-22.

Strupp, H. (1977). A reformulation of the dynamics of the therapist's contribution. In A. Gurmant & A. Rugin (Eds.), *Effective psychotherapy: A handbook of research.* Elmsdale, NY: Pergamon.

Susser, M. (1995). The tribulations of trials—Intervention in communities [Editorial]. *American Journal of Public Health, 85*(2), 156-158.

Szymanski, L. S. (1987). Prevention of psychosocial dysfunction in persons with mental retardation. Sterling D. Garrard Memorial Symposium: Community Health Care Services for Adults With Mental Retardation (1986, Auburn, MA). *Mental Retardation, 25,* 215-218.

Taylor, S. E. (1995). *Health psychology* (3rd ed.). New York: McGraw-Hill.

Van Ryn, M., & Heaney, C. A. (1992). What's the use of theory? *Health Education Quarterly, 19*(3), 315-330.

Weick, K. (1979). *The social psychology of organizing* (2nd ed.). New York: McGraw-Hill.

Weick, K. (1984). Redefining the scale of social problems. *American Psychologist, 39*(1), 40-49.

Weisz, J. R., & Weiss, B. (1993). *Effects of psychotherapy with children and adolescents*. Newbury Park, CA: Sage.

Wells, K., Hays, R. D., Burnam, M. A., Rogers, W., Greenfield, S., & Ware, J. E., Jr. (1989). Detection of depressive disorder for patients receiving prepaid or fee-for-service care: Results from the Medical Outcomes Study. *Journal of the American Medical Association, 262,* 3298-3302.

Wells, K., Stewart, A. L., Hays, R. D., Burnam, M. A., Rogers, W., Daniels, M., Berry, S., Greenfield, S., & Ware, J. E., Jr. (1989). The functioning and well-being of depressed patients: Results from the Medical Outcomes Study. *Journal of the American Medical Association, 262,* 914-949.

Wells, K. B., Sturm, R., Sherbourne, C. D., & Meredith L. S. (1996). *Caring for depression.* Cambridge, MA: Harvard University Press.

Wicker, A. W. (1969). Attitudes versus actions: The relationship of verbal and overt behavioral responses to attitude objects. *Journal of Social Issues, 25*(4), 41-78.

Wolfe, P., Kregel, J., & Wehman, P. (1996). Service delivery. In P. J. McLaughlin & P. Wehman (Eds.), *Mental retardation and developmental disabilities* (2nd ed., pp. 3-27). Austin, TX: Pro-Ed.

Zajonc, R. B. (1968). Attitudinal effects of mere exposure. *Journal of Personality and Social Psychology, 9*(2), 1-27.

CHAPTER 6

The Future of Psychotherapy in a Changing Health Care System

ROBERT W. PLANT

The practice of psychotherapy has been evolving slowly over the past hundred years. Today, psychotherapy faces a period of rapid change and serious challenges to its continued existence. The changes in the health care system being fueled by Managed Care and the cost-cutting agendas of business and government will impact the practice of psychotherapy in almost every conceivable way. How the field copes with these changes will determine if psychotherapy maintains its role as a central force in the treatment of psychiatric disorder, relief of emotional distress, and the enhancement of health and functioning. Psychotherapists must move beyond denial and outrage and consider where they fit in the evolving health care system and how they can position themselves to best serve the public good and maintain their professional identity.

Nearly every facet of psychotherapy is likely to undergo some degree of change in response to managed care and other system changes. The cost of psychotherapy, how it is financed, and the level of reimbursement are undergoing rapid change. The manner and setting in which services are delivered are likely to be transformed by market forces driven by cost containment, the availability of new technologies, and the need for improved integration of services. Recent trends suggest that the demographics, credentials, training, and status of psychotherapists will change significantly in the coming years. New models of service delivery and the nature of research into psychotherapy process and outcome will also need to evolve if the field is to remain viable. The length of treatment is already being impacted, and we can expect to see significant trends away from individual therapy as the primary treatment modality (e.g., increased group and family therapy, increase in "ecological" interventions). It is likely that the essential nature of therapy itself will undergo change as a function of cost-efficiency analyses, new definitions of "medical necessity," and an increased emphasis on immediate symptom reduction, rather than long-term health.

This chapter will review current trends in health care and psychotherapy research and extrapolate toward the future. It is intended to be speculative and thought-provoking (as any chapter on the future of anything must be) as much as a guide to decision making and a call to action.

A Selected History of Psychotherapy

Psychotherapy has been practiced for approximately one hundred years. Popularized by Freud in the form of psychoanalysis, psychotherapy was not readily accepted by the medical establishment of Vienna where it was first introduced (Shorter, 1997). By the end of World War II, Freud's psychoanalytic theory and technique had gained prominence in Europe and the United States. Psychoanalytic influence culminated in its recognition as the standard of care for the psychotherapeutic treatment of mental illness. In the years following World War II, the influence of psychoanalysis began to wane with the growth of biological psychiatry, ego-psychology, and the early development of schools of thought that are the dominant theories of contemporary psychotherapy. By the 1970s (Shorter, 1997), psychoanalysis was clearly in decline, replaced at first by psychodynamic variants of psychoanalysis and then later by the behavioral, cognitive, and family therapies that currently hold sway over psychotherapy as practiced today.

The history of psychotherapy has also been witness to the influence of economic factors on the nature and delivery of psychotherapeutic services. Private health insurance first appeared in the United States in 1930 with the creation of the first nonprofit Blue Cross program (Glueckauf, Frank, Bond, & McGrew, 1996; also see Day, Chapter 1, this volume). In the years to follow, health insurance gradually became more available with an acceleration in growth following tax advantages introduced after World War II. Prior to the rise of health insurance, psychoanalysis was primarily the province of the rich. Psychotherapy only became widely available as a covered medical benefit during the '60s and '70s. This period began largely unchecked growth in all facets of medicine, including the practice of psychotherapy. The numbers of individuals receiving care and the total costs of psychotherapy rose significantly. It is arguable that the excesses of this relatively unrestrained practice environment sowed the seeds of some of the current cost-containment efforts.

This era also saw the greatest infiltration of nonmedical practitioners (e.g. psychologists and social workers) into a marketplace that had been largely dominated by psychiatry (Humphreys, 1996). It was doctoral-level psychologists who first blazed the way for the nonmedical practice of psychotherapy. Psychology's challenge to psychiatry began in the years surrounding World War II and was bolstered by its strong position within the U.S. Veteran's Administration's health care service (Humphreys, 1996). By the 1950s, psychiatry's monopoly had been broken. The psychologist's ability to provide quality services without relatively expensive medical training opened the door for the acceptance of master's-level trained therapists, including psychiatric social workers and marriage and family therapists. The demedicalization of psychotherapy is evident when you observe recent trends in the growth of each professional group. Between 1975 and 1990, the number of psychiatrists increased by 10,000, psychologists by 27,000, marriage and family therapists by 34,000, and masters in social work by 55,000 (Humphreys, 1996). Unfortunately, this proliferation of psychotherapists coincides with the greatest period of cost containment—an unfortunate combination for the practitioners of psychotherapy.

What Is Managed Care and Where Is It Headed?

Managed care is a set of procedures and financial arrangements that function to limit or reduce the cost of health care services. In response to rapidly rising health care costs, managed care organizations (MCOs) or managed care departments within insurance companies have stepped between providers and consumers to regulate the delivery of care. While few can argue with the need to control costs, many are dissatisfied with the manner in which managed care has been pursuing its cost-savings agenda.

In 1996, approximately 168.5 million Americans, or 75% of those with health insurance, were enrolled in some form of managed behavioral health program, according to a survey conducted by *Open Minds,* a newsletter that covers the health care industry (Psychiatric Services, 1997b). Value Behavioral Health, a Virginia-based mental health carve-out company, had the highest enrollment, 24.4 million or approximately 11% of the insured population and 14.5% of the market share for managed behavioral health. The incredible growth of this industry over the past 10 years has occurred with little or no government guidance or oversight (Patterson, McIntosh-Koontz, Baron, & Bischoff, 1997). Neither has there been significant input or direction from health care providers or researchers. Humphreys (1996) reports that since the late 1980s, the driving force has been cost containment. Howard and Mahoney (1996) argue that managed care is really managed cost, since MCOs devote little or no attention to the quality of service. Miller (1996) states that managed care's emphasis on limiting the number of sessions amounts to hidden rationing, and a publication of the American Psychiatric Press (Group for the Advancement of Psychiatry, 1992) characterizes this as a national sociomedical experiment without full disclosure to the American people of the substantial risks involved.

Although the primary objective of all MCOs is to reduce or limit health care expenditures, they have organized themselves in a variety of forms to achieve this objective. MCOs' principal forms are described below.

- *HMO: Health Maintenance Organization* is a legal entity that finances and furnishes health care for a prepaid or capitated dollar amount. The *group model HMO* contracts with a network of providers and achieves cost savings by shifting a portion of the financial risk to providers. The *staff model HMO* employs providers on a salaried basis, retaining tight control over practice patterns and eliminating the financial incentive to over treat.
- *PPO: Preferred Provider Organization* is a legal entity that pays for health care services and contracts with a network of providers who

agree to accept lower fees for a higher volume of clients. Less regulation of care than the HMO but fewer cost savings.

- *PHO: Provider Hospital Organization* is a contracted agreement between a hospital and a group of providers creating an entity that bids to provide health care services. PHOs may contract with insurance companies or directly with large employers.
- *MHCOC: Mental Health Carve-Out Company* is a corporation that focuses on the management of mental health services, including psychotherapy and other psychiatric services.
- *MSO: Management Services Organization* is a legal entity owned by providers that provides contracting, billing, marketing, and other services. MSOs may be composed of large multispecialty groups that compete with MCOs to provide care while managing costs.

In the management of mental health benefits, MCOs employ several strategies that are designed to reduce costs. MCOs can (a) limit the number of providers through establishment of provider networks, (b) contract for lower fees, (c) require that services be authorized prior to delivery through a system of concurrent review, (d) establish fixed arbitrary limits on particular services (e.g., 20 sessions of outpatient psychotherapy), (e) withhold a portion of reimbursement based on failure to stay within service or financial limits, (f) contract services out on a fixed prepaid basis, or (g) hire service providers as staff to control practice patterns and eliminate financial incentives for high utilization.

In all their forms and with the various methods they employ, MCOs are indeed slowing the growth of health care expenditures. As noted above, they have been virtually free to set policy and develop practice guidelines without input from key stakeholders, including consumers, practitioners, and government representatives (Newman & Tejeda, 1996). Barlow (1996) argues that psychotherapy researchers must establish minimal standards of care and reliable treatment guidelines, otherwise MCOs will adopt guidelines based solely on cost savings. Only recently have we begun to see legislation to monitor and regulate managed care and current public opinion favors such action (Reuters, 1997).

Recently, health care analysts have noted that declining behavioral health care premiums and increased competition from integrated service delivery systems point to an uncertain future for managed care (Psychiatric Services, 1997a). Once provider groups reach a critical mass that provides them with the financial resources to accept risk, they are in a position to cut out the managed care middleman and contract directly with employers. The success of these provider-sponsored plans will depend on their capacity to replicate managed cares cost containment and network management practices.

In the future we can expect to see an increase in regulations governing managed care and in providers managing their own care. Even if MCOs disappear completely, they will have dramatically changed the way health care, including psychotherapy, is provided. By forcing the creation of large health care conglomerates and reversing the financial incentives that once rewarded service provision and will now reward service restriction, managed care has dramatically altered the health care landscape. In the absence of national health care reform, these changes will resonate throughout the system for some time to come.

Is There a Need for Psychotherapy?

If we presume that the future of a service is driven, in part, by need, then epidemiology should tell us something about the future demand for psychotherapy services. In the past 13 years, two large scale national studies have been completed with the purpose of determining the prevalence and incidence of psychiatric disorders (Howard et al., 1996). The Epidemiologic Catchment Area study, also know as the ECA (Regier, 1984) and the National Comorbidity Survey (NCS) interviewed large representative samples of adults to determine rates of psychiatric illness and the degree of comorbidity of disorders. Lifetime prevalence (the percentage of people who will suffer from some form of psychiatric illness within their lifetime) was estimated to be between 30% and 40% by the ECA and nearly 50% by the NCS. Both studies found that within any year, roughly one third (30%) of all adults in the United States will experience a mental illness (Howard et al., 1996). Let me repeat that: *nearly one in three individuals will have a diagnosable mental illness during any given year.* If we estimate the adult population of the United States to be roughly 200 million, then approximately 67 million Americans suffer from a mental illness in any given year. Seventy percent of those with a disorder do not receive any form of treatment—medical, psychotherapeutic, or otherwise. Thus, every year approximately 46.9 million Americans with a diagnosable psychiatric condition do not receive any form of treatment. Howard et al. (1996) note that strong resistance to obtaining mental health services remains, including ignorance of mental illness and available treatment, and fear of the stigma associated with mental illness. They note that receptivity to services is lowest among the very old, the very young, the less educated, and the poor. Receptivity is highest among the most highly educated, who, ironically, are the least likely to suffer from a mental illness. Howard and his colleagues concluded that mental illness is widespread and chronic. Most sufferers never receive care. The need for psychotherapy and other treatment interventions far exceeds the current capacity. This situation has remained essentially unchanged since Albee first recognized the problem in 1959.

Is Psychotherapy Effective?

Since Eysenck's (1952) much cited study in the 1950s, the question of the effectiveness of psychotherapy has been raised again and again. Certainly it is a valid question to ask, and just as certainly the answer matters greatly to the future of psychotherapy. Since Eysenck's controversial analysis, which claimed, among other things, that the rate of psychotherapeutic cure was no better than the rate of so-called spontaneous remissions, a tremendous body of research has demonstrated that psychotherapy is highly effective (Lambert & Bergin, 1994; Seligman, 1995; Smith, Glass, & Miller, 1980). In fact, eminent scientists (Barlow, 1996) have gone as far as stating that there is "incontrovertible evidence that effective psychological interventions exist for a large number of psychiatric disorders" (p. 1051). What is anomalous is that questions regarding psychotherapy's effectiveness are asked again and again (Strupp, 1997). The profession is continually "asked to defend the validity or value of its service based on the results of empirically conducted outcome research" (Kocsis, 1996, p. 303). Kocsis argues effectively that similar to other professions (e.g., surgery, law, and teaching), the practice of psychotherapy is based on principles derived primarily from anecdotal case material with partial empirical support. Yet teachers, lawyers, and surgeons are rarely asked to defend the validity of their professions.

While the vast majority of outcome research has focused on psychotherapy with adults, a major meta-analysis of 75 studies conducted by Casey and Berman (1985) found that therapy also benefits children. Based on their meta-analytic technique, the authors concluded that treated children are 76% better off at the end of therapy than the untreated child (Casey & Berman, 1985). Subsequent researchers have criticized Casey and Berman's analysis, claiming that many of the studies included in their review were seriously flawed and that their meta-analytic technique was only as good as the studies it was based on (Pearsall, 1997). Pearsall cites a recent review by Kazdin in which he concludes that psychotherapy with children is better than no treatment and that the effects appear to be about as strong as those observed in the treatment of adults. He concludes that when treatment differences are observed, they tend to favor behavioral techniques. (The issue of which approach to psychotherapy is most effective will be revisited later in this chapter.)

That psychotherapy is proven effective does not guarantee its survival in the health care system of the future, although it certainly strengthens its position. What seems clear is that psychotherapy will not be drummed out of existence on the grounds that it does no good. There is just too much good evidence to the contrary. Although questions about effectiveness continue to be raised, the more common argument offered by managed care is that psychotherapy is no more effective and less cost effective than its principal alternative, psychopharmacology.

Will Psychotherapy Be Replaced by Psychopharmacology?

Psychotherapy and psychopharmacology are the two primary interventions for the treatment of psychiatric disorder. Perhaps the greatest achievement of biological psychiatry in the past hundred years has been the development of powerful psychotropic drugs that alter mood, quell anxiety, reduce hyperactivity, and moderate psychotic symptoms. The use of psychotropic drugs has undoubtedly reduced human suffering and helped to improve the functioning of countless numbers of people around the world. The dark side of this shining star in the short history of psychiatry is that managed care policy and procedures appear to desire to replace psycho-therapy with psychopharmacology, and do so in the name of cost containment and the public good.

The simplest form of the argument is that since drugs are less expensive than psychotherapy and as or more effective, they should be provided in lieu of psychotherapy whenever possible. If psycho-therapy adds nothing of value to the mix, then dispense with it and focus attention on the development of safer, more powerful, and more effective drugs. While these arguments appear logical, coher-ent, and well formed on the surface, they are in fact flawed in several important ways.

To begin, it has yet to be determined if psychopharmacology is equal to or more effective than psychotherapy. Despite the lack of sufficient empirical evidence, practice guidelines published by the American Psychiatric Association for the treatment of depression emphasize treatment with medication and de-emphasize the role of psychotherapy (Barlow, 1996). When it comes to outcome research, psychotherapy is at a significant disadvantage when you consider that the National Institute of Mental Health funds the vast majority of psychotherapy research worldwide at a total cost that pales in comparison to what is spent to research and support the efficacy of psychotropic drugs (Kocsis, 1996). Clarkin, Pilkonis, and Ma-gruder (1996) cite six studies (selected on the basis of sound methodology) that demonstrate that psychotherapy is equal to medication in the treatment of acute phase mild to moderate depression. Several well-controlled studies demonstrate that the recipients of cognitive therapy show fewer depressive symptoms and lower rates of relapse than patients treated by acute phase pharmacotherapy. Also, the recipients of cognitive therapy did not require maintenance phase treatment, as is often provided in the treatment of depression. Ostrowski (1997) cites evidence for the effectiveness of a range of psychotherapeutic procedures that equal or surpass pharmacological approaches, including forms of cogni-tive, behavioral, family systems, interpersonal, and psychodynamic psychotherapies.

As effective as psychopharmacological drugs may be, substantial numbers of nonresponders exist. Barkley (1990) reported that approximately one third of children with ADHD do not benefit from treatment with stimulants. Similarly, Plant (1991) reports that approximately 40% of adults with obsessive-compulsive disorder (OCD) do not respond to treatment with selective serotonergic reuptake blockers, the principal form of medication treatment for OCD. Nonresponders need alternative treatments, and psychotherapy is the best known alternative. In addition, 5% to 10% of individuals refuse medication, and another 10% to 15% who attempt it cannot tolerate the side effects (Barlow, 1996). When you add to this the substantial number of individuals who cannot take medications because of other life circumstances, potential drug interactions, or medical conditions (e.g., pregnant women; pilots who fear grounding; individuals with liver disease, heart disease, etc.) it is clear that psychotherapy must remain available. While patient choice should not necessarily dictate treatment, the role of the patient's attitude has been found to be a significant factor in adherence to medication regimens. Patients who do not take their medication as prescribed cannot reap the potential benefits.

Psychotherapy will remain as a viable treatment of mental illness because it is equally or more effective than medication. Those who do not respond to medication, who cannot use it, or who choose not to use medication must have an alternative.

Who Will Provide the Service?

Managed care and other market forces are changing the face of the psychotherapy practitioner. As noted above, psychiatry and doctoral-level psychology are in a state of decline relative to the tremendous increase in numbers of masters' level practitioners. Rotheram-Borus (see Marelich & Rotheram-Borus, Chapter 5, this volume) points out that approximately 56% of psychiatrists now operate in private practice. She argues that the future marketplace will be unable to support this number of private practice psychiatrists. At the same time, based on data from a study of CHAMPUS utilization, the American Psychiatric Association predicts that nonpsychiatrist medical providers will increase their billing for psychotherapy to offset falling practice income (Group for Advancement of Psychiatry, 1992). Reports are that the number of primary care providers is roughly equivalent to the number of mental health specialty providers. In accordance with their numbers, primary care medical practitioners provide roughly half of all psychotherapy services (Group for the Advancement of Psychiatry, 1992).

According to a report completed by the American Psychiatric Association (Group for the Advancement of Psychiatry, 1992), the number of females entering psychiatry has increased significantly at a time when the number of men entering the profession is declining. If you also consider that women are predominant within the fastest growing practitioner groups (e.g., social work and marriage and family therapy), it is clear that in the future overwhelming majority of psychotherapy will be provided by women. The implications of this trend are difficult to predict.

As psychologists replaced psychiatrists, and are themselves being replaced by master's-level clinicians, the trend may continue toward the replacement of master's-level clinicians by bachelor's-level practitioners or other paraprofessionals. On a strict cost analysis, this makes good sense since lesser trained practitioners can deliver the service less expensively. This might also expand the number of practitioners to better address the unmet need for services. Considering the trend toward the "manualization" of treatment (Strupp, 1997), it is arguable that broadly trained clinicians who treat all types of disorder will be replaced by lesser trained practitioners who treat particular diagnoses according to a highly structured, manualized treatment protocol.

However, the argument that it is advantageous to treat psychiatric disorder with lesser trained paraprofessionals contains several important lacunae. To begin, this strategy may not produce the expected cost savings over the long run. One way that managed care has effectively reduced costs is by limiting the number of providers that can provide service within their networks. The fewer providers, the less care provided, and with higher caseloads, there is less of a financial incentive to prolong treatment. A proliferation of lesser trained practitioners may lower reimbursement rates but increase total dollars spent through increased volume of service. *If* focused manualized treatments provided by paraprofessionals can deliver outcomes equivalent to those achieved by broadly trained master's, doctoral, or medically trained mental health professionals, then perhaps the public good would be served by utilizing the lesser trained practitioner. More people would receive care and the costs to government, business, and the consumer would be lowered.

The important question is whether or not the paraprofessional can achieve the same results and outcomes as more highly trained professionals. Although it has been historically difficult to prove, there is a growing body of literature that demonstrates that training and experience do positively relate to the outcome and effectiveness of psychotherapy (Barlow, 1996). Frank, Kupfer, Wagner, McEachran, and Cornes (1991) and Frank and Spanier (1995) have shown that clients treated by more highly trained and experienced clinicians had better treatment outcomes than clients treated by lesser trained practitioners. A large survey of psychotherapy patients conducted by Consumer Reports ("Mental Health: Does Therapy Help?" 1995) also found that training and licensure requirements have a positive impact on the effectiveness and outcome of psychotherapy (Barlow, 1996).

Several models of therapy that are eclectic combinations of family systems theory, developmental psychopathology, and cognitive behavioral approaches (Hengeller, Melton, & Smith, 1992; Hoberman, Clark, & Saunders, 1996) are showing great promise. Hengeller et al. (1992) suggest that when working with children and adolescents, a systemic approach that allows the flexibility to adapt and apply proven treatments from other schools has the best likelihood of success. Outcome research supports the effectiveness of their approach with a population that is traditionally difficult to treat, adolescents with conduct and behavior problems. Such an approach requires broad training and sophisticated practitioners who adapt their techniques to the family and the problem. There is strong empirical support for the effectiveness of this approach and its superiority over typical treatment approaches (Hengeller et al., 1992). Paraprofessionals do not have the training to deliver such a treatment effectively.

The use of paraprofessional providers also requires an accurate diagnosis, because the treatment approach is "locked in" once the initial diagnosis is made. The process of reaching an accurate diagnosis is a complex and sophisticated clinical skill that is not easily mastered even by practitioners with advanced training. No one expects a paraprofessional to be able to provide an accurate diagnosis. Clinical settings that utilize paraprofessionals as the service providers will require more highly trained diagnosticians who will make all initial contacts with clients and then refer them on to highly specialized paraprofessional providers. Under this model, the need to switch providers after the initial diagnostic contact could seriously interfere with the development of the therapeutic relationship. This approach also allows very little room for error in the diagnostic process since the knowledge necessary to make major midcourse treatment corrections is not expected to be part of the paraprofessionals' clinical repertoire.

The possibility of utilizing paraprofessionals as the first line of treatment providers depends in part on the effectiveness and generalizability of the manualized treatments they are expected to use. A great deal of debate has been focused on this trend in psychotherapy research, with criticisms of the "manualization" of psychotherapy coming from several camps (Silverman, 1996; Strupp, 1997). This debate is complex and critically important, and warrants further discussion in the section that follows.

What can we conclude about the face of the psychotherapy practitioner of the future? Most likely she will be female and hold a master's degree. It will become less and less likely that she will be a psychiatrist or a psychologist. At the same time, we may see the continuation of a trend where primary care physicians provide half or more of psychotherapy services. The effectiveness of psychotherapy when provided by GPs or family physicians is generally unknown, although there is some evidence that it is inferior to the service provided by specialty practitioners (Clarkin et al., 1996). The replacement of master's-level clinicians by lesser trained paraprofessionals seems unwise and appears unlikely to occur. There may be resistance from managed care due to the potential increase in numbers of practitioners. Also, the continued success of multisystemic approaches will require broadly trained practitioners and cannot be sustained by paraprofessionals who employ highly structured, inflexible, manual-based treatments.

Will Treatment Manuals
Dictate How Psychotherapy Is Practiced?

Over the past 5 to 10 years, psychotherapy outcome research has seen a significant increase in the use of treatment manuals. Manuals were originally intended as a means to improve research design by clearly explicating a particular therapeutic approach or technique, but the "manualization" of treatment has itself become a standard by which treatment approaches are evaluated. Several influential literature reviews used to establish practice guidelines have been exclusively limited to the review of studies employing manualized treatments (Silverman, 1996). This trend toward manualization of treatment has been controversial and has important implications for the future of psychotherapy.

While the use of treatment manuals may improve the research psychotherapist's adherence to the therapeutic technique being evaluated and thus provide a "purer" scientific test, some have argued that manualization unjustifiably elevates technique to a level of predominance over other factors that influence treatment outcome (Silverman, 1996; Strupp & Andersen, 1997). Strupp (1997) contends that manualization is driven by managed care and researchers without clinical experience who believe that slavish application of a treatment manual is all that is necessary to achieve positive treatment outcomes. He notes that such an argument assumes that the influence of clinical skill on treatment outcome is negligible. Differences in clinical skills across therapists are treated as "error variance" rather than as important factors in understanding the effectiveness of treatment. Strupp (1997) concludes that the clinical literature supports the fact that there are marked individual differences in clinical skills, even between experienced clinicians. These skills relate positively to therapy outcome. Therapists are not interchangeable, negligible factors, and patients are not passive recipients of treatments delivered to them (Silverman, 1996). Technique is not the "be-all and end-all of psychotherapy" (Silverman, 1996, p. 209). An overemphasis on treatment manuals implies that technique is king and that, manual-in-hand, an inexperienced paraprofessional can deliver a treatment as successfully as a highly trained professional. As reported by Silverman (1996, p. 209), when Strupp and colleagues attempted to enforce a strict manualized treatment in a study of therapy outcome effectiveness, they concluded that "treatment was delivered, but therapy did not occur" (Silverman, 1996, p. 209). Perhaps "therapy did not occur" because the essential elements of a successful therapeutic relationship, including honesty, trust, genuineness, empathy, and the client's perception of these qualities in the therapist (Rogers, 1965) were not present.

One rationale for the use of treatment manuals is that it will allow for a reduction in the range of accepted and approved therapeutic interventions based on empirical evidence of what works and at what cost (Barlow, 1996). Barlow argues that it is highly questionable to assume that the effectiveness of highly structured treatment manuals applied in controlled research settings will generalize to the more flexible application and diverse settings in which therapy is typically delivered. The real-world application of treatment manuals is untested and could have negative as well as positive effects (Strupp & Andersen, 1997). Treatment manuals may be valuable, but their value is limited and must be seen in relation to the contributions of clinical skill and patient characteristics to the outcome of psychotherapy.

Although the field appears to be "advancing" toward a "cookbook" or "paint-by-numbers" (Silverman, 1996, p. 207) approach that would be attractive to managed care and allow paraprofessionals to replace highly trained (and more expensive) practitioners, it seems unlikely that such an intensely human activity will be reduced to a simple formula. In the words of Dostoyevsky's Underground Man,

> If you say that everything, chaos, darkness, anathema, can be reduced to mathematical formulae, that it is possible to anticipate all things and keep them under the sway of reason by means of an arithmetic calculation, then man will go insane on purpose so as to have no judgement and behave as he likes. (Dostoyevsky, quoted in Berdyaev, 1974, p. 53)

In other words, individuals receiving psychotherapy want to be understood as individuals and will resist being processed according to a manual.

In What Settings Will Psychotherapy Be Practiced?

At present, roughly half of all treatment of mental illness occurs in general health care settings (Barlow, 1996). The other half takes place in specialty mental health clinics or the private offices of mental health specialty providers. Knesper (1997) found that outside of the care provided in general health care settings, 72% of psychotherapy patients are seen in private offices, 16% in the community mental health clinic, 4% in medical school clinics, and

4% in public hospitals. As noted above, we can expect a trend toward improved integration of mental health and physical health services. We can also expect changes in the nature of the settings that will provide the care. Some of these changes may significantly impact the nature of the care itself.

With the concerns over rising costs and the growing influence of managed care over the practice of psychotherapy (Psychiatric Services, 1997a), there is a movement to bring economies of scale to bear on the practice of psychotherapy (Group for the Advancement of Psychiatry, 1992). Behavioral health care management companies are merging and acquiring smaller companies at an accelerating rate (Psychiatric Services, 1997b). Forces are being combined to consolidate market share, reduce overhead, increase negotiating power, and improve profits.

This movement seems to parallel developments in other industries such as banking, home-improvement centers, and pharmacies. In these and many other industries, superstore chains dominate the marketplace and force the closing of smaller companies. In sophisticated health care markets within the United States, there is a trend toward large multispecialty provider groups that enter the marketplace in competition with managed care, accepting risk through capitation, and contracting directly with employers. These large providers eliminate the managed care middleman by establishing a direct relationship between employers and providers.

There is also a trend toward agencies and private practice groups merging and/or forming strategic alliances to survive in an increasingly competitive environment. Large regional networks increase their negotiating power with managed care and ensure their participation in networks and contracts essential to their continued survival.

Mergers, acquisitions, strategic alliances, and multispecialty groups will alter the practice of psychotherapy. For many years the business of psychotherapy had existed primarily in the form of a cottage industry of independent private practitioners. More recently there has been speculation that the solo private practitioner is a dinosaur nearing extinction. Managed care companies are said to prefer large groups or agencies because that reduces the number of offices that have to be dealt with on a regular basis. The solo practitioner, unable to accept risk, could be locked out of capitated contracts that could cover the majority of mental health care services provided in future. In the absence of health care reform and the creation of a national single payer system, a two-tiered system is likely to emerge in which those who can afford to pay for services will seek out private practitioners and the rest will receive care from large health care conglomerates. In such a scenario, private practice will be greatly reduced from its current share of the market, but a few practitioners will survive outside the mainstream.

With the shift away from the private office and toward large, bureaucratic health care entities, we can expect psychotherapists to receive less pay, have less status, and have reduced autonomy. Consumers may have fewer choices and less personalized and conveniently located treatment options. Innovation and flexibility are likely to decline. Services will become more homogeneous. Expected declines in income and status may impact the quality of students entering the field. While monitoring and oversight will improve, and standardization may reduce negligent and irresponsible care, the overall impact suggests a decline in the quality of service.

With the growth of mammoth mental health provider entities and the decline of the private office, we may also see an increase in the number of mental health specialty providers practicing in general health care settings (see section on the integration of mental and physical health). Also, expect to see continued growth of school-based health centers, an increasingly popular and effective service delivery model for children and youth (see Dryfoos, Chapter 4, this volume). School-based health centers provide medical, mental health, and dental services in an easily accessible and naturalistic setting, the neighborhood school. A review of the treatment of adolescent depression suggests that school-based or school-adjacent clinics may be the best settings to provide mental health care (Hoberman et al., 1996).

Another trend in service delivery is the provision of care in the home. Targeted toward lower socioeconomic groups who encounter various barriers to clinic attendance (e.g., transportation problems, lack of child care, mistrust and apprehension regarding services, etc.), home-based care has been found to improve the effectiveness of services that had previously been available only in clinic settings (Hengeller et al., 1992).

It is not hard to imagine that small franchise-based multispecialty groups consisting of nursing, social work, psychology, psychiatry, pediatrics, obstetrics-gynecology, and family or general practice will emerge in the near future. Such "franchises" could be locally owned but part of a larger corporate structure that could contract to accept risk and provide marketing, administrative support, and purchase needed goods and services at "wholesale" rates. The clinic would retain a small locally based, comfortable feel but provide services within a truly integrated biopsychosocial model. Such a model could combine the best of the private office with the economic advantages of a large health care corporation.

I believe that in the future, psychotherapy will be more likely to be provided within large corporate health structures, primary care settings, the home, in school-based or school-linked clinics, or perhaps in small multispecialty franchised groups. Psychotherapy will be less likely to be provided in the private office of a solo practitioner or small mental health specialty group. Certain settings provide the advantage of improved access (school-based or home-based) or increased collaboration among providers (franchised group or general health care setting), while others may reduce the cost of services at the expense of reduced quality (large mental health care corporation).

Will Psychotherapy Be Limited to Brief Intervention?

Managed care has cut costs associated with psychotherapy, primarily by limiting the length of treatment. HMOs and other managed care entities "recommend short-term treatment for all comers regardless of diagnosis or acuity and based solely on cost containment" (Group for the Advancement of Psychiatry, 1992, p. 47). MCOs argue that brief treatment is as or more effective than longer term care and justify their policies on the basis of this argument. Within the mental health field, the typical practitioner has also been convinced that long-term treatment is wasteful, extravagant, and no better than brief therapy. Psychotherapists of all persuasions seem to be accepting this opinion as fact and conceding defeat without "a sober examination of what the [our] field may be sacrificing" (Strupp, 1997, p. 93). According to Strupp (1997), "it is wrong to create the impression within the field or in the public view that brief forms of treatment are comparable or even superior to more intensive or extended forms of psychotherapy" (p. 94).

The psychotherapy outcome literature is often cited as the source of evidence supporting the contention that brief treatment is as effective as longer term psychotherapy. Miller (1996) disputes the conclusions of several previous reviews that claim to demonstrate the equivalence of brief and longer-term approaches. Miller distinguishes between clinically determined treatment (CDT) and time limited treatment (TLT). In CDT, the therapist and client come to an agreement about the length of treatment based on an analysis of client functioning and progress toward goals. In TLT, the length of treatment is predetermined and arbitrary. Miller reports that his review of the literature reveals that CDT is significantly more effective than TLT. Howard, Kopta, Krause, and Orlinsky (1986) report that there is a significant dose-related effect of psychotherapy with improvements in outcome with longer-term treatment (up to 26 sessions). A similar result was reported by a large survey of psychotherapy recipients completed by Consumer Reports ("Mental Health," 1995). This evidence lead Miller (1996) to conclude that "general time limits imposed by third parties are likely to harm therapeutic outcome" (p. 575).

Managed care operates to maximize short-term profitability. Brief treatment fits with its short-term profit-making agenda. Strupp and Anderson (1997) wonders if "providing minimal care to resolve symptoms of a current depressive episode is the most cost effective in the long-term" (p. 163). In a similar vein, Newman and Tejeda (1996) use an analogy to physical health care to highlight the absurdity of managed care's arbitrary limits on length of treatment: "90 percent of your tumor is gone but you have reached the 20-session limit for radiation treatment. Please come back next year when your eligibility has been renewed" (p. 1040).

Despite the research evidence supporting clinically determined treatment, managed care continues to limit the length of care as its primary cost-savings tool. The practice continues because the financial incentives support it, it remains largely unregulated, the public has not been educated, and policymakers remain ignorant about the price of sacrificing quality for the sake of short-term savings. The hope for a rational policy on the length of treatment rests with national health care reform and the ability of researchers to show that effective psychotherapy saves money through reduced general health care expenditures, improved productivity, better educational outcomes, and other economic advantages arising from a population with good emotional health.

In What Form Will Psychotherapy Be Practiced?

As managed care has gained control over the practice of psychotherapy, there has been a movement away from insight-oriented, emotive, and dynamic psychotherapies and toward shorter term, action-oriented behavioral and solution-focused treatment. Managed care has been co-opting the psychotherapy outcome literature to support its cost-saving and profit-making agendas and efforts to restrict the practice of psychotherapy to those forms it deems acceptable (Strupp, 1997). Unfortunately, many practitioners and mental health administrators are buying into managed care's limited view of what constitutes cost-effective psychotherapy despite significant evidence supporting the effectiveness of a wider range of interventions (Barlow, 1996).

A large body of literature supports the effectiveness of behavioral and cognitive behavioral interventions for the treatment of adults (Barlow, 1996; Strupp & Anderson, 1997) and children (Kazdin, 1993). Meta-analytic reviews often suggest that where there are differential treatment effects, results favor cognitive and behavioral approaches. While practitioners and policymakers should not ignore these findings, it is equally irresponsible to reach the erroneous conclusion that these are the only valid techniques and others should be abandoned given their "inferior" empirical support. Pearsall (1997) argues that behavior therapies have fared well in outcome effectiveness in part because behaviors are easier to measure than thoughts, emotional processes, or personality changes. Just because the technology of measurement has not evolved to the point that these elusive concepts can be measured does not lead to the conclusion that what can be more easily measured is therefore the best.

Articles by Barlow (1996) and Pearsall (1997) on psychotherapy practice cite literature that supports a wide range of treatment interventions. Family therapy has demonstrated some effectiveness with the treatment of schizophrenia (Falloon, Boyd, & Mcgill, 1985), drug abuse (Barlow, 1996), anxiety disorders (Barlow &

Lehman, 1996), and adolescent behavior disorders (Hengeller et al., 1992). Barlow (1996) reports that complex psychological treatment is the only from of intervention that has been shown to be effective in the treatment of borderline personality disorder. He also cites evidence indicating that such treatment is cost effective over the long term because of a reduction in the utilization of general health care services. Barlow also cites a trend away from schools of therapy and toward a more eclectic blend of psychotherapeutic approaches. Hengeller et al.'s (1992) Multisystemic Therapy and Hoberman et al.'s (1996) Multi-Dimensional Developmental Psychotherapy are two examples of this trend toward systematic eclecticism. Interpersonal psychotherapy has shown effectiveness in the treatment of depression that is equal to the success of cognitive-behavioral approaches. Brief psychodynamic psychotherapies have also proven to be effective techniques in the treatment of depression and other psychiatric disorders (Barlow, 1996).

Despite what managed care might have us believe, effective psychotherapy is not limited to cognitive-behavioral approaches. The field is experiencing the growth and refinement of a number of different schools of thought and a substantial degree of cross-fertilization among approaches. I believe that with support from this eclectic movement the development of more formalized systems will continue that will guide psychotherapists toward the most effective combinations of techniques.

How Will Psychotherapy Relate to Medical Practice?

Psychotherapy was developed within the medical profession as a treatment for mental disease (Pearsall, 1997). Over time, with the demedicalization of psychotherapy, increasing specialization within the medical community, and the influence of the biopsychosocial model, psychotherapy has become somewhat divorced from its roots. With the exception of the practice of psychotherapy by general medical practitioners, who are generally untrained in psychotherapeutic technique, most psychotherapy is practiced in specialty clinics or the private offices of mental health specialty providers. The philosophical duality of mind and body finds its expression in the current disconnection between practitioners of "physical" health care and "mental" health practitioners. While volumes of research have shown us how biological factors influence mental states and psychological factors impact physical health, the artificial division between these professions remains. Half of all referrals for outpatient psychotherapy originate from medical doctors. However, the relationship between these practitioners seldom goes beyond the passing of the baton.

Miller and Farber (1997) report that the medical model has not integrated psychological services into practice in the primary care setting. They argue that doing so would produce several health enhancing effects. To begin, integration of psychological services into primary care would facilitate the early detection and treatment of psychiatric conditions. This would benefit patients and managed care groups through reduced suffering and should lower costs over the long term. We have known for some time that psychological and psychosocial variables play very important roles in the prevention and treatment of disease (Kiecolt-Glaser & Glaser, 1995). Psychotherapeutic interventions that change health-related behavior, lifestyles, and attitudes are a very promising area in the growing field of health promotion (Humphreys, 1996). Psychotherapists are the experts in behavioral change, and behavioral change is what drives many health outcomes. Adherence to medical regimens is notoriously poor, and brief therapy-based interventions can improve follow-through on treatment recommendations. Brief interventions can also help people stick to diets and exercise programs, stop smoking, practice safe sex, and reduce risks for serious illness (Miller & Farber, 1997).

Positioning mental health specialty providers in primary care settings such as pediatric clinics, family practice settings, internal medicine centers, and obstetrics offices would encourage collaborative care and enhance all areas of practice. Cummings, Pallak, Dorken, and Henke (1993) have shown that the provision of psychotherapy reduces distress and overall health costs in a Medicaid population. The integration of medical and mental health services is good practice that saves money. Despite this reality, managed care systems are often structured in a fashion that provides disincentives for this kind of collaboration. The current trend in managed care is to "carve out" mental health services into a separate benefit management system. Unfortunately, a mental health carve-out company will not benefit from a reduction of general health care utilization created by improved collaboration between medical and mental health providers. However, a mental health carve-out will bear the costs of increased mental health service provision. Until mental health and medical care are integrated at the level of clinical practice *and* benefit management, the cost-savings achieved through improved collaboration will not be realized.

If cost savings are truly driving health care reform, then it is only a matter of time before policymakers begin to see the value of a health care system that encourages the kind of collaboration described above. The future will see a family health care team providing integrated biopsychosocial services in primary care settings (Clarkin et al., 1996). Involvement of the patient's family will be an important factor in promoting adherence to treatment regimens and implementing the treatment care plan. Elements of this model have already been implemented in school-based health clinics (Dryfoos, Chapter 4, this volume), large multispecialty medical practice groups (G. Sternstein, Grove Hill Medical Center, Department of Psychiatry, New Britain, CT; personal communication, 1998), and progressive, staff-based HMOs (Miller & Farber, 1997).

How Will Technology Influence the Practice of Psychotherapy?

We are in the midst of a technological revolution fueled largely by the personal computer and widespread application of microchip technology. It is unlikely that psychotherapy will escape the influence of this technology, and there have already been forays into various applications. The computer's capacity to manage and organize information and make it easily accessible in an interactive format could advance the field. Although the computer has been unable to "duplicate the kind of dialogue typically utilized in clinician administered therapy" (Wright & Wright, 1997), computer administered therapy has been developed and found to be accepted by patients and effective in the treatment of several disorders (Ahmed, Bayog, & Boisvert, 1997; Greist, 1995; Newman, Kenardy, Herman, & Taylor, 1997). Palm-top computers with a cognitive-behavioral treatment program have been used as an adjunct in the treatment of panic disorder with some promising results (Newman et al., 1997). Ahmed et al. (1997) used computer transcripts of sessions as an adjunct to the psychotherapeutic treatment of schizophrenia. They suggest that the computer, "by visually representing words, may facilitate communication by compensating for deficits in auditory processing, information processing, attention and memory often found among patients with schizophrenia" (p. 1334).

While other health-related fields, such as those that work with the blind or disabled, make good use of assistive technologies, psychotherapists have generally neglected their use. The computer's capacity to interact with clients and to provide programmed feedback in multiple modalities has tremendous potential for the delivery of cognitive and behavioral treatment protocols. As technology advances and more computing power can be packed into ever smaller devices, I believe we will see an increase in the use of assistive technologies in the psychotherapeutic treatment of mental illness.

The computer can also be used to collect data for use in treatment planning, diagnosis, and outcome assessment. When used directly with clients, it improves the efficiency of data collection and may become an essential tool in the collection of background information, symptom severity, and outcome-related measures of functioning and well-being.

It is also likely that Internet access to the psychotherapy literature, practice guidelines, and updated diagnostic information will keep the practicing psychotherapist current with the field. Communication on the Internet via chat modules, telephone emulators, and videophones could increase access to psychotherapy and provide anonymity that would enhance self-disclosure. While psychotherapy performed via the Internet is completely untested, it may be an effective and convenient way to provide a segment of service. The computer also has tremendous potential to improve the efficiency of record keeping associated with psychotherapy. Programs already exist to assist in the development of treatment plans, and the next generation of products may someday contain built-in practice guidelines (broader and more flexible than current guidelines), decision trees, and other devices to improve efficiency and enhance the treatment planning process.

The computer interface is unlikely to replace face-to-face psychotherapy. As noted above, the therapeutic relationship appears to be an important factor in the effectiveness of psychotherapy. Because technology places a machine between individuals, it may interfere with the therapeutic relationship and the transmission of important information through nonverbal communication. However, technological aids are likely to become an increasingly important adjunct to psychotherapy in the manner described above.

Will Psychotherapy Outcome Research Influence Health Care Policy?

Over the past 5 years, policy regarding the delivery of psychotherapy has come to be dominated by managed care. During this same period the scientific research on psychotherapy has failed to have a significant impact on health care policy (Newman & Tejeda, 1996). If psychotherapy is to survive the current challenges being forged by managed care, it must better utilize research to inform public policy.

To begin, psychotherapy researchers must do a better job of making their work more accessible and relevant to the typical practitioner. Research needs to demonstrate the effectiveness of interventions in real-world settings, not the sterile but well-controlled university clinic. As research designs achieve greater internal validity and scientific purity, it must be recognized that they move farther away from the typical situation in which most psychotherapy is actually practiced. While there should be a reciprocal relationship between practice and research, it is clear that those in the lab often have little understanding of what is happening out in the field (Strupp, 1997).

Psychotherapy research must also do a better job of evaluating functional outcomes and the costs and cost-benefits associated with particular interventions. In order to determine the ultimate value of psychotherapy to society, researchers need to determine how it impacts job performance, school performance, marital satisfaction, and parenting skills (Barlow, 1996). Cost analyses would help to justify psychotherapy on economic grounds. The Administration of Health Care Policy Research (AHCPR) and the National Institute of Health (NIH) are beginning to include such cost analyses in research efforts.

Psychotherapists also need to take more responsibility for the funding and completion of psychotherapy outcome research (Kocsis, 1996). As noted earlier, the amount of dollars allocated for the empirical validation of pharmacological agents far exceeds that which is funded by NIMH, the principal funding agent for psychotherapy research. The formation of local research practice networks that evaluate interventions in real-world settings would provide much needed support for the value of psychotherapy (Barlow, 1996). "The future of psychotherapy rests largely on how well research will define and justify psychotherapy's utility to major stakeholders" (Ostrowski, 1997, p. 2). Private foundations and corporations interested in improving health and well-being through improved mental health treatment will need to step forward and supplement the funding of psychotherapy outcome research.

What Ever Happened to Health Care Reform?

At the beginning of his first term in office, President Clinton began a campaign for national health care reform. His attempt at reforming the health care system failed. For a variety of reasons, conflicting public concerns could not create the national consensus needed to overcome the special interests that saw their livelihood threatened by the prospect of socialized medicine. As a result, managed care emerged as a very powerful force in shaping the delivery of health care, including psychotherapy.

In the absence of government sponsored health care reform, the U.S. system has settled for a set of technical fixes that lack any vision or coherent rationale for the changes being implemented other than short-term cost savings (Sabin, 1995). Within the current mental health system there are significant disincentives to provide quality care. In Connecticut, for example, 10 or 11 MCOs compete within the state's Medicaid Managed Care program. Medicaid recipients are given the choice as to which company they wish to manage their health care. Consider two plans, one that provides excellent mental health care and one that provides substandard care. Assuming other factors are equal, who is most likely to achieve the most cost savings and the greatest profit? Since, over time, the plan that provides the best care will attract the most expensive members (those who utilize such care on a regular and long-term basis), the plan that provides the worst care will profit most.

A second flaw in the current managed care system is how it allows and encourages cost shifting to the government. For example, consider a case where managed care denies appropriate intensity and duration of treatment to a child with a serious emotional disturbance. As the result of the failure to receive appropriate care, the school system provides hundreds of thousands of dollars of special education services to help this child succeed in school. Despite the allocation of resources, the educational interventions fail and the child drops out of school at age 16. With few job prospects and a lack of structure, he is at increased risk for substance abuse and related criminal activity. He is arrested and incarcerated. In this way, the costs of restricting psychotherapy are temporarily hidden, only to reemerge in the budget of the educational, criminal justice, social welfare, and general health care systems. Ultimately, the taxpayer bears the cost.

In the past, the provision of mental health services in the United States was largely unregulated. This was due to the availability of free or donated care and services provided under state grant funded initiatives. With the advent of third-party payers, regulation increased, first to assure quality, and increasingly of late to contain costs. These days, practitioners are forced to be concerned with cost issues and have been left out of the struggle to "balance individual and population oriented concerns" (Sabin, 1995, p. 994).

Sabin (1995) describes the British and U.S. health care systems as representing Jekyll-and-Hyde care, two very different faces of the same effort to deliver service and contain costs. In Hyde care, the restriction of access, reduction of benefits, and the creation of administrative hassles are designed to cut costs and reduce the profits of providers. In contrast, Jekyll care utilizes research-based practice guidelines, clear priorities, and efficient management to "increase the total benefit for an insured population" (p. 994). Thus, within a national health care, single-payer system, the goal is the equitable distribution of limited medical benefits. Cost containment remains, but so do concerns about the impact of limits and restrictions. There are no longer disincentives to treat or shift costs. By contrast, in the unregulated free market health care economy, corporate profitability is the bottom line and outweighs concerns for the societal good. Health care expenditures are reduced but at a great cost to society.

Given President Clinton's recently failed attempt at health care reform, it seems unlikely that reform will occur in the near future. However, it seems equally likely that policymakers and the public will someday recognize the true impact of managed care and take steps to correct it. Initially there will be efforts to regulate and legislate managed care without making fundamental changes in the underlying system. I believe that, eventually, consumer and governmental dissatisfaction will peak and a national health care system will be created. How long it takes, and how much damage is done in the interim, will depend on the ability of researchers and practitioners to inform public opinion and educate the legislature.

Summary

In the absence of a national health care system, managed care has grown to become the dominant force in shaping the delivery of health care in the United States. Changes in the way psychotherapy is practiced are already occurring, and more dramatic change is expected due to the influence of managed care and its impact on the health care marketplace. What will the future hold?

Epidemiological surveys demonstrate a need for psychotherapy that exceeds the current treatment capacity. Under a managed care system this disparity will worsen as increased competition, declining income, and lowered status of psychotherapy practitioners begin to impact their availability. Research will continue to demonstrate the effectiveness of psychotherapy, but is unlikely to alter the practice of managed care unless it can impact social policy and spur reform. Managed care will continue to show a preference for pharmacotherapy over psychotherapy, based on cost analysis. However, psychotherapy will be shown to be equal or superior to pharmacotherapy and will remain as an option for those who cannot or choose not to use medication.

The psychotherapist of the future will most likely be female and hold a master's degree. Relatively fewer psychiatrists and psychologists will provide psychotherapy, although primary care physicians may continue to provide a large portion of the service. Attempts to replace master's-level practitioners with lesser trained paraprofessionals will not be successful due to the trend toward more eclectic treatment models requiring a higher degree of training.

Treatment manuals will help to explicate specific psychotherapeutic techniques, but their prominence will decline as researchers and practitioners play closer attention to therapist variables, the acquisition of clinical skills, and healing aspects of the therapeutic relationship. The advance toward a cookbook approach will be replaced by a reconsideration and renewed appreciation of the human factors in the provision of psychotherapy.

In the future, psychotherapy will be more likely to be provided within large corporate health structures, primary care settings, the home, in school-based or school-linked clinics, or perhaps in small multispecialty franchised groups. Psychotherapy will be less likely to be provided in the private office of a solo practitioner or small mental health specialty group.

While research supports the value of psychotherapy beyond the minimal brief treatment approved by managed care, length of treatment will continue to be limited as a primary means of cost containment. Longer term treatment will remain available to the wealthy, outside of the mainstream of practice. There may be an increase in intermittent psychotherapy across the life span.

Psychotherapy will move beyond the current bias toward behavioral and cognitive-behavioral approaches as measurement technology improves and the efficacy of family systems, brief psychodynamic, interpersonal, and eclectic or multisystemic approaches is more clearly demonstrated.

In the future, psychotherapy will be better integrated into primary care. The biopsychosocial model will progress from theory to practice and achieve reductions in general health care utilization and improved adherence to medical regimens.

Technological advances will result in an increase in the use of assistive technology, computer aided communication (the Internet, videophones, etc), computer-based record keeping and treatment planning, and computer-based adjuncts to psychotherapy.

Research on psychotherapy will become more relevant to practitioners and policymakers by examining "real-world" applications of therapeutic techniques and including cost- and functional analyses. Practitioners of psychotherapy will need to do a better job at marketing the effectiveness of their interventions to those who will influence and structure the mental health systems of the future.

Mental health specialty practitioners will also need to diversify and move beyond psychotherapy per se. They must learn to use their considerable skills to create and deliver preventive programs, contribute to social policy, and move beyond the treatment of mental illness to improving health and functioning. In economic terms, psychotherapists will need to find new markets for their skills.

A rational policy on how to limit the cost of psychotherapy while maintaining high-quality effective services will not emerge until managed care has run its course and a national health care plan is adopted. A nationally sponsored single-payer plan is the only way to avoid the short-term thinking, cost shifting, and Band-Aid fixes that plague the current system. Given recent history, it may take more than 10 years to achieve fundamental change in the U.S. health care system. How long it takes, and the degree of damage done in the interim, will depend on how well the practitioners and researchers make their case for the value of psychotherapy.

References

Ahmed, M., Bayog, F., & Boisvert, C. M. (1997). Computer-facilitated psychotherapy for inpatients with schizophrenia. *Psychiatric Services, 48,* 1334-1335.

Albee, G. W. (1959). *Mental health manpower trends.* New York: Basic Books.

Barkley, R. A. (1990). *Attention deficit hyperactivity disorder: A handbook for diagnosis and treatment.* New York: Guilford.

Barlow, D. H. (1996). Health care policy, psychotherapy research, and the future of psychotherapy. *American Psychologist, 51*(10), 1050-1058.

Barlow, D. H., & Lehman, C. (1996). Advances in the psychosocial treatment of anxiety disorders: Implications for national healthcare. *Archives of General Psychiatry, 53,* 727-735.

Berdyaev, N. (1974). *Dostoyevsky, The underground man.* New York: Meridian Books.

Casey, R. J., & Berman, J. S. (1985). The outcome of psychotherapy for children. *Psychological Bulletin, 96,* 388-400.

Clarkin, A. H., Pilkonis, R. N., & Magruder, E. R. (1996). Psychotherapy of depression. *Archives of General Psychiatry, 53,* 717-722.

Cummings, N. A., Pallak, M. S., Dorken, H., & Henke, C. J. (1993). Medicaid managed mental health care and medical cost offset. *Behavioral Healthcare Tomorrow, 7,* 15-20.

Eysenck, H. J. (1952). The effects of psychotherapy: An evaluation. *Journal of Consulting Psychology, 16,* 319-324.

Falloon, I. R. H., Boyd, J. L., & McGill, C. W. (1985). Family management in the prevention of morbidity of schizophrenia: Clinical outcome of a two-year long study. *Archives of General Psychiatry, 42,* 887-896.

Frank, E., Kupfer, D. J., Wagner, E. F., McEachran, A. B., & Cornes, C. (1991). Efficacy of interpersonal psychotherapy as a maintenance treatment of recurrent depression. *Archives of General Psychiatry, 48,* 1053-1059.

Frank, E., & Spanier, C. (1995). Interpersonal psychotherapy for depression: Overview, clinical efficacy, and future directions. *Clinical Psychology: Science and Practice, 2,* 349-369.

Glueckauf, R. L., Frank, R. G., Bond, G. R., & Mcgrew, J. H. (1996). *Psychological practice in a changing healthcare system.* New York: Springer.

Greist, J. H. (1995). Computers and psychiatry. *Psychiatric Services, 46*(10), 989-991.

Group for the Advancement of Psychiatry. (1992). *Psychotherapy in the future.* Washington, DC: American Psychiatric Press.

Hengeller, S. W., Melton, G. B., & Smith, L. A. (1992). Family preservation using multisystemic therapy: An effective alternative to incarcerating serious juvenile offenders. *Journal of Consulting and Clinical Psychology, 60,* 963-961.

Hoberman, H. M., Clarke, G. N., & Saunders, S. M. (1996). Psychosocial interventions for adolescent depression: Issues, evidence, and future directions. *Programs of Behavioral Modification, 30,* 25-73.

Howard, K. I., Cornville, T. A., Lyons, J. S., Vessey, J. T., Lueger, R. J., & Saunders, S. M. (1996). Patterns of mental health service utilization. *Archives of General Psychiatry, 53,* 696-702.

Howard, K. I., Kopta, S. M., & Orlinsky, D. E. (1986). The dose-effect relationship in psychotherapy. Psychotherapy research [Special issue]. *American Psychologist, 41*(2), 159-164.

Howard, K. I., & Mahoney, M. T. (1996). How much outpatient therapy is enough? *Behavioral Healthcare Tomorrow, 5,* 44-50.

Humphreys, K. (1996). Clinical psychologists as psychotherapists: History, future, and alternatives. *American Psychologist, 51*(3), 190-197.

Kazdin, A. E. (1993). Psychotherapy for children and adolescents: Current progress and future research directions. *American Psychologist, 48,* 644-657.

Kiecolt-Glaser, J. K., & Glaser, R. (1995). Psychoneuroimmunology and health consequences: Data and shared mechanisms. *Psychosomatic Medicine, 57*(3), 269-274.

Knesper, D. J. (1997). *Primary care psychiatry.* Philadelphia: W. B. Saunders.

Kocsis, J. H. (1996). Practice guidelines and professional challenges: What psychotherapists need to do. *Archives of General Psychiatry, 53,* 303-304.

Lambert, M. J., & Bergin, A. E. (1994). The effectiveness of psychotherapy. In A. E. Bergin & S. L. Garfield (Eds.), *Handbook of psychotherapy and behavior change* (pp. 143-189). New York: Wiley.

Mental health: Does therapy help? (1995, November). *Consumer Reports,* pp. 734-739.

Miller, B., & Farber, L. (1997). Delivery of mental health services in the changing health care system. *Professional Psychology Research and Practice, 27,* 527-529.

Miller, I. J. (1996). Time-limited brief therapy has gone too far: The result is invisible rationing. *Professional Psychology: Research and Practice, 27*(6), 567-576.

Newman, F. L., & Tejeda, M. J. (1996). The need for research that is designed to support decisions in the delivery of mental health services. *American Psychologist, 51*(10), 1040-1049.

Newman, M. G., Kenardy, J., Herman, S., & Taylor, C. B. (1997). Comparison of palmtop-computer-assisted brief cognitive-behavioral treatment to cognitive-behavioral treatment for panic disorder. *Journal of Consulting and Clinical Psychology, 65*(1), 178-183.

Ostrowski, M. (1997). *The future of psychotherapy in the era of managed care: The importance of research that addresses the needs of stakeholders.* Unpublished manuscript, Antioch New England Graduate School.

Patterson, J. E., McIntosh-Koontz, L., Baron, M., & Bischoff, R. (1997). Curriculum changes to meet challenges: Preparing MFT students for managed care settings. *Journal of Marital and Family Therapy, 23*(4), 445-459.

Pearsall, D. F. (1997). Psychotherapy outcome research in child and adolescent psychiatric disorders. *The Canadian Journal of Psychiatry, 42,* 595-600.

Plant, R. W. (1991, October 20). Treating obsessive-compulsive behavior. *New York Times,* Connecticut Q&A.

Psychiatric Services. (1997a). Behavioral health care companies challenged by costs, competition. *Psychiatric Services, 48*(10), 1352.

Psychiatric Services. (1997b). 75 percent of insured Americans now enrolled in managed behavioral care programs. *Psychiatric Services, 48*(8), 1094-1095.

Regier, D. A. (1984). The NIMH Epidemiologic Catchment Area program: Historical context, major objectives, and study population characteristics. *Archives of General Psychiatry, 41,* 934-941.

Reuters. (1997). HMO's: Legislation likely to continue. Reuters Health Information Services, Inc. *Yahoo News,* 1997.

Rogers, C. R. (1965). *Client-centered therapy, its current practice, implications, and theory.* Boston: Houghton Mifflin.

Sabin, J. E. (1995). Lessons for U.S. managed care from the British National Health Service: I. "The vision thing." *Psychiatric Services, 46*(10), 993-994.

Seligman, M. E. P. (1995). The effectiveness of psychotherapy: The Consumer Reports study. *American Psychologist, 50,* 956-974.

Shorter, E. R. (1997). *A history of psychiatry.* New York: John Wiley.

Silverman, W. H., (1996). Cookbooks, manuals, and paint-by-numbers: Psychotherapy in the 90's. *Psychotherapy, 33*(2), 207-215.

Smith, M. L., Glass, G. V., & Miller, T. I. (1980). *The benefits of psychotherapy.* Baltimore, MD: Johns Hopkins University Press.

Strupp, H. H. (1993). The Vanderbilt Psychotherapy Studies: Synopsis. *Journal of Consulting and Clinical Psychology, 61*(3), 431-433.

Strupp, H. H. (1997). Research, practice and managed care. *Psychotherapy, 34*(1), 91-95.

Strupp, H. H., & Andersen, T. (1997). On the limitations of therapy manuals. *Clinical Psychology: Science and Practice.*

Wright, J. H., & Wright, A. S. (1997). Computer-assisted psychotherapy. *Journal of Psychotherapy Practice and Research, 6*(4), 315-329.

CHAPTER 7

Behavioral Medicine: The Cost-Effectiveness of Primary Prevention

NANCY J. KENNEDY

> Clinical medicine is "a science of uncertainty and an art of probability."
>
> *Osler (1961, p. 129)*

Our current medical system, with few exceptions, is a sickness care system and not a health care system. The medical model, in contrast to the public health model, has embraced a narrow biological viewpoint of disease (more recently accepting of biopsychosocial factors) and has devoted sometimes excessive efforts to curing individuals of afflictions. Although the causative factors in disease have changed dramatically from acute afflictions with identified pathogens to chronic disorders that have a web of causation, the core culture of American medicine has remained relatively constant and tenacious. Throughout the 20th century, the medical system has continued emphasizing the individual perspective with success measured by cures, if possible, and, if not, by longevity of life.

Managed care is our newest opportunity and risk. Experts and practitioners in behavioral medicine and health savor the opportunity to integrate psychosocial with biomedical approaches to health and illness. The impetus for these approaches emanates from primary prevention and the efforts to change factors influencing health or well-being, especially lifestyle and the attitudes, beliefs, and moods that influence adaptation to stressors or illness. Seventy percent of today's illnesses or disorders are preventable (Fries et al., 1993). That statistic is the basis for instituting strategies that focus on systematically reducing the need and thus the demand for medical services. Health care costs in the United States are almost 15% of the gross domestic product, the highest of any country in the world (Fries et al., 1993). There exist extraordinary opportunities within this changing health care environment. "Health promotion is (or should be) characterized by efforts to link actions at different social levels in some coherent way" (Labonte, 1994).

Interventions directed at entire populations or targeted segments of the population are traditionally referred to as primary prevention. The public health model is not the antithesis of the medical model; in fact, most of traditional medicine can be characterized as secondary prevention with the purpose of addressing the prevalence of diseases or disorders. Medicine has also moved into the realm of tertiary prevention, especially in reducing the disability associated with all diseases or disorders. Nonetheless, with the exception of behavioral medicine, a discipline whose intervention techniques are based on learning theory (Gordon, 1982), few physicians are interested in primary preventive strategies. The goal of primary prevention is to prevent the occurrence of disease, disorder, or events that are deleterious to health. The major objectives of primary prevention are to promote health and provide specific protection where pathogens have been identified. Primary prevention also includes the promulgation of public policies, for example, mandatory education, fluoridation, restaurant inspection, and other social interventions and legislative policies, to address or eradicate epidemics that threatened the populace. There is a paucity of health care agencies, especially those predominated by clinical medicine, that would assume or are interested in primary preventive interventions. There are, of course, exceptions to this statement. For example, most health care agencies provide specific protective interventions where the disease-causing agents have been identified and units of service, for example, immunizations or vaccinations, can be administered.

Health care in this country is dramatically changing—that change is not totally attributable to managed care. Communication technologies are, as Tom Ferguson, M.D. (1996) writes, turning the treatment pyramid upside down. Health information systems are creating health-activated consumers. Why should health care providers, especially physicians, be advocating for this change? As Ferguson writes:

> As health information flow becomes widely available to all, we are seeing the medical equivalent of the toppling of the Berlin Wall that once separated lay healthcare from professional medicine. Some of our widely held assumptions are now in question. We have assumed that we can safely ignore our own health until it breaks down, then count on a doctor to bail us out, and that medicine is something only doctors know about. Consumer health information provides citizens with the tools, skills, information, and support they need to play the role of primary practitioners in the emerging healthcare system. The biggest challenge for a health professional is to see that consumers are not only people with problems but also resources for information about those problems. (p. 3)

Not only consumers but also purchasers of health care services are demanding and are increasingly insisting that providers and organizations be held accountable for providing the needed interventions and the outcomes of those interventions. Nearly all of a physician's training is devoted to acquiring technical skills associated with medicine. Technical intervention may reverse or palliate biologic illnesses, but have little effect on the factors influencing health/wellness or disease/disorder.

In a primary care medical practice, while 10% to 20% of presenting patients have a diagnosable psychiatric disorder, the remaining 80% have significant psychological distress (Barsky, 1981; Stoeckle, Zola, & Davidson, 1964). However, traditional treatment is not necessarily what is required. In fact, several studies document that providers' offering services to address the psychosocial problems decreased subsequent utilization without problem resolution (Mumford, Schlesinger, Glass, Patrick, & Curedon, 1984; Schlesinger et al., 1983). Rather than medical interventions or verbal admonitions to change lifestyles by adopting behaviors that either never existed or are culturally disharmonious, what is necessary are the primary preventive strategies associated with behavioral medicine. The subsequent measures of success may become quality of life in lieu of "cures."

Models: Public Health Versus Medical Model

People in health care represent different disciplines, different occupations, different institutional affiliations. All are interested in the issue of children and health, but unless we have common understanding of terminology, our collective interest will easily be dissipated by our individual differences. We must have an operational context that encompasses our differences, integrates them, and permits us to realize that the power of a group is greater than the sum of its parts.

Medicine, as science and art dealing with the prevention and cure or alleviation of disease, is an integral part of the public health model. The biological sciences are the theoretical bases of the medical model. Information is structured within the framework of signs, symptoms, cause, pathology, and treatment, course, prognosis, and the sequelae or abnormal conditions that result from either the problem or the treatment. The focus of the medical model is individual care, and the major assumption is that man has a right to live. The medical model is now being utilized more when planning health services for the population (either private or public sector) and is conceptualized as a three-tiered system (see Figure 7.1).

Providers of primary medical care services are now the gatekeepers of our managed care system; that is, these services should meet the health needs of most people and be the entry point into the medical care system. Primary care providers can include physicians, nurse practitioners, physician assistants, and several other professional groups recognized by the accrediting organizations. Secondary medical care services require a certain degree of sophistication and use specialized resources. As this is a three-tiered model, obviously the degree of sophistication is greater than primary but less than tertiary. Secondary care usually occurs after the diagnosis is established and the patient's illness or disorder requires the services of a specialist or specialized care. Tertiary medical care services are services that, because of the degree of sophistication of the resources required to provide them and because of the low

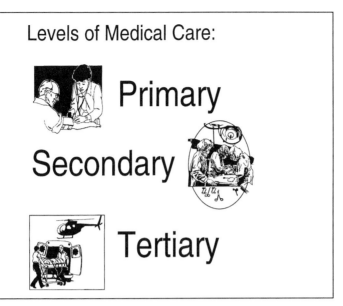

Figure 7.1. Medical Model

frequency with which conditions requiring these services occur, should be centralized and grouped within units emphasizing efficiency, effectiveness, and continuity. One of the best examples of tertiary medical care services is a shock trauma center.

As with any model, the medical model is fraught with problems. There is no systematic approach to dealing with the sequelae associated with disease and/or treatment. Similarly, there is no systematic approach to psychosocial conditions. Finally, there is no systematic approach to addressing community- or population-based health.

The public health model (Figure 7.2) structures information within the framework of environmental, social, economic, and biological conditions affecting health or well-being. Thus, one of the theoretical bases of the public health model is, like the medical model, that of the biological sciences. Other bases of public health include the physical sciences, the humanities, and its two cornerstones—epidemiology and biostatistics. Unlike the medical model, the focus of the public health model is the health of the community—

	Primary Prevention	Secondary Prevention	Tertiary Prevention
PURPOSE	Prevent the Occurrence	Reduce the Duration	Limit Impairment and Prevent Sequelae
ACTIVITIES	Promote Health	Detection and Screening	Optimize Coping Skills and Adjustment
	Specific Protection	Early Diagnosis and Treatment	Rehabilitation

Figure 7.2. Public Health Model

or, the health of the people—and the major assumption of the public health model is that man has a right to an environment that promotes health or well-being. The individual is not relegated within the model, for individuals constitute the community. Public health seeks to promote health and to control the development and presence of illnesses or disorders in populations by utilizing methods and activities that are designated as primary prevention, secondary prevention, and tertiary prevention.

The most familiar type of activity in the public health model is secondary prevention. The goal of secondary prevention is to discover, diagnose, and treat illnesses or disorders as soon as possible in order to prevent, control, minimize, or lessen the serious impact of the identified problems. Secondary prevention is expressed by prevalence measures—for example, point prevalence, period prevalence.

Activities under the aegis of secondary prevention are classified in two general ways. First, there are activities designed to screen and detect problems, that is, efforts that lead to the discovery of specific illnesses, diseases, or disorders within members of the population. Examples include: breast self-examination, routine physical examinations that are mandatory at various stages throughout life, and specific tests such as urine and blood screening examinations to detect diabetes. The second major grouping of secondary prevention activities are those efforts to provide early diagnosis and treatment of illnesses as soon as those illnesses occur.

These activities are usually referred to as medical care services, especially primary and secondary medical care. Here is the primary intersection of the medical model with the public health model. Activities and settings for early diagnosis and treatment include first aid, industrial clinics, employee assistance programs, community hospitals, and community mental health centers.

The goal of tertiary prevention is to prevent the sequelae or abnormal conditions resulting from illnesses or disorders and/or treatments rendered. Conditions illustrating the latter have several designations. *Iatrogenic illnesses/disorders* result from side effects associated with treatment, frequently medications, or from direct maltreatment. *Nosocomial infections* are contracted in the environments where treatments are provided, with hospitals still being commonplace (Brecker, 1982).

Tertiary prevention activities also have two major groupings. First, there are activities to limit the sequelae associated with the illnesses or the treatment. Examples of such activities include early ambulation after surgery or childbirth; timely release from inpatient hospital care to prevent the social breakdown syndrome of institutionalization; and programs designed to maintain family, social, vocational, and community ties during and after illnesses. The other major grouping of tertiary prevention is rehabilitation. Examples of rehabilitation include physical medical treatment to restore functioning, vocational rehabilitation for jobs training or retraining, and sheltered workshops and halfway houses.

One of the most important, least costly, and most effective aspects of disease control is those activities designated primary prevention or preventive intervention. Primary prevention activities seek to promote health and prevent the occurrence of new cases of illness or disease or disorder. In contrast to prevalence, the measurement associated with primary prevention is incidence. As with the other types of prevention, primary prevention activities have two major groupings. Examples of primary prevention activities that promote health include: family planning programs; premarital, vocational, and retirement counseling; anticipatory guidance; seat belts and infant car seats; media campaigns; and antismoking classes. These activities are part of traditional school and community education agendas and are directed to problems of living. That is, those events, expected or unexpected, during life that in the absence of sufficient ability to cope, may lead to deleterious behavior and/or disease or disorder. In addition, public policy of the Federal government and State and local governments mandate programs that have as a major objective the promotion of health. Examples include mandatory education; adequate housing; Synar tobacco amendment; recreation programs and parks; and income maintenance, including retirement and disability payments.

The other major primary prevention grouping of activities is specific protection. When a pathogen has been identified or a segment of population is acknowledged to have a higher statistical probability of developing an illness, disease, or disorder, prevention activities have been developed to stop or delay the onset of the problem or lessen the impact. Examples include: immunization against diseases such as smallpox, rubella, or polio; industrial accident prevention, including the wearing of hard hats or eye goggles; highway safety prevention, including the wearing of seat belts, infant car seats; limits on excessive and/or aggressive programs; and well-baby clinics. Here, too, like the other objective of primary prevention, public policy programs exist. Examples include pure food and drug laws, fluoridation, and meat and restaurant inspection; surveillance system for identified infectious diseases; and sewage and garbage collection.

The public health model also has its problems. There is no systematic approach to rehabilitation outside of the medical model. A similar deficiency exists relative to home health care. Public health is less responsive than the medical establishment to managed care. Finally, with Medicaid and Medicare recipients increasingly organized and financed by managed care entrepreneurs, the lack of a coordinated community-based health service system threatens the existence of the critical safety net for the public sector.

Factors Influencing Health/ Wellness or Disease/Disorder

There are major factors that influence, in a positive or a negative manner, health or well-being (see Figure 7.3). Genetics encompasses, in a varying and unique mixture, the biological inheritance of the individual and possible predisposition to specific diseases or disorders—for example, sickle cell anemia and Tay-Sachs disease. Heredity is considered the internal (host) variable of health status.

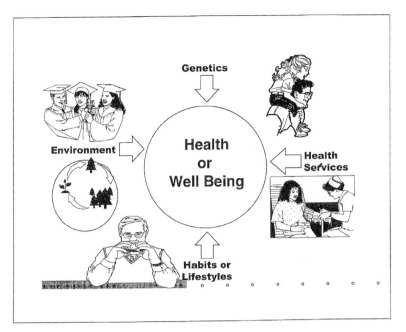

Figure 7.3. Factors That Influence Health

The genetic inheritance of the individual influences such easily recognizable characteristics as eye, hair, and skin colors; texture of hair; height; and, to a certain degree, weight. Genetic inheritance also determines such aspects of individuality as metabolism, susceptibility to disease, and patterns of behavior.

Another major factor influencing health is the environment; this is characterized as external, in contrast to genetics as internal. Under this heading are included such factors as the physical environment, purity of air and water, health, chemical pollution, infectious agents, and the quality and quantity of housing including the presence and absence of plumbing, heating, and other factors that enhance or divest individual dignity in the ability to maintain self-respect. Also included are such factors as the social environment: the ways in which we work, the people with whom we interact, and the environmental factors that enhance or deter the gratifications received from this socialization (or lack of such). The social environment is the major determinant of an individual's psychological constitution (Denham, 1978).

Another external cause or factor of health or well-being is the availability and quality of health services. Some individuals have equated this factor with that of the *medical* care system, a system currently undergoing rapid and dramatic changes. Thus, discussion of what constitutes this factor is a description of medical care personnel, facilities, and interventions. Yet even with a narrow conceptualization of health services, individual health is affected when services are accessible and appropriately utilized. Inappropriate utilization occurs when either an individual or providers "medicalize" an individual's life, reducing all problems to medical terms and risking the onset of iatrogenic disorders or nosocomial infections.

The significant impacts of the managed care industry are being experienced at both the micro- and the macro level. As managed care systems grow and assume responsibility for larger segments of the population, especially those financed with public funds such as the recipients of Medicaid and Medicare, community-based approaches need to be a critical component with clinical interventions in comprising health care services (Kennedy, 1998).

Under the headings of habits or lifestyle are behavioral factors such as amount and quality of diet, exercise, sexual activity, work, reaction to stress, and use of alcohol, tobacco, and other drugs. An individual can be made ill by the way he or she lives; both behavioral excesses and deficiencies are factors determining health, wellness, disorder, or disease.

With repetition, behaviors become habitual. Those behaviors become a categorical lifestyle when they dominate as normative behaviors. However, as the body cannot be separated from the mind, so behavior is intrinsically linked to the psyche. Thus, attitudes and values are even more influential than knowledge in determining behavior. The evidence for learning, which is also an internal process, is behavioral change that can be observed or measured. Thus, we infer that learning has occurred with changes in behavior, ushering in a new lifestyle or reclaiming a previous lifestyle. This seemingly simplistic explanation is not meant to give a specious appearance to the complexities of human behavior. Instead, the purpose is to establish the premise that behavior, especially deleterious behavior, can be changed.

There is also consensus that culture is a significant factor in the context of personal and public health. Culture is not restricted to racial or ethnic identification or heritage; instead, culture is the customs, beliefs, values, knowledge, and skills that guide a people's behavior along shared paths (Linton, 1947). In fact, cultures even define differently the concepts of health/wellness and disease/disorder. Nonetheless, culture is pervasively intertwined among all factors of health/wellness and disease/disorder. However, the four major factors influencing health—genetics, environment, health services, and habits/lifestyle—need to be congruent with cultural and linguistic norms and mores.

Epidemiological Approach to Morbidity and Mortality

As previously stated, epidemiology and biostatistics are the cornerstones of public health. There is a need to quantify all problems in order to assess their magnitude, characterize the populations involved, identify the possible causes underlying the problems, and propose resolutions. By definition, epidemiology is the study of the distribution and factors of health-related states and events in a defined population (Last, 1987). How the population is defined often determines the information and data collected. Epidemiology is the major vehicle for evaluating health status, describing the natural history of diseases/disorders, identifying risk and protective factors, aiding in the process of clinical analysis and decision making, and developing and evaluating the continuum of care.

Having its origin in ancient Greece (Smith, 1979), epidemiology emerged as a method to identify the source of illness and disease by characterizing its occurrence in terms of person, place, and time. These characteristics reflect the basic paradigm of epidemiology, which involves the relationship among host, agent, and environment. When considering the history of epidemiology, public health historians have identified distinct phases and eras.

Modern epidemiology developed in response to a need to measure the extent and characterize the occurrence of infectious diseases such as cholera and hepatitis. These diseases were the predominant cause of illness and death, primarily due to a lack of sanitation, poor nutrition, and an absence of medical technology such as vaccinations and antibiotics. Poor sanitation contributed to the occurrence of diseases such as cholera, while poor nutrition contributed to host susceptibility and subsequent clinical manifestation of disease.

In infectious disease, the focus of attention is the agent, without which the disease would not occur. Infectious disease seems to result from a relatively straightforward cause-and-effect relationship, making epidemiological methods for describing the occurrence of disease apparently simple. In many cases, however, the mere presence of the agent in a host does not necessarily initiate the disease process in the host. Thus, host susceptibility and environment are determinants of whether or not disease will occur.

In addition to its primary focus on the agent, transmission of an agent to a susceptible host further distinguishes infectious disease epidemiology from other types of epidemiology. An important aspect for characterizing the occurrence of disease involves identifying the source and spread of the agent to a susceptible host. Another distinguishing characteristic of investigations of infectious disease relates to identification and enumeration of cases and the population at risk. Almost all infectious disease cases come to the attention of the medical care system. Visits to physicians, clinics, or other facilities such as jails and almshouses in the late 19th century, provide documentation of the diseases. These records become the primary source for enumerating the number of people experiencing the diseases or at risk of developing the diseases. Statistics began to be collected to demonstrate the clustering of morbidity and mortality.

The identification of the pathogens for the infectious diseases provided the necessary clues to developing interventions such as isolation rooms, vaccinations, and, eventually, antibiotics. Physicians now had interventions to treat or prevent the majority of the morbidity and mortality during the 19th century. While these interventions brought major improvements in health, not all infectious diseases were eradicated. Some infectious diseases are not subject to lifelong immunity. For example, the infectious disease gonorrhea can develop again upon engaging in behavior that subjects the individual to reexposure. In addition, in spite of all of our technological advances, in many countries, particularly developing countries, or even in certain segments of the U.S. population, infectious diseases continue to be the fundamental problems affecting the health status of individuals. An example of such a problem in the United States is mycobacterium tuberculosis (Jereb, Kelley, Dooley, Canthen, & Snider, 1991).

A natural result of decreasing infectious diseases was an increase in longevity. As a result, chronic diseases are more prevalent and the focus of epidemiologists. For the past 40 years in the United States, heart disease, cancer, stroke, chronic lung diseases, and accidents have been the leading causes of death (Centers for Disease Control [CDC], 1995). Eighty-eight and a half million noninstitutionalized Americans (46% of individuals who had identified a health condition associated with medical care use or disability days) had one or more chronic conditions in 1987 (Hoffman, Rice, & Sung, 1996). And, while the rates of chronic disorders are highest among the elderly, one in four children younger than 18 years also has a chronic condition (Hoffman et al., 1996; Newacheck & Stoddard, 1994).

Epidemiological research reveals that chronic diseases have multiple causes leading to a single effect. This makes case identification and prevention more problematic, because the inability to isolate a chemical or physical agent increases the difficulty of establishing the link between exposure and onset of disease. The metaphor of a "web of causation" (MacMahon, Pugh, & Ipsen, 1960) explains the complexity of chronic diseases. As for the classic paradigm of agent, host, and environment, Morris (1975), in postulating a paradigm for chronic diseases, replaced the term *agent* with *behavioral factors*. Etiologic research involving the chronic diseases reveals the importance of behavioral risk factors. This prospective allows chronic diseases to be classified as diseases of lifestyle. However, many of these behaviors are established during adolescence and young adulthood. More recent research (Pentz, 1985) suggests that host susceptibility is the most important factor in the paradigm. Subsequently, the preventive and treatment approaches for chronic diseases are to address the factors that influence health/ wellness or disease/disorder.

Table 7.1 identifies and quantifies the major external (not genetic) factors that contribute to the 1990 U.S. deaths (McGinnis & Foege, 1993). Approximately half of all deaths that occurred in 1990 are attributed to the factors identified. Moreover, tobacco and diet/activity patterns are the two most influential factors, outpacing each of the other factors by a tremendous magnitude.

Table 7.1   Actual Causes of Death in the United States in 1990

Causes	Deaths	Estimated Number*
Tobacco	400,000	19
Diet/Activity patterns	300,000	14
Alcohol	100,000	5
Microbial agents	90,000	4
Toxic agents	60,000	3
Firearms	35,000	2
Sexual behavior	30,000	1
Motor vehicles	25,000	1
Illicit use of drugs	20,000	< 1
Total	1,060,000	50

SOURCE: From McGinnis & Foege, 1993.
NOTE: * Composite approximation drawn from studies that use different approaches to derive estimates, ranging from actual counts (e.g., firearms) to population attribute risk calculations (e.g., tobacco). Numbers over 100,000 rounded to the nearest 100,000; over 50,000 rounded to the nearest 10,000; below 50,000, rounded to the nearest 5,000.

In a recent survey (Clements & Hales, 1997), 90% of participants agreed with this statement: My physical well-being is in my hands. In spite of this affirmation, 57% of respondents described themselves as overweight, 52% did not exercise, and 26% smoked cigarettes. In addition, the most common health problems cited by the survey respondents who were 18 years and older were arthritis (25%), high blood pressure (23%), and depression (14%). These paradoxical statements are further evidence of the need for a new model applicable to the complexity of the emerging 21st century.

Epidemiology has been seen as an important research method for identifying factors associated with a variety of social and health problems, such as violence, accidents, mental disorders, and addiction, and has assumed an important role in understanding these conditions and behaviors (Kozel, Sanborn, & Kennedy, 1990). While each of these conditions has unique characteristics, they all share a common trait involving the inability to cease a behavior, which has or could have a deleterious effect on health or well-being. Similar to chronic disease, the focus of attention in the epidemiology of behavioral disorders is on environment and host susceptibility. While basic research has demonstrated clear biochemical and neurophysiological changes that occur with some disorders, such as alcoholism and schizophrenia, a common element among the diseases appears to be a significant psychosocial dimension.

The conditions or precursors that lead to these disorders are generally more voluntary, and, to some extent, there is more knowledge of the consequences than with either infectious or chronic disease. The sensitive nature of the data associated with almost all of these disorders presents unique measurement problems. Traditional data sources fail to capture most of the afflicted population. Veracity of self-report also presents a challenging methodological problem. People with these problems or disorders generally avoid contact with facilities or systems through which their behavior can be identified, including health care systems. Often primary care providers are not cognizant of these problems or disorders as a potential cause of trauma and/or disease, and thus, important data may not be recorded.

Finally, the emergence of Acquired Immunodeficiency Syndrome (AIDS) as a major international health problem highlights the interrelationship among infectious, chronic, and behavior diseases and the epidemiology used in their study. The Human Immunodeficiency Virus (HIV), which causes the disease, is transmitted principally through sexual contact and/or sharing of syringes among intravenous (IV) drug users. When the epidemic first was recognized, the population at greatest risk for contracting the disease included those who engaged in unprotected sex with multiple partners, especially homosexual and bisexual males. As the epidemic has shifted, a growing percentage of AIDS victims are IV drug users who share needles, those who engage in unprotected sexual contact with IV drug users, and the offspring of IV drug users. The AIDS issue is the most recent example of the importance of epidemiology in public health and chronicles the need for continually adapting effective methods of investigation to accommodate both changes in human behavior and changing conditions of life.

Behavioral Disorders Through the Life Cycle

Neither behavioral disorders nor preventive interventions are restrictive as to who may be affected, or why, when, where, and how the problems can be averted or alleviated. Medicine is as much an art as it is a science. Thus, the wisdom of one of our foremost mentors can provide the artistry for this section.

The Seven Ages of Man

All the world's a stage,
And all the men and women merely players:
They have their exits and their entrances;
And one in his time plays many parts,
His acts being seven ages. At first the infant,
Mewling and puking in the nurse's arms.
And then the whining school-boy, with his satchel,
And shining morning face, creeping like snail
Unwillingly to school. And then the lover
Sighing like furnace, with a woeful ballad
Mads to his mistress' eyebrow. Then a Soldier,
Full of strange oaths, and bearded like the pard,
Jealous in honour, sudden and quick in quarrel,
Seeking the bubble reputation
Even in the cannon's mouth. And then the justice,
In fair round belly with good capon lined
With eyes severe, and beard of formal cut,
Full of wise saws and modern instances;
And so he plays his part. The sixth age shifts
Into the lean and slipper'd pantaloon,
With spectacles on nose and pouch on side,
His youthful hose well sav'd a world too wide
For his shrunk shank; and his big manly voice,
Turning again toward childish treble,
And whistles in his sound. Last scene of all,
That ends this strange evently history,
Is second childishness and mere oblivion
Sans teeth, sans eyes, sans taste, sans everything.

(William Shakespeare, *As You Like It*, 1599)

The etiology, treatment, and prevention of physical illnesses and mental and addictive disorders raise unique issues and challenges at each stage of the life cycle to which the Bard made reference. Educators, sociologists, and psychologists, like their other professional colleagues in medicine, recognize the importance of the developmental stages of life. While specific ages may vary, the life cycle has six distinct phases: infancy and early childhood; middle childhood; adolescence; early adulthood; middle age; and later life. Important health issues are associated with specific stages of life. Prevention, treatment, and psychosocial adjustment to diseases of the 20th and impending 21st centuries require the development and implementation of behavioral interventions that are culturally appropriate, including age and gender.

Behavior may

1. be a cause of illness or a risk factor arising through the adoption of health-damaging behaviors, such as alcohol and other drug use/abuse, diet, high-risk sexual practices, or tobacco;

2. serve as a cofactor in the progression of disease by modifying the course of illness;

3. be altered as a consequence of illness, with co-occurring depression, anxiety, substance abuse, and other psychosocial complications of chronic or acute illness; and

4. serve as a component of treatment and prevention (Blumenthal, 1993b).

By the late 1970s, behavioral factors had gained national recognition for their role in the promotion of health and the prevention of disease. The landmark 1979 publication *Healthy People: The Surgeon General's Report on Health Promotion and Disease Prevention* provided the foundation for the first national health promotion and disease prevention initiative. Broad national goals were set for each of the major stages of life: namely, infants (under 1 year of age); children (1-14 years of age); adolescents and young adults (15-24 years of age); adults (25-64 years of age); and elderly (65 years of age and over; U.S. Department of Health, Education and Welfare, 1979).

The National Health Interview Survey (NHIS) reports that 69% of children between the ages of 5 and 16 years had a physical examination once at ages 5 and 6 and once every 2 years from ages 7 to 16. The percentage was lower for children with family incomes below the poverty level (62%), but higher for children with Medicaid (83%; Newacheck & Halfon, 1988). For children younger than 6, 65% of all medical care visits are to pediatricians. Developmental, learning, and emotional problems are among the most common chronic conditions for both children and adolescents (National Center for Health Statistics [NCHS], 1990). Among children ages 3 to 17, 4% have a developmental delay, 6.5% have a learning disability, and 13.4% have an emotional or behavioral problem. Diagnosis of these problems is more difficult at early ages and, without attention, can easily go undetected until after age 6, when children are already in the second or third grade.

Early intervention is of critical importance during the infancy-to-preschool period when brain development is more rapid and extensive, and much more vulnerable to environmental influences. Research provides evidence that stressful experiences during these early years of life negatively affect brain development and place children at risk for developing a variety of cognitive, behavioral, and emotional difficulties ("Starting Points," 1994). Early intervention programs that target children while their personality and adaptive capacity are still forming, rather than when the personality structure has become less malleable, can be very effective (Meisels & Shonkoff, 1990).

Use of preventive health services is a critical problem among school-aged children in families living below the poverty level (Children's Defense Fund [CDF], 1994; U.S. Congress, Office of Technology Assessment [OTA], 1991). In Medicaid's Early and Periodic Screening, Diagnostic, and Treatment (EPSDT) program, States are required to provide or arrange for "comprehensive, periodic assessments of the physical and mental health and follow-up services for Medicaid-eligible children under age 21 and to diagnose and treat any problems discovered as part of the screening process." Pediatricians and other primary care providers are often the first health care professionals to be consulted or present when behavioral and/or emotional problems are manifested.

An estimated 12 million children—20% of all children—experience some substance abuse or mental health problems while they are growing up (Center for Mental Health Services [CMHS], 1996; Committee to Identify Research Opportunities, 1989; U.S. Department of Health and Human Services [DHHS], 1991; U.S. Congress, Office of Technology Assessment [OTA], 1994). By the age of 11, one in five children has smoked cigarettes and 1 in 11 children has had their first drink of alcohol (Elster & Kuznets, 1994; Johnston, Bachman, & O'Mallet, 1997). Among adolescents aged 12 to 17 years, the likelihood of engaging in behaviors that increase risk for chronic disease is inversely related to socioeconomic status (SES), with the greatest level of risk behaviors found among adolescents from families in which the parent or other responsible adult was less educated and financial resources are limited (Lowry, Kann, Collins, & Kolbe, 1996).

As children reach adolescence, they enter a stage of greater developmental and emotional changes resulting in a need for psychosocial support. Because many of the health problems of adolescents arise from environmental factors and risk-taking behavior, they need anticipatory guidance programs to address "problems of living." By ages 16 to 20, only 8% of visits were to pediatricians, with 10% to internists and 16% to obstetricians/gynecologists (Elster & Kuznets, 1994). An estimated 84% of pregnancies of teenagers ages 15 to 19 are not intended (DHHS, 1991). In addition, about 25% of all births to teenagers are not first births (Alan Guttmacher Institute, 1993). Counseling adolescents is further important because life-long health patterns, such as physical activity, diet, or smoking, solidify during this age.

Given the preceding information on unintended pregnancies, the dramatic change in what constitutes the American family is far from surprising. While two-parent families still predominate, divorced families, never-married single-parent families, step-families, and cohabiting heterosexual and homosexual families now constitute the myriad families with children (U.S. Bureau of the Census, 1992). These familial arrangements are now the substance of research as to the impact on children's health and behavior. A significant proportion of the work is directed at the fact that one in four families is single-headed and 50% to 60% of children born today will spend part of their childhood or adolescence in single-headed, primarily female-headed, families (Theil, 1994). Children who live apart from one or both parents appear to be disadvantaged across a range of outcomes, which increases the long-term risk of poverty and economic dependence (National Institute of Child and Human Development [NICHD], 1991).

The typical American spends approximately one third of his or her day working (Greene & Simons-Morton, 1984). Therefore, both work and the workplace have significant impact on health. Among people aged 20 to 34, one third of all injuries (National Center for Health Statistics [NCHS], 1985) and one sixth of all injury deaths occur on the job (Baker, O'Neill, & Ginsburg, 1992). Stress in the workplace has a negative impact on both individuals and organizations. Of the 550 million days lost due to absenteeism every year in the United States, 54% are stress-related (Cooper & Cartwright, 1994).

Quite naturally, most morbidity, as well as mortality, is concentrated in the geriatric population. The population of the United States is aging (Schneider & Guralnik, 1990). At the beginning of the 20th century, individuals aged 65 and older constituted 4% of the population; today, that percentage has risen to 13% and is projected to be 20% by 2030 (Satariano, 1997). Just like the other age segments, the question for individuals late in life is how to prevent and/or postpone disease, disorder, and disability and maintain the quality of health or wellness. Although mortality is inevitable and much premature death can be prevented, the predominant investment in behavioral medicine may be associated with morbidity and the therapeutic alliance of achieving self-care and quality of life.

This section would not be complete with recording the leading causes of death by age and considered the extent to which those deaths can be prevented (Ventura, Peters, Martin, & Maurer, 1997) (see Table 7.2). The groups are similar to the aforementioned ones, except adults are separated into two categories: 25 to 44 years of age and 45 to 64 years. Data are based on a continuous file of records received from the States. Rates are per 100,000 population in specified group.

Overall, mortality rates have steadily been declining during the 20th century. However, U.S. rates continue to compare poorly with those of other industrialized nations. In addition, significant disparities for mortality, morbidity, and health status exist in this country between racial and ethnic populations, individuals with different income levels, and people with disabilities (Lillie-Blanton, Parsons, Gayle, & Dievler, 1996; Tusler, 1993).

Direct and Indirect Costs of Chronic Disorders

Escalating health care costs are the major factor forcing the reexamination of our entire health care system. Both public and private purchasers are aware of the costs of chronic diseases and

Table 7.2 Leading Causes of Death by Age

Ages	Cause of Death	Number	Rate (per 100,000)
1-4	Accidents & adverse effects	2,155	13.9
1-4	Congenial abnormalities	633	4.1
1-4	Malignant neoplasms	440	2.8
1-4	Homicide & legal intervention	395	2.5
1-4	Diseases of heart	207	1.3
5-14	Accidents & adverse effects	3,521	9.2
5-14	Malignant neoplasms	1,035	2.7
5-14	Homicide & legal intervention	513	1.3
5-14	Congenital abnormalities	456	1.2
5-14	Diseases of heart	341	0.9
15-24	Accidents & adverse effects	13,872	38.2
15-24	Homicide & legal intervention	6,548	18.1
15-24	Suicide	4,369	12.1
15-24	Malignant neoplasms	1,642	4.5
15-24	Diseases of heart	920	2.5
25-44	Accidents & adverse effects	26,554	31.7
25-44	Human immunodeficiency virus infection	22,795	26.4
25-44	Malignant neoplasms	22,147	26.4
25-44	Diseases of heart	16,261	19.4
25-44	Suicide	12,536	15.0
45-64	Malignant neoplasm	132,805	247.2
45-64	Diseases of heart	102,510	190.8
45-64	Accidents & adverse effects	16,332	30.4
45-64	Cerebrovascular disease	15,526	28.9
45-64	Chronic obstructive pulmonary diseases	12,849	23.9
65 & over	Diseases of heart	612,886	1,810.0
65 & over	Malignant neoplasms	386,092	1,140.2
65 & over	Cerebrovascular diseases	140,938	416.2
65 & over	Chronic obstructive pulmonary diseases	91,624	270.6
65 & over	Pneumonia and influenza	73,968	218.4

SOURCE: Ventura, Peters, Martin, & Maurer, 1997.

the subsequent disproportionate use of health care resources by a segment of the population. For example, in the Medicare population, 10% of beneficiaries account for 70% of medical expenditures

(Health Care Financing Administration [HCFA], 1995). This realization has contributed in part to the emergence of managed care.
However, managed care, as it is currently operationalized, is still a
system firmly entrenched in rendering acute, ambulatory services.
This is an oxymoron, given the health-seeking behavior of individuals with chronic illnesses.

In 1967, national health expenditures were $51 billion or 6.3%
of the gross national product. Computing these national expenditures to per person equals $247 in 1967. By 1995, the total Health
Care Financing Administration (HCFA) program outlays were
$248.9 billion or 16.4% of the Federal budget (Health Care Financ-
ing Administration [HCFA], 1996). This is a 21-fold increase. In
terms of dollars expended per person, the figure has grown to
$3,510. There were an estimated 697.1 million visits to office-
based physicians in 1995, or about three visits per person (Woodwell, 1997).

In the past 30 years, from 1965 to 1995, there has been a
significant change in the proportion of total expenditures for health
care by private and public sources (HCFA, 1996; see also Table 7.3).
What accounts for the dramatic difference from 1965 to 1980 is
that the Federal proportion of public sources was 11.7% in contrast
to 13.3% of State/local resources. Fifteen years later, those proportions had dramatically shifted, with the Federal level now consti-
tuting 29.1% and State/local resources remaining the same, 13.3%.

Determining the economic costs of behavioral disorders is not as
straightforward as it appears. There are few sources of data that
enable the estimation of both direct and indirect costs. Direct costs
are considered annual personal health expenditures. These expenditures include hospital stays, visits to physicians and other health
care providers, emergency room visits, home health care services,
dental and eye visits, medication, and medical equipment and
supplies. Indirect costs are societally determined, such as lost or
diminished productivity and premature death.

The costs of health services and supplies for noninstitutionalized
persons with chronic conditions totaled $272.2 billion in 1987.
While almost half of noninstitutionalized individuals reported
chronic conditions, they account for 78% of the direct medical care
costs (Hoffman et al., 1996). More than three quarters of all
mortality in 1990 was attributed to chronic conditions. Moreover,
morbidity for individuals with chronic disorders in 1990 amounted

Table 7.3 Proportion of Total Expenditures for Health Care by Private and Public Sources

Calendar Year	Private Source of Funds (%)	Public Source of Funds (%)
1965	75.0	25.0
1980	57.6	42.4
1994	55.2	44.8
1995	53.8	46.2

SOURCE: Health Care Financing Administration, 1996.

to 4.5 million years of productivity loss (this figure is determined by applying average annual income to the number of years of lost work for individuals with chronic conditions as well as assigning a dollar value for homemaker services for those not working and unable to perform those activities because of the chronic conditions). Adding the mortality and morbidity costs amounts to $234 billion in total indirect costs (Hoffman et al., 1996). Direct and indirect costs for individuals with chronic conditions are over $500 billion. Obviously, the economic costs are profound and the human costs are limitless.

Consumers and their families are the primary caregivers in chronic illness (Clark et al., 1991; Lorig, 1993; Sobel, 1995), practicing self-care. Because of the nature of chronic disorders, traditional medical interventions are not sufficient. Managed care is an opportunity yet to be realized. Health care providers can be effective change agents because of the importance of behavioral factors in the development of chronic disorders and/or the building of collaborative relationships to maintain or improve health or well-being. According to Von Korff, Gruman, Schaeffer, Curry, and Wagner (1997), "Within an overall strategy of chronic illness and preventive care, efforts to improve services for one condition also improve care for other conditions by building general health care system capabilities" (p. 1100).

Behavioral Medicine

Behavioral medicine is primarily concerned with the prevention and treatment of diseases and disorders through recognizing that behavioral factors affect both health/wellness and disease/disorder. Similar to Health Psychology and Health Education, Behavioral Medicine is multidisciplinary, an amalgam of medicine, nursing, psychology, social work, sociology, and education. One product of the 1977 Yale Conference on Behavioral Medicine was a recommended definition of behavioral medicine as: "concerned with the development of behavioral science knowledge and techniques relevant to the understanding of physical health and illness and with the application of this knowledge and human techniques to prevention, diagnosis, treatment and rehabilitation" (Goodwin, 1993). Because of the mention of physical health, there is a need to differentiate psychosomatic from behavioral medicine. While the latter is the targeted use of behavioral techniques to prevent and treat diseases or disorders, psychosomatic medicine "stresses the etiology and pathogenesis of physical disease" (Gordon, 1982). Behavioral medicine has assisted individuals with psychosomatic complaints (Hellman et al., 1990).

In 1978, the Academy of Behavioral Medicine Research was founded under the auspices of the National Academy of Sciences and, later that year, the more broadly based Society of Behavioral Medicine was founded (Krasnegor, 1990). In 1980, a joint Alcohol, Drug Abuse and Mental Health Services Administration (ADAMHA) and a National Institutes of Health (NIH) committee convened six conferences examining the behavioral factors of major public health problems (Blumenthal, 1993a). In addition, the Committee provided Federal funding for an Institute of Medicine (1981) report examining in depth the influence of stress in health and behavior. The material from that report and the six conferences formed the genesis of another IOM report the following year that became the seminal work of behavioral health.

Behavioral medicine is destined to engender cynicism and other disputes, not dissimilar to psychiatry. Psychology grew up in the shadow of psychiatry. Despite the obvious difference that psychiatrists can prescribe medications and psychologists cannot (although that continues to be debated), there are more similarities between the two disciplines than there are differences. The term *medical psychology* is described sometimes in a narrow context with almost exclusive concern with individuals having psychiatric problems. If medical psychology is broadened, then all problems involving behavior (see Blumenthal categorization) could be within the scope of the discipline. How does the medical profession benefit? According to Rachman and Philips (1980),

> they [medical profession] would receive additional assistance in dealing with certain types of clinical problem . . . the theory of medicine might be enriched. . . . It could help doctors to establish more satisfactory personal relationships with their patients and to develop their important educational functions. Patients . . . would be encouraged to become less dependent on their doctors and to play an active part in their own health. (p. 13)

Not unlike most areas of medicine, most attention is within the clinical arena. The following are examples of the plethora of diseases, disorders, and conditions within the scope of behavioral medicine (Sobel, 1995): self-care for minor injuries and acute illnesses, psychosomatic and stress-related disorders, chronic pain, chronic diseases, surgery, compliance with medication, and childbirth. Given that change is constant and life is synonymous with change, it is critical that the approach of behavioral medicine focus on life's major transitions (Valliant, 1993).

Stress is one of the most common "problems of living." Hollister's (1976) stress model, developed over two decades ago, is a conceptual model used by change agents because everyone experiences stress. All individuals are surrounded by influential forces and must respond to these stimuli in order to: survive, maintain the integrity of the personality, and meet profound needs. Throughout life, when these stimuli strike, survival or emotional security is threatened, plans or expectations are defeated, and individuals' ability to cope is precarious.

The forces that contribute to these negative results are called stressors. Responses include use and abuse of mind-altering substances, aggression, social withdrawal, and the like. All stimuli are not stressors for all individuals. One individual's stimulus to grow is another individual's stressor causing social withdrawal. However, some forces or events of life seem to affect the majority of human beings—such as loss of loved ones, serious illnesses or debilitating injuries, natural disasters, too many demands and expectations, or serious emotional conflicts. Fortunately, resources for preventive intervention exist: self, family, friends, community helpers such as faith leaders and indigenous healers, and professionals, especially physicians. There are four categorical strategies that the different resources for preventive intervention use to assist individuals experiencing stress—stressor avoidance, stress resistance building, stressor management (interception), and stress reaction management. Medical behaviorists may not have familiarity with these strategies. Once learned, however, they become important tools in their armamentarium.

Behavioral medicine is obviously well suited to the rapidly changing health care system and its emphasis on consumerism, consumer satisfaction, and reduction of inappropriate utilization of providers—especially physicians—and facilities. While the majority of dialogue about our rapidly changing health care system is focused on financing and organization of services, there has been little discourse about the context of health care delivery and the pursuit of quality of life. Behavioral medicine is not restricted to clinical settings, and a visionary integrated delivery system will be inclusive of all venues in which preventive interventions can produce measurable outcomes.

Continuum of Care

As frequently as the public health model is expounded, the misunderstanding of that model just as frequently occurs. There exists the need for a model that will be applicable for both the business orientation of the health care system and also the altruism of providers working to improve health and empower people. The model that accomplishes that is the framework proposed by the Institute of Medicine (IOM; 1994). It is referred to as either the IOM model or the continuum of care model. Prevention, treatment, and maintenance activities are clearly delineated along a dynamic continuum with all parts interconnected. The relationship among prevention, treatment, and maintenance is visually displayed to better understand the semantics. With the continuum of care model (Figure 7.4), prevention has three components that more finitely describe the interventions appropriate for designated populations and/or individuals.

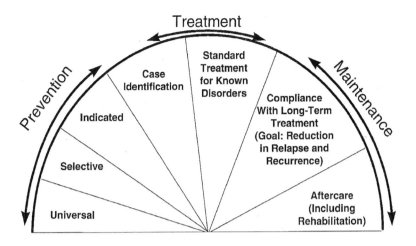

Figure 7.4. Continuum of Health Care
SOURCE: Reprinted with permission from *Reducing Risks for Mental Disorders: Frontiers for Preventive Intervention Research.* Copyright 1994 by the National Academy of Sciences, Courtesy of the National Academy Press, Washington, D.C.

Universal Preventive Interventions

Universal prevention, not dissimilar to primary prevention of the public health model, targets either the entire population or a designated segment of the population, such as adolescents, women, or a special racial/ethnic group. Everyone in the designated population shares the same general risks (speaking in terms of probability of disease occurrence and not as a negative label), although the magnitude of risk may vary among individual members of the population. For example, all prospective parents can benefit from parenting classes or learning about child development.

Universal prevention is not new. The purpose is to increase health and wellness by providing the information and skills necessary to avoid behaviors that may be deleterious. Universal preventive interventions are considered when the prevention effort (National Institute on Drug Abuse [NIDA], 1997c, p. 16):

- Targets all eligible members . . . without regard either to their member in an at-risk subgroup or their individual risk factors
- Targets populations that are expected to benefit as a group from the prevention programs
- Is considered to be desirable for everyone in the eligible population

As the intent is to reach large segments of the population, the venues of delivery are often media, schools, and other community settings. When determining the designated population for the preventive intervention, implementers do not explicitly petition the participation of the population. The appeal is for universality and, thus, marketing is critical to the success of universal preventive interventions. Consequently, the interventions can be expensive and, if designed appropriately, very comprehensive. However, the programs are both less intensive and less intrusive. Fewer staff are usually required for administering universal programs, and the staff are not always experts in behavioral health. The effects of universal programs are difficult to measure because it is difficult to determine the recipients of the interventions. Because universal preventive interventions target the general population or subgroups, it is difficult to isolate the effects of the program from other universal influences (see Figure 7.5).

Many managed care organizations (MCOs) and other health care facilities use various aspects of universal preventive interventions. For example, Kaiser Permanente provides copies of the book *Healthwise for Life* (Mettler & Kemper, 1992) to all enrollees. To be culturally sensitive, the book has been translated into Spanish. Most health care systems and health insuring organizations distribute quarterly newsletters that contain many prevention articles and often a listing of health education classes. The waiting areas in all facilities are replete with a variety of brochures, booklets, charts, and signs such as those prohibiting smoking.

The most frequent, and perhaps critical, component of universal preventive interventions within the health care system is the communication that occurs between providers and consumers. A vital function of health care providers, especially physicians, is to teach individuals when and how to use self-care. The Latin word for *doctor* means "teacher" (Harlem, 1977). To most Americans, physicians are still trusted and respected professionals whose words can

---

- *Universal Preventive Interventions:* General public or a segment of the entire population with average risk of a disorder.
- *Selective Preventive Interventions:* Populations whose risk of a disorder is significantly higher than average, either imminently or over a lifetime.
- *Indicated Preventive Interventions:* Populations who have minimal by detectable signs or symptoms suggesting a disorder or who carry biological markers for a disorder; often referred to as high risk.

Figure 7.5. Types of Prevention and Population Targets
SOURCE: Reprinted with permission from *Reducing Risks for Mental Disorders: Frontiers for Preventive Intervention Research.* Copyright 1994 by the National Academy of Sciences, Courtesy of the National Academy Press, Washington, D.C.

convince consumers to change, modify, and/or adopt different behaviors (Fleming et al., 1997).

Notwithstanding, few physicians demonstrate the ability to teach disease prevention and health promotion (Blumenthal & Their, 1996). This limitation of physicians diminishes hope that consumers can control their environments (Adler, Boyce, Chesney, Folkman, & Syme, 1993). Considering that 25% of physician office visits are for problems that consumers could treat themselves (Vickery et al., 1983), managed care organizations need to urge their physicians to teach self-care. In addition to reducing inappropriate utilization, the inevitable result of this instructional communication is an increase in individuals' self-confidence. Ornstein and Sobel (1989) postulate that there is a biology of self-confidence that may be as important to health as specific behavioral medicine interventions.

Selective Preventive Interventions

Selective preventive interventions are used for specific subgroups of the general population whose risk or probability of a disorder, disease, or behavioral occurrence is significantly higher than average, either approaching (because of an expected life event) or over a lifetime (because of some biological or environmental factor). In keeping with the public health orientation, and in contrast to the medical model, the entire subgroup of individuals receives the selective preventive intervention. As the entire subgroup receives the intervention, it is not necessary to assess or identify a specific individual's magnitude of risk. Belonging to the subgroup presumes risk of particular diseases, disorders, or problematic behaviors.

The purpose of selective preventive interventions is to deter the onset of a diagnosable disorder either by reducing those risk factors amenable to change and/or by strengthening those protective or resiliency factors to cope with risk factors not amenable to change. Tapping resiliency can "ignite innate potential for full and healthy development" (Benard & Marshall, 1997).

The subgroups targeted for selective preventive interventions include the following, defined by various types of risk factors (National Institute on Drug Abuse [NIDA], 1997a):

- Demographic risk factors such as age, gender, race/ethnicity, income, socioeconomic status, employment, education, location of residence, and population density of community of residence.
- Psychosocial risk factors such as family disruption and/or dysfunction, divorce, death of a loved one, incarceration, low income, lack of family or social support, unemployment, family substance abuse and parental emotional disturbance, dysfunctional within school or work environment, lack of support for positive values, attitudes, and behaviors, and low morale of authority and/or peers.
- Environmental risk factors such as community values and attitudes that [are] tolerant of deleterious behaviors, a school or work climate that provides little encouragement and support, lack of active community institutions and community support resources, and community dysfunction such as high rates of crime and violence, high rates of drug abuse, and rampant harmful behavior in non-family owned residence.
- Biological and genetic risk factors such as a genetic predisposition for obesity, alcoholism, severe mental disorders, hyperactivity, pain sensitivity, neurological problems, developmental disabilities, and fetal damage in utero due to drug exposure that can lead to biological problems such as mental retardation, hyperactivity, and attention deficit disorders (pp. 8-9)

Selective preventive interventions are generally more costly to operate per participant than universal preventive interventions. Several variables account for this fact. The interventions are tailor-made as they differ in content and form on the particular subgroup that is targeted. While that may also be applicable for universal preventive interventions, there is greater complexity involved for both planners and providers given the existence of risk factors and the goal to reduce those objectives or counteract them by increasing protective factors or engendering individuals' innate resiliency. In addition, recipients of selective interventions are recruited to participate. Selective preventive interventions generally operate for longer periods of time and require more time and effort from participants. The daily lives of participants are often affected, as behavioral change is absolutely necessary. Selective preventive interventions require staff who have the knowledge and skills necessary to work with individuals, usually youth, and their families enmeshed in problems and not necessarily motivated to change.

Research confirming the effectiveness of selective preventive interventions, especially in health care settings, is limited. Only recently has the prevention field begun to target subgroups of the general population and follow the groups long enough to document changes in behavior. One example of such a program is the Strengthening Families Program (SFP) (Kumpfer, DeMarch, & Child, 1989; Kumpfer, Molgaard, & Spoth, 1996). The SFP targets children of a major risk group—children of parents who are substance abusers. The impetus for the program came from parents enrolled in a methadone treatment program who desired improved parenting skills to help their children avoid substance abuse. The SFP also has been used with at-risk youth who already exhibit behavioral and/or emotional risk factors for drug and other substance abuse. The SFP has been implemented in a variety of diverse settings, such as community centers, mental health centers, churches, public housing communities, drug treatment centers, and hospitals.

The following is an example of a selective preventive intervention that Salzman (1998) utilizes for illustrative purposes in presenting a tool for assessing the relationship among preventive interventions and expectations by MCOs. The activity is a psychoeducational group for adolescents, primarily between 14 and 18 years of age, whose parent(s) abuse alcohol or other drugs. Obviously, the intervention can be used in venues other than MCOs, such as school systems, faith communities, and juvenile justice systems. The clinical outcomes are: reduced incidence of precursors for mental health and behavioral problems compared to nonintervention control groups; strengthening of protective factors for individual group members served (e.g., higher academic achievement, fewer associations with socially deviant peers, and increased social skills); and preventing the onset of diagnosable conditions, including substance dependency. With Salzman's selected intervention, one full-time-equivalent clinician can deliver the intervention on a cost-reimbursement basis with $35 cost reimbursement per person per unit served. This intervention is targeted to a group, which may increase the level of reported satisfaction due to the nature of group work, that is, providing connectivity and breaking down isolation.

Indicated Preventive Interventions

Indicated preventive strategies involve high-risk individuals who have minimal or detectable signs or symptoms foreshadowing a diagnosable disease or disorder. Depending upon the specific behavioral manifestations, screening or detection methodology is available to verify, if they exist, any biological markers warning of an impending problem. Although indicated preventive interventions are appropriate for all high-risk individuals regardless of age, gender, or other variables, infancy, childhood, and adolescence are critical periods for intervention (National Institute on Drug Abuse [NIDA], 1997b). Adolescence is the time when the inevitable trajectory of socioeconomic status, probably the most consistent predictor of morbidity and mortality, can be most modified because of school attendance and other intervening factors. The following examples of indicated preventive interventions illustrate the range and diversity available for individuals who need assistance or early intervention either to prevent a current problem from worsening or to enhance resiliency to endure the circumstances of life.

Broussard's (1977) Pittsburgh First-Born Preventive-Intervention Program was designed to provide indicated information for infants at high risk. The services making up the intervention include individual interviews with parents or mother alone, participation in mother-infant groups, and home visits. Supplementary parenting leaves the child's relationship with the primary mother intact, supplementing for the child what the mother cannot be now. Concurrently, the intervention assists the mother with her depression and low self-esteem. The providers become a surrogate extended family system. Growth in the mothers and infants occurs with the provision of a new invested relationship that provides a safe learning environment. One programmatic goal is to provide mothers with a new vision of a potential relationship through the staff's parenting of the mother. As she feels valued and respected and her child valued and respected, she can begin to modify her self-perception and her perception of the child.

Webster-Stratton and Herbert (1994) and her colleagues at the University of Washington developed the Partners Parent Training program to help families with young children identified as having conduct disorders and who were referred to a mental health clinic. The aim of the Partners curriculum is to promote parent competence, child social competence, and home-school connections in order to enhance protective factors and reduce the risk of early onset of oppositional defiant behavioral and other forms of antisocial behavior. The Parent Training is characterized by:

- Parent meetings for 8 or 9 weeks
- Use of video-taped culturally diverse vignettes as the basis for active group discussion and exercises (e.g., the vignettes address helping children play and learn, and teaching parents to use praise and encouragement)
- Training Head Start family service staff (and sometimes parent program "graduates") as coleaders of parent groups
- Providing a shortened training for the teachers to increase consistency between home and Head Start
- Rigorous evaluation strategies

Service workers reported the program was like the "hub of a wheel," fostering trust and a supportive network among all families and extending to the community. They redefined this role to focus on providing effective comprehensive parent programs rather than acting as in the caseworker role of making referrals to support services.

A large proportion of individuals seen by primary care providers are at high risk because of a sedentary lifestyle. Obesity and non-insulin-dependent diabetes are increasing in prevalence despite universal preventive interventions (King, Rewers, & WHO Ad Hoc Diabetes Reporting Group, 1993; Kuczmarski, Flegal, Campbell, & Johnson, 1994). When visiting primary care providers, most patients expect a written prescription. Rather than writing a prescription for a medication, primary care providers can write a prescription on which exercise goals have been jointly set by the practitioner and the patient (Neale, 1992). This approach seems very feasible in noting that "diet/activity" patterns constitute the second most important factor, behind tobacco, contributing to U.S. mortality (Swinburn, Walter, Arroll, Tilyard, & Russell, 1998).

Silverman (1977) is credited with developing the Widow-to-Widow program, mutual help groups to assist in the grieving process. Grief is a normal human experience but is also sometimes viewed as an illness for which providers are sought to provide "recovery" services. However, bereavement is a part of the developmental life cycle involving a series of stages—namely, impact, recoil, and accommodation. Other widowed persons as resources for preventive intervention can provide a selective intervention by providing the newly widowed with a reference group to help them accept what they are experiencing and find hope to live without the deceased. Prevention is not simply preventing an emotional problem, but improving individuals' capacity to master in a positive way another dilemma of life, possibly the most stressful. Mutual help is a mechanism for providing assistance and does not require the individual to define himself or herself as "sick" and become a patient to be "treated" or "cured." Mental health providers can assume various roles with mutual support groups—such as making referrals to groups, becoming a consultant, or developing new support groups.

Health care systems can easily identify individuals who are labeled "high utilizers" of health care services. Harvard Community Health Plan in Boston developed interventions for those "high utilizers" who experienced physical symptoms accompanied by significant psychosocial components (Hellman et al., 1990). The interventions focused on the mind-body relationship and emphasized cognitive restructuring. Another study conducted at the Department of Behavioral Medicine at Hohf Clinic and Hospital in Victoria, Texas (Gonik et al., 1981) structured indicated preventive interventions for inpatients having stress-related disorders. The intervention was an inpatient program and included medical management, training in biofeedback, structured self-study and self-management, and psychotherapy with outpatient follow-up. In the 2 years after the indicated preventive intervention, average hospital days dropped 68%.

Cost-Effectiveness of Preventive Interventions

In today's climate of fiscal accountability, empirical evidence of the costs and benefits of preventive interventions is needed to demonstrate to legislatures, government agencies, employers, and others that investing in prevention is worth while. Disease prevention/health promotion can minimize the direct personal burdens imposed by illness or injury; reduce the indirect impacts, such as lost productivity or premature death; and may ultimately permit a societal reallocation of resources from the medical/health sector to other sectors.

Relatively few preventive interventions, especially primary or universal, include formal quantitative methods to determine economic and/or social costs. Economic costs may be thought of as "opportunity costs" (Donnermeyer, 1977)—that is, money that could be used if the behavior did not exist and financial resources did not have to be allocated to address the behavior and its sequelae. Social costs are more difficult to determine for they relate to qualities of life often defined in terms of human interactions. Although a distinction can be made, the costs of behavioral problems and subsequent interventions are financial as well as human investments.

There are various types of economic evaluation methods, including costs offsets, cost-minimization, cost-benefit, cost-utility, cost-effectiveness, and willingness to pay. Some interventions are more amenable to one method than another. After costs are estimated, the next step is to combine cost estimates with the outcomes of the intervention and perform an economic evaluation. Several evaluations are related to costs and outcome analyses—namely, cost-benefit, cost-utility, cost-minimization, and cost-effectiveness (Drummond, Stoddart, & Torrance, 1987; Haddix, Teutsch, Shaffer, & Dunet, 1996; Plotnick, 1994). Obviously, these economic evaluation methods have similarities as well as differences.

Cost-benefit analysis (CBA) translates all benefits of the intervention into common unit dollars. Although substantial data are needed for CBA, this method is advantageous for measuring the extent of the social gain (i.e., net benefits) directly for each preventive intervention. Many cost-benefit studies measure the costs of screening for particular diseases or disorders (Tolley & Rowland, 1991). Studies evaluating preventive interventions deploy CBA when multiple outcomes are possible. Cost-utility analysis converts an entire array of health improvements into a single common unit, making comparison of alternative programs easier. Quality-adjusted life years gained is the preferred unit. Although cost-utility analysis is used frequently in the medical literature, this method is probably less relevant for evaluating preventive interventions.

Cost-minimization is the most direct type of economic evaluation. If two preventive interventions have the same capability for producing the outcomes of interest (e.g., decreasing the purchase of tobacco products by youth), then the cheaper intervention is preferred, merely because the costs are minimized. Cost-effectiveness analysis (CEA), which includes cost-minimization as a special case, is the most common form of economic evaluation related to health (Zarkin & Hubbard, 1997). CEA is the ratio of the difference in costs between two or more programs relative to the difference in effectiveness. This computation yields ratios such as incremental costs per case of disease/disorder prevented or treated.

Cost-effectiveness of preventive interventions is the economic evaluation method discussed in greater detail for several reasons. First, *cost-effectiveness* is a term widely used by professionals and laypersons. However, sometimes the only area of agreement by parties using the terminology is the notion of "value for money." Other than that, the meaning of cost-effectiveness is as disparate as the groups using the term. Second, cost-effective analysis (CEA), an evaluative measurement tool used for almost three decades, is also replete with imprecision. Evaluators using CEA come from different academic disciplines, including economics, medicine, psychology, public health, medical sociology, and operations research; thus each discipline, allied with a particular set of concepts and unique language, created an intermixture often lacking clarity. Consequently, and the final reason for concentration on CEA, was the desire to obtain a sound methodology that improved CEA's quality, comparability, and utility for making decisions about the allocation of resources, especially public. The Public Health Service, U.S. Department of Health and Human Services convened in 1993 the Panel on Cost-Effectiveness in Health and Medicine (Gold, Siegel, Russell, & Weinstein, 1996). This panel not only assessed the current science of CEA but also identified unresolved methodological issues.

Immunization programs targeting childhood diseases that can result in permanent disability or impairment have left little doubt as to their economic value. Williams and Sanders (1981) recommend four childhood vaccinations that not only yield favorable CE (cost-effectiveness) but produce cost savings as well. They include vaccinations for pertussis, poliomyelitis, measles, and rubella. The savings (including productivity gains) are estimated at $1.4 million, $0.9 million, $11.3 million, and $17.2 million, respectively. CEAs have determined that these vaccinations not only produce net health benefits, but they save medical costs as well. In the case of infectious diseases, the health status of an individual can affect the health of the population at large. Populationwide vaccination programs show continual increases in savings after being in place for many years because the proportion of people who are "carriers" of the disease at any given time is dependent upon the number of people who were immunized in the past. As the number of immune individuals in the population increases, susceptibility to a disease and the number of infectious cases decreases.

Smoking cessation is considered by many health economists to be one of the most economically successful preventive health measures that have been implemented in the United States. Eddy (1992) referred to it as the "gold standard" and estimated that it could yield a CE ratio of up to 7,000 person-years of life saved per $1 million spent. That would make it roughly 10 times more cost effective than the most effective cancer screening tests. Cummings, Rubin, and Oster (1989) estimated the CE of physicians' counseling patients to quit smoking; it cost $705 to $988 per year of life saved for men and $1,204 to $2,058 per year of life saved for women, assuming 2.7% of smokers quit as a result of counseling. (The variation in CE ratios between men and women is in part due to heavier smoking among men than women, and, therefore, greater benefits realized from smoking cessation among men.) Even if only 1% of smokers were affected, the intervention would still be more cost effective than many other common preventive practices, such as treatment for mild hypertension.

Recent research by Fiscella and Franks (1996) demonstrates that addition of the nicotine patch to physician-based counseling for men and women in primary care settings is largely cost-effective. The use of the patch produced one additional lifetime quitter at a cost of $7,332. The incremental CE of the patch by age group ranged from $4,390 to $10,943 per quality-adjusted life years (QALYs) saved for women. A clinical strategy involving limiting prescription renewals to patients successfully abstaining for the first 2 weeks improved the CE by 25%. Interestingly, the patch was contrasted with nicotine gum. The patch is about twice as cost-effective as the 2-mg gum and comparable to the 4-mg gum. The two physicians provided a strong rationale for coverage by third-party insurance payers as study recipients did not bear the cost of the patches, and other research demonstrates that self-payment for nicotine patch therapy discouraged use (Hughes, Wadland, Fenwick, Lewis, & Bickel, 1991). Reimbursement might improve the use of the patch by ethnic minorities, especially African Americans and Hispanics, who use the patch at one third the rate of Caucasians (Pierce, Gilpin, & Farkas, 1995). The key finding for behavioral medicine and preventive interventions is that observational data from the California tobacco survey suggest that the nicotine patch may not be effective when it is provided without provider counseling (Pierce et al., 1995).

Exercise as a preventive health measure is still a largely unexplored area of health economics. However, one study provides some evidence of its cost effectiveness. Hatziandreu, Koplan, Weinstein, Caspersen, and Warner (1988) estimated the effects of exercise on coronary heart disease (CHD) using cohorts of one thousand 35-year-old-men that were drawn from the Framingham Heart Study. Thirty years of data were adjusted to compare the number of CHD events, life expectancy, and quality-adjusted years of life of men who exercised and men who did not. They estimated that exercise costs $11,313 per year of quality-adjusted life gained, $27,851 per year of life gained, $76,760 per case of CHD averted, and $250,836 per death averted. The investigators acknowledge that the costs may seem high. Nevertheless, exercise is a cost-effective preventive health measure relative to other CHD interventions, for example, coronary artery bypass surgery and treatment of hypertension.

White, Urban, and Taylor (1993) reviewed four studies on the cost-effectiveness of mammography. Depending on the model of reference, screening can be viewed as an early intervention strategy for either a selective or an indicative preventive intervention. They found that estimates of the CE ratios of screening for breast cancer in women over 50 ranged from $5,400 to almost $14,000 per year of life saved, varying with the screening strategy used and baseline estimates of effectiveness. They concluded that the most reliable CE estimate may be $36,000 for an annual mammography, derived by Eddy (1989). While there is general agreement that mammography is cost-effective compared to other strategies for detecting and treating breast cancer, it is not a cost-saving technology. Nevertheless, the CE ratios indicate that mammography may yield health outcomes that justify its costs. The costs of screening seem more reasonable compared to the cost of treatment alternatives required at a later stage of development.

In an ambitious attempt to compare the cost-effectiveness of a variety of preventive interventions across sectors of society, Tengs et al. (1995) reviewed approximately 1,200 documents. They then calculated CE ratio, expressed in cost per life-year saved, for 587 interventions. The investigators found that primary prevention in medicine yielded a median cost-effectiveness estimate of $5,000 per life-year saved, versus $23,000 per life-year saved for secondary prevention and $22,000 for tertiary prevention. These figures support that the cost effectiveness of primary prevention surpasses that of secondary and tertiary prevention.

A new issue associated with the changing health care paradigm pertains to funding prevention programs. All preventive interventions do not save costs. Nonetheless, purchasers are interested both in short-term costs as well as in being convinced that savings from preventive strategies are future oriented and impact morbidity and mortality. If the need and demand is reduced for health care services, especially medical services, then health care costs will be reduced. Health promotion strategies, referred to as either primary prevention or universal prevention, can be cost-effective if part of the strategies is the goal of cost reduction (Fries et al., 1993). The reasons that reducing the demand for medical services is feasible has heretofore been discussed—most morbidity is preventable; today's habits and lifestyles, including smoking, poor nutrition, lack of exercise, violence, drinking, and driving, costs money to the individual, insurer, employer, and society; and informed consumers make better health care decisions, including using self-care and other resources for preventive intervention.

All professionals responsible for administering preventive interventions, especially primary care physicians, need to broaden the concept of promoting health and wellness to include financial health. The latter is as important to consumers as it is to providers and purchasers. As there is little history of insurance coverage for universal preventive interventions, cost-effectiveness data may be the key to the future for obtaining reimbursement.

Conclusion

Population Demography and Cultural Factors

Health care is evolutionary. Today's system of managed care is still predominated by medical care. The last evolutionary stage of health care moves the locus from the individual to the population. A health care delivery system requires attention to the population of "covered lives" in addition to individual patients. Managed care was formerly confined mostly to middle-class populations but now envelops many more diverse and vulnerable groups, including Medicaid, Medicare, and minority populations (Fisher, 1994).

A sizable proportion of the population (close to 41,000,000 individuals) has no health insurance (Employee Benefit Research Institute, 1994). While managed care systems may serve the majority of individuals who have either private or public funding, the greatest fear in our newest transformation of the health care system is the disappearance of the safety net and the dramatic increase of individuals with no insurance. The absence of health insurance is a critical challenge, for it is "adults of color" who suffer disproportionately in not having such insurance (Taylor, 1994).

Approximately 37 million Americans 15 years of age or older (Batvia, 1993), or 15% (and this is likely an underestimation because of the paucity and difficulties associated with epidemiological research) of the population, have some sort of physical, mental, or emotional disability, creating one of the largest minorities in the country. In addition, at some point in people's lives, 70% of all people will endure a condition lasting at least 6 months that interferes with activities of daily living, earning them the medical "label" of permanent disability (Cherry & Gillespie, 1991).

The occurrence of many diseases, injuries, and other public health problems is disproportionately higher in some racial/ethnic populations in the United States. Understanding the differential distribution of adverse health consequences in racial groups is essential to developing effective solutions to these problems. Race is a societally constructed taxonomy reflecting the intersection of a variety of factors, including racism (Williams, 1993).

Concurrent with the rapid changes in health care is a similar situation with the demographic characteristics of the United States. In less than 3 years, about one quarter of the U.S. population will be members of "minority" groups (U.S. Bureau of the Census, 1995). Projections suggest that by the year 2050, ethnic subpopulations will make up 47.5% of the total U.S. population, and that by the year 2056, whites will probably be a minority group (*Time*, 1990).

The Nation's Hispanic population continues to grow faster than the rest of its population. Among the reasons for the rapid increase in the Hispanic population are

- A higher birthrate for Hispanics
- High levels of immigration

Today, about 1 in 10 Americans are Hispanic. By 2050, nearly 1 in 4 American may be Hispanic (U.S Bureau of the Census, 1995).

Geographically, 70% of Hispanic Americans are concentrated in six of the nation's most populous States: California, Texas, New York, Florida, New Jersey, and Illinois. The managed care situation, especially for the Medicaid population, varies dramatically in each of these states. Eli Ginzberg (1991), of Columbia University's Eisenhower Center for Conservation of Human Resources, reports that

> the concentration (of Hispanics) in (these) six states indicates that the health policies of these states are first order determinants of the availability of health care to the Hispanic poor through their Medicaid programs, public hospitals, and special programs such as compensatory reimbursement to the providers of uncompensated care. (p. 238)

Hispanics are younger than their counterparts. Their median age was 26 years in 1994, 10 years less than non-Hispanic whites. Among Hispanic groups, the median age ranged from 24 years for persons of Mexican origin to 43 years for those of Cuban descent. Close to 40% of Hispanics were born outside the United States, compared with 3% of non-Hispanic whites. For decades, ethnographic researchers have noted that immigrants and their children are subjected to psychological stresses as a result of the social, psychological, and cultural processes inherent in moving from one social and cultural environment to another (Vega et al., 1994). Unless there is linkage between the Hispanic community and the managed care organization, there will never be a successful integrated delivery system for this segment of the population, and substance abuse and mental health problems will worsen and chronicity be almost inevitable.

Prevention of Behavior Disorders Within Managed Care

Less than 10 years ago, very few Americans with private health insurance received care within managed care systems. Now, the overwhelming majority of employed individuals and their dependents have some form of managed care—such as Health Maintenance Organizations (HMOs), Preferred Provider Organizations (PPOs), or Point-of-Service (POS) plans. Only small proportions of individuals who have private insurance are still in fee-for-service (FFS) arrangements. HMOs, with their different types as well, are still the most recognizable to individuals and account for the largest enrollment when private and public enrollees and beneficiaries are totaled. Like all types of MCOs, the market penetration of HMOs varies geographically (Marion Merrell Dow, 1994). HMOs are the most responsive to behavioral preventive interventions.

As States have increasingly enrolled Medicaid populations into managed care systems, schools have, quite naturally, been affected, with school-based managed care programs beginning to proliferate throughout the country. This is critically important for preventive behavioral interventions. Schools, in concert with health care providers, could do more than perhaps any other institution in society to help young people (especially "those of color") and the adults they will become, to live healthier, longer, more satisfying, and more productive lives (Carnegie Council on Adolescent Development, 1995). America's youth are not only managed health care's most valuable population, but also ours (Rollins, 1996).

PCPs could assume responsibility for outreach and special access to services for traditionally disenfranchised populations that make up a disproportionate share of individuals having behavioral health problems. Most PCPs and the settings in which they practice are not disinterested in prevention. Most clinicians understand the benefits of certain preventive interventions, such as smoking cessation. In spite of their understanding, few clinicians make a serious effort to help consumers quit or not begin. Studies document that while 70% of smokers see a physician each year, only about half of the smokers are urged to quit during the clinical visit, and less than 20% are actually provided advice on how to quit and information on cost-effective interventions (Eisenberg, 1998). However, most primary care physicians practicing today did not receive academic or practice training emphasizing the psychological sciences necessary for behavioral change in consumers (Thompson, 1995). Nor do PCPs receive the evidence-based research supporting the cost effectiveness of such strategies. In addition, there is scant financial remuneration for providers to offer preventive behavioral interventions. Furthermore, most PCPs, especially physicians, assert that they have neither time nor energy to engage in the appropriate activities.

An example from Kaiser Permanente's three Bay Area primary health care sites concerning children's social development (Developmental Studies Center, 1986) illustrates the three components of prevention in the IOM continuum of care. A result study by the American Academy of Pediatrics reveals that 70% of mothers interviewed in pediatricians' offices were more concerned about parenting, social behavior, or child development issues than about their children's physical health (Hickson, Altemeier, & O'Connor, 1983). Thus, component one (universal) is to meet this need and prospectively provide child development information to all parents. The population for the second component (selected) narrows, based upon, for example, responses to the screening instrument or observations by staff, and might be suggestions to read specific materials or attend parenting classes. For the last component (indicated), some issue or problem has been noted and the parent, parents, or families receive a referral to rectify the situation.

And the Future Is . . .

Behavioral problems have their roots in the community; likewise, the community is the repository of solutions. The responsibility for the health and well-being of the community has often been relegated to the caregivers of the community. However, seldom do PCPs assume the leadership for community-oriented primary care. Nonetheless, Barbara Starfield (1992) asserts that the concept is now appropriate as the 21st century approaches.

Four decades ago, René Dubos (1959) wrote

> It is not impossible that in the future, as in the past, effective steps in the prevention of disease will be motivated by an emotional revolt against some of the inadequacies of the modern world . . . scientific medicine will certainly define the factors in the physical environment and the types of behavior which constitute threats to health in modern society. . . . Medical statesmanship cannot thrive only on scientific knowledge, because exact science cannot encompass all the human factors involved in health and in disease. Knowledge and power may arise from dreams as well as from facts and logic. (pp. 218-219)

As managed care systems grow and assume responsibility for larger segments of the population, especially those financed with public funds such as the recipients of Medicaid and Medicare, community-based approaches will be a critical complement to individual clinical interventions. The development of community-based prevention linked to community-level risk factor rating analyses is a more targeted approach for MCOs to achieve the final evolutionary step in maintaining community health or well-being.

The old thinking had hospitals and health care systems as institutions located within the community. The transformation of health care reform has hospitals and health care systems as organizers and participants within integrated delivery systems composed of community care networks. These networks can be the foundation for empowering healthier communities and assisting in the resolution of problems on a personal, local, state, and even national level.

Examples are starting to emerge. The Head Start Maine Collaboration Project (Leeman, 1994) was one of the first demonstrations initiated to build closer links between Head Start and the States. As part of a broad range to include Head Start in an integrated delivery system, staff of the collaboration project led efforts to better integrate the State's Medicaid program with Head Start and to use the Medicaid Preventive Health Care Program to pay for activities such as outreach, health education, case planning related to mental health, referral, screening, and counseling. A State team designated all Head Start Centers as Medicaid-reimbursable Preventive Health Programs. The State's Head Start health service money was used as the match for Medicaid services. Thus, the State's Head Start money is freed for other kinds of services. On the other coast, Ventura County, California, Head Start and the County Mental Health agency have joined forces to fund mental health services through Medicaid and systematically to screen children in Head Start through EPSDT for emotional and behavioral problems (Jordan & Hernandez, 1990). MediCal dollars are used in the area of prevention as well as treatment and include such services as classroom consultation for teachers working with children whose behaviors do not meet criteria for diagnosis, but who are nonetheless difficult and challenging.

The future of health care in this country bodes well for primary prevention of behavioral disorders. Despite the almost universal lack of reimbursement, a growing number of health professionals, including physicians, advocate the development of preventive interventions to improve the health of children, especially adolescents. The publication of the American Medical Association's (AMA) *Guidelines for Adolescent Preventive Services: Recommendations and Rationale* (Elster & Kuznets, 1994) is testimony of this forecast. The publication, known as GAPS, contains 24 recommendations of three major types (i.e., health guidance, screening, and immunization) directed at 14 separate health topics. Health guidance encompasses health education, health counseling, and anticipatory guidance. The acknowledgment that the AMA is recommending practice guidelines in this area to physicians provides the unprecedented opportunity to utilize the clinical visit for health promotion and disease prevention.

The implications for other health care and human service workers are obvious. Since the majority of health determinants are similar but with different behavioral manifestations, there must be a collaborative interdisciplinarian approach to address those factors so as to prevent the occurrence of the problem or lessen its impact. According to Pransky (1991),

Intervention and treatment are essential but do little if anything to change the conditions that initially caused the problem . . . conditions to which the clients usually return. Once "treated," these individuals again face the same difficult situations. If they have gained those missing self-perceptions and skills . . . they have a chance of recovery. If they have not, once they return to their old environments, they will often begin to manifest the same or a different problem once again. (p. 32)

Both accrediting associations and statutory and regulatory policies necessitate the release of specific information, including how satisfied individuals are with their policies. Maintaining enrollees and their beneficiaries, whether private or public, is the key to financial solvency.

Managed care is challenging the interrelationship between behavioral health and physical health that has existed for quite some time. Evidence has been presented that the provision of behavioral interventions, especially preventive interventions, can both be effective and reduce medical costs. Preventive behavioral interventions can shift much responsibility for health care from providers to consumers. Placing the onus for health and well-being back into the hands of individuals should increase more direct responsibility of health care status and, ultimately, reduce the demand for service utilization. These actions are not meant to obviate the responsibilities of providers, especially physicians. At the present time, however, many individuals view behavioral disorders as something beyond their control. Thus, the role of patients with behavioral disorders is characterized as a passive, sometimes negative role that, when accompanied by stigma, strips those individuals of their dignity and results in negative verbalizations against the providers and systems whose true aim is to help. Vigorous, well-designed programs of health promotion and prevention of behavioral disorders requires a therapeutic alliance and active participation by all parties. If the objective of an integrated delivery system is both to increase the quality of life and, concomitantly, to reduce the financial burden, then behavioral medicine is the vanguard. The measurement of ultimate success is the transformation of the current health care system from a focus on sickness to one on wellness.

References

Adler, N. E., Boyce, W. T., Chesney, M. A., Folkman, S., & Syme, S. L. (1993). Socioeconomic inequalities in health: No easy solution. *Journal of the American Medical Association, 269,* 3140-3145.

Alan Guttmacher Institute. (1993). *Facts in brief: Teenage sexual and reproductive behavior.* New York: Author.

Baker, S. P., O'Neill, B., Ginsburg, M. J., & Li, G. (1992). *The injury fact book.* New York: Oxford University Press.

Barsky, A. J. (1981). Hidden reasons some patients visit doctors. *Annuals of Internal Medicine, 94,* 492-498.

Batvia, A. (1993, Spring). Health care reform and people with disabilities. *Health Affairs,* pp. 40-56.

Benard, B., & Marshall, K. (1997). A framework for practice: Tapping innate resilience. *Research Practice, 5*(1), 9-15.

Blumenthal, S. J. (1993a). Introductory remarks: New frontiers in behavioral medicine research. In S. J. Blumenthal, K. Matthews, & S. M. Weiss (Eds.), *New research frontiers in behavioral medicine* (pp. 9-15). Rockville, MD: National Institutes of Health.

Blumenthal, S. J. (1993b). An overview of NIH behavioral medicine research programs. In S. J. Blumenthal, K. Matthews, & S. M. Weiss (Eds.), *New research frontiers in behavioral medicine* (pp. 41-60). Rockville, MD: National Institutes of Health.

Blumenthal, D., & Their, S. O. (1996). Managed care & medical education. *Journal of the American Medical Association, 276*(9), 725-727.

Brecker, D. J. (1982). *Hospital health education.* Rockville, MD: Aspen Systems.

Broussard, E. R. (1977). Primary prevention program for newborn infants at high risk for emotional disorder. In D. C. Klein & S. E. Goldston (Eds.), *Primary prevention: An idea whose time has come* (NIMH, ADAMHA, PHS, DHEW Publication No. [ADM] 77-447; pp. 63-68. Washington, DC: U.S. Department of Health and Human Services.

Carnegie Corporation of New York. (1994). *Starting points: Meeting the needs of our youngest children.* New York: Author.

Carnegie Council on Adolescent Development. (1995). *Great transitions: Preparing adolescents for a century.* New York: Author.

Center for Mental Health Services, Substance Abuse and Mental Health Services Administration, Department of Health and Human Services. (1996). *Mental, emotional, and behavior disorders in children and adolescents.* Rockville, MD: CMHS, Knowledge Exchange Network.

Centers for Disease Control and Prevention, National Center for Health Statistics. (1995). *Health, U.S., 1997* (DHHS Publication No. PHS 93-1232). Hyattsville, MD: U.S. Department of Health and Human Services.

Cherry, L., & Gillespie, J. (1991). *Discussion paper: Alcohol, drugs & disability* (National Policy & Leadership Symposium). Stanford, CA: Institute on Alcohol, Drugs and Disability.

Children's Defense Fund. (1994). *Protecting our children: State and federal policies for exempt child care settings.* Washington, DC: Author.

Clark, N. M., Becker, M. H., Janz, N. K., Lorig, K., Bakowski, W., & Anderson, L. (1991). Self management of chronic disease by older adults: A review and questions for research. *Journal of Aging and Health, 3,* 3-27.

Clements, M., & Hales, D. (1997, September 7). How healthy are we? *Parade Magazine,* pp. 4-7.

Committee to Identify Research Opportunities in the Prevention and Treatment of Alcohol Related Problems. (1989). *Prevention and treatment of alcohol problems: Research opportunities* (Institute of Medicine, National Research Council). Washington, DC: National Academy Press.

Cooper, C. L., & Cartwright, S. (1994). Healthy mind, healthy organization: A proactive approach to occupational stress. *Human Relations, 47*(4), 455-471.

Cummings, S., Rubin, S., & Oster, G. (1989). The cost effectiveness of counseling smokers to quit. *Journal of the American Medical Association, 26,* 1, 75-79.

Denham, J. (1978). *The role of medicine in health promotion.* Chapel Hill, NC: Health Sciences Consortium.

Developmental Studies Center. (1986, January). *Integrating social development into early pediatric care: A preventive approach.* San Ramon, CA: Developmental Studies Center.

Donnermeyer, J. F. (1977). The economic and social costs of drug abuse among rural populations. In E. B. Robertson et al., (Eds.), *Rural substance abuse: State of knowledge and issues* (NIH Publication No. 97-4177, pp. 220-245). Washington, DC: U.S. Department of Health and Human Services.

Drummond, G. W., Stoddart, G. L., & Torrance, G. W. (1987). *Methods for the economic evaluation of health programmes.* Oxford, UK: Oxford University Press.

Dubos, R. (1959). *Mirage of health.* New York: Perennial Library.

Eddy, D. M. (1989). Screening for breast cancer. *Annals of Internal Medicine, 111,* 389-399.

Eddy, D. M. (1992, July). David Eddy ranks the tests. *Harvard Health Letter,* pp. 10-11.

Eisenberg, J. (1998, February 10). *Statement on smoking cessation.* Administrator, Agency for Health Care Policy and Research, Senate Labor and Human Resources Committee, February 10, 1998.

Elster, A. B., & Kuznets, N. J. (Eds.). (1994). *Guidelines for adolescent preventive services: Recommendations and rationale.* Chicago: American Medical Association.

Employee Benefit Research Institute. (1995). *March 1994 current population survey.* Washington, DC: Author.

Ferguson, T. (1996, February). Consumer health informatics: Turning the treatment pyramid upside down. *Behavioral Healthcare Tomorrow,* pp. 35-37.

Fiscella, K., & Franks, P. (1996, April 24). Cost-effectiveness of the transdermal nicotine patch as an adjunct to physicians' smoking cessation counseling. *Journal of the American Medical Association, 275*(16), 1247-1251.

Fisher, M. S. (1994). Medicaid managed care: The next generation? *Academic Medicine, 69,* 317-322.

Fleming, M., et al. (1997). Brief physician advice for problem alcohol drinkers: A randomized controlled trial in community-based primary care practices. *Journal of the American Medical Association, 277*(13), 1039-1045.

Fries, J. F., Koop, C. E., Beadle, C. E., Cooper, P. P., England, M. J., Greaves, R. F., Sokolov, J. J., Wright, D., & the Health Project Consortium. (1993, July 29). Reducing health care costs by reducing the need and demand for medical services. *The New England Journal of Medicine, 329*(5), 321-325.

Ginzberg, E. (1991). Access to health care for Hispanics. *Journal of the American Medical Association, 265*(2), 238-241.

Gold, M. R., Siegel, J. E., Russell, L. B., & Weinstein, M. C. (Eds.). (1996). Cost-effectiveness in health and medicine. New York: Oxford University Press.

Gonik, U. L., et al. (1981). Cost-effectiveness of behavioral medicine procedures in the treatment of stress-related disorders. *Journal of Clinical Biofeedback, 4*(1), 16-24.

Goodwin, F. (1993). Welcome to participants. In S. J. Blumenthal, K. Matthews, & S. M. Weiss (Eds.), *New research frontiers in behavioral medicine* (pp. 3-7). Rockville, MD: National Institutes of Health.

Gordon, L. B. (1982). *Behavioral interventions in health care.* Boulder, CO: Westview.

Greene, W. H., & Simons-Morton, B. G. (1984). *Introduction to health education.* New York: Macmillan.

Haddix, A. C., Teutsch, S. M., Shaffer, P. A., & Dunet, D. O. (Eds.). (1996). *Prevention effectiveness: A guide to decision analysis and economic evaluation.* New York: Oxford University Press.

Harlem, O. K. (1997). *Communication in medicine: A challenge to the profession.* New York: Karger.

Hatziandreu, E., Koplan, J., Weinstein, M., Caspersen, C., & Warner, K. (1988). A cost-effectiveness analysis of exercise as a health promotion activity. *American Journal of Public Health, 78*(11), 1417-1421.

Health Care Financing Administration. (1995, February). *Medicare: A profile* (Chart PS-11). Washington, DC: Author.

Health Care Financing Administration. (1996, September). *1996 HCFA statistics* (HCFA Publication No. 03394). Washington, DC: Author.

Hellman, C. J., Budd, M., Borysenko, J., et al. (1990). A study of the effectiveness of two group behavioral medicine interventions for patients with psychosomatic complaints. *Behavioral Medicine, 16*, 165-173.

Hickson, G. B., Altemeier, W. A., & O'Connor, S. (1983). Concerns of mothers seeking care in private pediatric offices: Opportunities for expanding services. *Pediatrics, 72*(5), 619-624.

Hoffman, C., Rice, D., & Sung, H. Y. (1996). Persons with chronic conditions. *Journal of the American Medical Association, 276*, 1473-1479.

Hollister, W. (1976). *Basic strategies in designing primary prevention programs.* Paper presented at Pilot Conference on Primary Prevention, Philadelphia.

Hughes, J. R., Wadland, W. C., Fenwick, J. W., Lewis, J., & Bickel, W. K. (1991). Effect of cost on the self-administration and efficacy of nicotine gum: A preliminary study. *Preventive Medicine, 20*, 486-496.

Institute of Medicine. (1981). *Research on stress in human health.* Washington, DC: National Academy Press.

Institute of Medicine. (1994). New directions in definitions. In P. J. Mzarek & R. J. Haggerty (Eds.), *Reducing risks for mental disorders*. Washington, DC: National Academy Press.

Jereb, J. A., Kelley, G. D., Dooley, S. W., Canthen, G. M., & Snider, D. E. (1991). Tuberculosis morbidity in the United States: Final data, 1990. *Morbidity and Mortality Weekly Report, 40,* 23-27.

Johnston, L., Bachman, J., & O'Mallet, P. (1997). *Cigarette smoking may have peaked in younger teens* (Press release, Monitoring the Future Project, Institute for Social Research). Ann Arbor: University of Michigan News.

Jordan, D. D., & Hernandez, M. (1990). The Ventura planning model: A proposal for mental health reform. *The Journal of Mental Health Administration, 17*(1), 26-47.

Kennedy, N. J. (1998). Approaches to change. In V. De La Cancela et al. (Eds.), *Community psychology: Empowerment for diverse communities* (p. 85). New York: Routledge.

King, H., Rewers, M., & WHO Ad Hoc Diabetes Reporting Group. (1993). Global estimates of diabetes mellitus and impaired glucose tolerance in adults. *Diabetes Care, 16,* 157-177.

Kozel, N. J., Sanborn, J. S., & Kennedy, N. J. (1990, November). *A conceptualization of addictive disease epidemiology as compared to infectious and chronic disease epidemiology.* Paper presented at the Symposium, Drug Dependence: From the Molecular to the Social Level, Escuela Militar de Granduados de Sandidad, Mexico City, Mexico.

Krasnegor, N. A. (1990). Health and behavior: A perspective on research supported by the National Institutes of Health. *Annals of Behavioral Medicine, 12,* 72-78.

Kuczmarski, R. J., Flegal, K. M., Campbell, S. M., & Johnson, C. L. (1994). Increasing prevalence of overweight among U.S. adults: The National Health and Nutrition Examination Surveys, 1960-1991. *Journal of the American Medical Association, 272,* 205-211.

Kumpfer, K. L., DeMarsh, J. P., & Child, W. (1989). Strengthening Families Program: Children's skills training curriculum manual (Preventive Services to Children of Substance-Abusing Parents). Salt Lake City, UT: University of Utah, Graduate School of Social Work, Social Research Institute.

Kumpfer, K. L., Molgaard, V., & Spoth, R. (1996). Family interventions for prevention of delinquency and substance use with special populations. In R. Peters & R. McMahon (Eds.), *Proceeding of the 1994 Banff International Conference.* Thousand Oaks, CA: Sage.

Labonte, R. (1994). *Health promotion and empowerment: Practice frameworks.* Toronto, Canada: Center for Health Promotion.

Last, J. (1987). *Public health and human ecology.* East Norwalk, CT: Appleton & Lange.

Leeman, C. A. (1994). *The Maine experience: Head Start's participation in the Medicaid EPSDT program.* Augusta: Maine Department of Human Services, State Office of Head Start.

Lillie-Blanton, M., Parsons, P. E., Gayle, H., & Dievler, A. (1996). Racial differences in health: Not just black and white, but shades of gray. *Public Health, 17*(Annual review), 411-448.

Linton, R. (1947). *The study of man.* New York: Appleton Press.

Lorig, K. (1993). Self management of chronic illness: A model for the future. *Generations, 12,* 11-14.

Lowry, R., Kann, L., Collins, J. L., & Kolbe, L. J. (1996). The effect of socio-economic status on chronic disease risk behaviors among U.S. adolescents. *Journal of the American Medical Association, 276*(10), 792-797.

MacMahon, B., Pugh, T. F., & Ipsen, J. (1960). *Epidemiological methods.* Boston: Little, Brown.

Marion Merrell Dow, Inc. (1994). *Managed care digest, HMO edition, 1994.* Kansas City, MO: Marion Merrell Dow, & Chicago, IL: SMG Marketing Group.

McGinnis, J. M., & Foege, W. H. (1993). Actual causes of death in the United States. *Journal of the American Medical Association, 270,* 2207-2212.

Meisels, S. J., & Shonkoff, J. P. (Eds.). (1990). *Handbook on early childhood intervention.* New York: Cambridge University Press.

Mettler, M., & Kemper, D. W. (1992). *Healthwise for life.* Boise, ID: Healthwise.

Morris, J. N. (1975). *Uses of epidemiology.* Edinburgh: Churchill Livingstone.

Mumford, E., Schlesinger, H. J., Glass, G. V., Patrick, C., & Curedon, T. (1984). A new look at evidence about reduced cost of medical utilization following mental health treatment. *American Journal of Psychiatry, 141,* 1145-1158.

Mrazek, P. J., & Haggerty, R. J. (Eds.). (1994). *Reducing risks for mental disorders.* Washington, DC: Institute of Medicine, National Academy Press.

National Center for Health Statistics. (1985). *Persons injured and disability days due to injuries: United States 1980-1981.* Washington, DC: Author.

National Center for Health Statistics. (1990). *Developmental, learning, and emotional problems: Health of our nation's children: United States, 1988* (Advanced data from Vital and Health Statistics, No. 190). Hyattsville, MD: Author.

National Institute of Child and Human Development. (1991). *An evaluation and assessment of the state of the science.* Rockville, MD: U.S. Department of Health and Human Services, Public Health Service, National Institute of Health.

National Institute on Drug Abuse. (1997a). *Drug abuse prevention for at-risk groups* (NIH Publication No. 97-4114). Rockville, MD: U.S. Department of Health and Human Services.

National Institute on Drug Abuse. (1997b). *Drug abuse prevention for at-risk individuals* (NIH Publication No. 97-4110). Rockville, MD: U.S. Department of Health and Human Services.

National Institute on Drug Abuse. (1997c). *Drug abuse prevention for the general population* (NIH Publication No. 97-4113). Rockville, MD: U.S. Department of Health and Human Services.

Neale, A. V. (1992). Behavioral contracting as a tool to help patients achieve better health. *Family Practitioner, 8,* 336-342.

Newacheck, P. W., & Halfon, N. (1988). Preventive care use by school-aged children: Differences by socioeconomic status. *Pediatrics, 82,* 462-468.

Newacheck, P. W., & Stoddard, J. J. (1994). Prevalence and impact of multiple childhood chronic illnesses. *Journal of Pediatrics, 124,* 40-48.

Ornstein, R., & Sobel, D. (1989). *Healthy pleasures.* Reading, MA: Addison-Wesley.

Osler, W. (1961). *Aphorisms from his bedside teachings and writings* (R. B. Bean & W. B. Bean, Eds.). Springfield, IL: Charles C Thomas.

Pentz, M. A. (1985). Social competence and self-efficacy as determinants of substance abuse in adolescence. In S. Shifman & T. A. Wills (Eds.), *Coping and substance use.* Orlando, FL: Academic Press.

Pierce, J. P., Gilpin, E., & Farkas, A. J. (1995). Nicotine patch use in the general population: Results from the 1993 California tobacco survey. *Journal of the National Cancer Institute, 87,* 87-93.

Plotnick, R. D. (1994). Applying benefit-cost analysis to substance use prevention programs. *The International Journal of the Addictions, 29*(3), 339-359.

Pransky, J. (1991). *Prevention: The critical need.* Springfield, MA: Burrell Foundation.

Rachman, S. J., & Philips, C. (1980). *Psychology and behavioral medicine.* New York: Press Syndicate of the University of Cambridge.

Rollins, R. (1996). *America's youth: Managed care's most valuable population.* Presentation at Working with America's Youth Conference, St. Louis, MO.

Salzman, P. (1998). *The matrix handbook.* Sudbury, MA: Advocates for Human Potential.

Satariano, W. A. (1997). The disabilities of aging—Looking to the physical environment [Editorial]. *American Journal of Public Health, 87,* 331-332.

Schlesinger, H. J., Mumford, E., Glass, G. V., et al. (1983). Mental health treatment and medical care utilization in a fee-for-service system: Outpatient mental health treatment following the onset of a chronic disease. *American Journal of Public Health, 73,* 422-429.

Schneider, E. L., & Guralnik, J. M. (1990). The aging of America: Impact on health care costs. *Journal of the American Medical Association, 263,* 2335-2340.

Shakespeare, W. (1960). "The seven ages of man," from *As you like it.* In O. Williams (Ed.), *Immortal poems of the English language* (p. 73). New York: Washington Square Press.

Smith, B. C. (1979). *Community health.* New York: Macmillan.

Silverman, P. R. (1977). Mutual help groups for the widowed. In D. C. Klein & S. E. Goldston (Eds.), *Primary prevention: An idea whose time has come* (NIMH, ADAMHA, PHS, DHEW Publication No. [ADM] 77-447, pp. 76-78). Washington, DC: U.S. Department of Health and Human Services.

Sobel, D. S. (1995). Rethinking medicine: Improving health outcomes with cost-effective psychosocial interventions. *Psychosomatic Medicine, 57,* 234-244.

Starfield, B. (1992). *Primary care.* New York: Oxford University Press.

Stoeckle, J. D., Zola, I. K., & Davidson, G. E. (1964). The quantity and significance of psychological distress in medical patients. *Journal of Chronic Disease, 17,* 959-970.

Swinburn, B. A., Walter, L. G., Arroll, B., Tilyard, M. W., & Russell, D. G. (1998). The Green Prescription Study: A randomized controlled trial of written exercise advice provided by general practitioners. *American Journal of Public Health, 88*(2), 288-291.

Taylor, H. (1994). *National Comparative Survey of Minority Health Care, 1995.* The Commonwealth Fund, One East 75th Street, New York, NY 10021 (phone: 212-535-0400).

Tengs, T., Adams, M., Pliskin, J., Safran, D., Siegel, J., Weinstein, M., & Graham, J. (1995). Five hundred life-saving interventions and their cost-effectiveness. *Risk Analysis, 15*(3), 369-390.

Theil, K. S. (1994). Family characteristics and health. In *Proceedings of the 1993 Public Health Conference on Records and Statistics: Toward the year 2000* (DHHS

Publication No. 94-1214, pp. 121-123). NCHS, CDC, PHS. Hyattsville, MD: National Center for Health Statistics.

Thompson, R. S. (1995, September 21). *Primary and secondary preventive services in clinical practice: Twenty years' experience in development, implementation and evaluation.* Paper presented at "From Managed Care to Managed Health" Conference, Bloomington, MN.

Tolley, K., & Rowland, N. (1991). Identification of alcohol-related problems in a general hospital setting: A cost-effectiveness evaluation. *British Journal of Addictions, 86*(4), 429-438.

Tusler, A. (1993). Disability as a cultural issue. *Alcohol, drugs and disability: Summary Report.* Washington, DC: U.S. Department of Health and Human Services, Substance Abuse and Mental Health Services Administration, Center for Substance Abuse Prevention.

U.S. Bureau of the Census. (1992). *Housing of single-parent families. Statistical brief* (Current Population Reports, Series P-20, No. 458, Household and family characteristics). Washington, DC: Government Printing Office.

U.S. Bureau of the Census. (1995). *Statistical abstract of the United States, 1992.* Washington, DC: Government Printing Office.

U.S. Congress, Office of Technology Assessment. (1991). *Adolescent health: Vol. 2. Background and the effectiveness of selected prevention and treatment services* (OTA-H-466). Washington, DC: Government Printing Office.

U.S. Congress, Office of Technology Assessment. (1994). *Technologies for understanding and preventing substance abuse and addiction* (OTA-HER-597, September). Washington, DC: Government Printing Office.

U.S. Department of Health, Education and Welfare. (1979). *Healthy people: The Surgeon General's report on health promotion and disease prevention.* Washington, DC: Public Health Service.

Valliant, G. E. (1993). Behavioral medicine over the life span. In S. J. Blumenthal, K. Matthews, & S. M. Weiss (Eds.), *New research frontiers in behavioral medicine* (pp. 37-40). Rockville, MD: National Institutes of Health.

Von Korff, M., Gruman, J., Schaeffer, J., Curry, S. J., & Wagner, E. H. (1997). Collaborative management of chronic illness. *American College of Physicians, 127*(12), 1097-1102.

Vega, W. A., et al. (1964). The role of cultural factors in mental health problems of Hispanic adolescents. In C. Telles & M. Karno (Eds.), *Latino mental health* (NIMH Monograph, 41-61). Washington, DC: U.S. Department of Health and Human Services.

Ventura, S. J., Peters, K. D., Martin, J. A., & Maurer, J. D. (1997). Births and deaths: United States, 1996. *Monthly Vital Statistics Report, 46*(1), Suppl. 2. Hyattsville, MD: National Center for Health Statistics.

Vickery, D. M., et al. (1983). Effects of a self-care education program on medical visits. *Journal of the American Medical Association, 250*(21), 2952-2956.

Webster-Stratton, C., & Herbert, M. (1994). *Troubled families—Problem children: Working with parents: A collaborative process.* New York: John Wiley.

White, E., Urban, N., & Taylor, V. (1993). Mammography utilization, public health impact, and cost effectiveness in the United States. *American Review of Public Health, 14*, 605-633.

Williams, D. R. (1993, June 26). Race in the heart of America: Problems, issues and directions. Use of race and ethnicity in public health surveillance. *Morbidity and Mortality Weekly Report, 42,* RR-10, 8-10.

Williams, J. S., & Sanders, C. R. (1981). Cost-effectiveness and cost-benefit analyses. *Journal of Infectious Diseases, 166,* 486-493.

Woodwell, D. A. (1997). *National Ambulatory Medical Care Survey, 1995 summary* (Advance data from Vital and Health Statistics: No. 286). Hyattsville, MD: National Center for Health Statistics.

Zarkin, G. A., & Hubbard, R. L. (1997). Analytic issues for estimating the benefits and costs of substance abuse prevention. In *Cost-benefit/cost-effectiveness research of drug abuse: Implications for programming and policy.* Rockville, MD: National Institute on Drug Abuse.

CHAPTER 8

Developing Integrated Service Delivery Systems for Children and Families: Opportunities and Barriers

GARY M. BLAU

DAVID A. BRUMER

This chapter describes the development and implementation of integrated service delivery systems across the United States. To date, each state is at a different evolutionary stage. Some states do not have much experience in this arena, some have partially implemented systems, and some are highly developed. The authors contend that these child and adolescent service systems, often referred to as systems of care, will continue to emerge and expand into the next century. The system of care models presented in this chapter are rooted in theory and research, and have the support of state and national associations, as well as state and federal funding sources. These models, and the specific example of Connecticut, describe a multilevel, multidisciplinary approach to

AUTHOR'S NOTE: This chapter is dedicated to the memory of David Brumer. During the writing of this chapter David passed away, and his passion, leadership, and commitment to children's services will be sorely missed. He leaves his wife, Arlene, and his two children, Mark and Melissa. In addition to developing integrated service delivery systems in Connecticut, David was considered a national expert on children's mental health, and on behalf of the federal Center for Mental Health Services, he served as a consultant across the United States. On a professional level, the state of Connecticut and the country have lost a quality human being. On a personal level, I have lost a friend, and I will miss him.

meet the most complex needs of children and families. For children and adolescents with serious disturbances, the authors believe that this approach will continue to receive support, and will guide service delivery efforts into the future.

Epidemiology

According to national estimates, between 14% and 20% of all children and adolescents have some type of emotional or behavioral disturbance (Brandenburg, Friedman, & Silver, 1990). This means that, in a classroom of 25 children, 4 youngsters probably suffer from a diagnosable mental health condition. These conditions could be mild anxiety or depression, or more severe disorders such as post traumatic stress or reactive attachment.

Recent data indicate that between 9% and 13% of all children have a serious emotional disturbance (Center for Mental Health Services, 1997). Those with Serious Emotional Disturbance (SED), as defined by the Center for Mental Health Services (CMHS),

> are persons from birth to eighteen years of age, who currently or at any time during the past year have had a diagnosable mental, behavioral, or emotional disorder of sufficient duration to meet diagnostic criteria within DSM III-R that resulted in functional impairment which substantially interferes with or limits the child's role or functioning in family, school, or community activities. (Center for Mental Health Services, 1997, p. 5213)

Whereas children and families with mild conditions can often be served by an individual provider or service type, youth with serious emotional disturbances often require intervention that must be integrated and coordinated across providers and agencies. In fact, Friedman, Katz-Leavy, Manderscheid, and Sondheimer (1996) write that services to children with significant mental health difficulties should be delivered in a coordinated system of care.

Background

The need to identify an array of services and to integrate these services into broader systems of care began to receive national attention in 1982 when the National Institute of Mental Health

(NIMH) and the State Mental Health Representatives for Children and Youth (SMHRCY) met to explore the needs of youth with severe emotional disturbances. These meetings corresponded with Jane Knitzer's (1982) seminal work *Unclaimed Children,* which documented the failure of children's services to meet adequately the needs of youth with severe emotional disturbances. Knitzer identified that children's mental health services were fragmented and uncoordinated, and she called for a fundamental change in service delivery. From these activities came recommendations that included defining the target population, developing a community-based approach to service delivery, and establishing an appropriate continuum of care for children with serious emotional disturbances.

Recommendations such as these were not new. In 1969, for example, the Joint Commission on the Mental Health of Children recommended that coordinated networks be developed to serve youth and their families, and in 1978 the President's Commission on Mental Health highlighted the need to develop integrated service delivery systems. Unfortunately, despite such recommendations, few service delivery systems were implemented before the mid-1980s.

Recognizing the need to provide an impetus for change, in 1984, the U.S. Congress funded an initiative to build locally based child-serving systems that would provide comprehensive and coordinated service delivery. Under the auspices of the Center for Mental Health Services (CMHS), The Child and Adolescent Service System Program (CASSP) was established. Renamed the Child and Family Branch, this federal initiative has been responsible for the development of these systems of care across the country.

The CASSP initiative was created to promote systems change, assist states and communities in the development of comprehensive community-based systems of care, and encourage collaboration among service providers, parents, advocates and policymakers. During the first several years of CASSP, 24 states received grant money to promote these concepts and strategies. Based on the experiences of those states, Stroul and Friedman (1986, 1988) developed a comprehensive approach that focused on system development. These authors found that a system of care must include a coordinated array of services (ranging from residential to nonresidential care) in order to meet the individualized needs of youth and families requiring services. As defined by Stroul and Friedman (1986), "a system of care is a comprehensive spectrum of mental health and other necessary services which are organized into a coordinated network to meet the multiple and changing needs of severely emotionally disturbed children and adolescents" (p. iv). In a recent grant application, the Child and Family Branch of CMHS defined a system of care as being:

> A comprehensive spectrum of mental health and other support services which are organized into a coordinated network to meet the multiple and changing needs of children and adolescents with serious emotional disturbances and their families. The creation of such system of care involves a multi-agency, public/private approach to delivering services, an array of service options, and flexibility to meet the full range of needs of children, adolescents and their families. Mechanisms for managing, coordinating, and funding services are necessary.

These definitions provide the framework for integrated service delivery systems.

Integrated Service Delivery Systems

The framework to develop integrated service delivery systems must be grounded in program theory. This theory can then serve to guide practice and research. While a system of care approach, with an emphasis on collaboration and partnership, has appeal, the model must clearly articulate values, principles, and goals.

Core Values and Guiding Principles

What evolved during the 1980s was the establishment of a philosophical framework for systems of care consisting of two core values and 10 guiding principles. These guiding principles were developed by CASSP participants in collaboration with numerous advisory groups and interested parties. The first core value was that systems of care be child and family focused, with the needs of each child and family dictating the provision of services. This is significant because it is not the availability of services that is important, but rather what the child and family need—even if that means creating services or providing nontraditional services. The 50-minute therapy hour may not be what a family needs or wants to get better. In fact, the family may prefer respite care or mentoring, and a respectful system of care engages families in the treatment-planning and decision-making process. A child-centered, family-focused treatment philosophy means that service providers, in partnership with children and families, find the way to provide "whatever it takes" to improve functioning and health outcomes.

The second core value is that the system of care be community based, with the locus of services and decision-making authority housed at the community level. The idea is simple. Children and adolescents are part of families, families are part of communities, and by empowering communities, families are empowered. The inclusion of families in the service-planning process is viewed as a hallmark of any successful system of care, and systems must develop family-friendly terminology and a "customer-driven" service philosophy. The following 10 principles were described by Stroul and Friedman (1986):

1. Children with emotional disturbance should have access to a comprehensive array of services that address the child's physical, emotional, social and educational needs.
2. Children with emotional disturbance should receive individualized services in accordance with the unique needs and potentials of each child, and guided by an individualized service plan.
3. Children with emotional disturbance should receive services within the least restrictive, most normative environment that is clinically appropriate.
4. The families and surrogate families of children with emotional disturbance should be full participants in all aspects of the planning and delivery of services.
5. Children with emotional disturbance should receive services that are integrated, with linkages between child-caring agencies and programs and mechanisms for planning, developing and coordinating services.
6. Children with emotional disturbance should be provided with case management or similar mechanisms to ensure that multiple services are delivered in a coordinated and therapeutic manner, and that they can move through the system of services in accordance with their changing needs.

7. Early identification and intervention for children with emotional problems should be promoted by the system of care in order to enhance the likelihood of positive outcomes.

8. Children with emotional disturbance should be ensured smooth transitions to the adult service system as they reach maturity.

9. The rights of children with emotional disturbance should be protected, and effective advocacy efforts for emotionally disturbed children and youth should be promoted.

10. Children with emotional disturbance should receive services without regard to race, religion, national origin, sex, physical disability or other characteristics, and services should be sensitive and responsive to cultural differences and special needs. (p. vii)

Service System Goals

In the context of these guiding principles, Stroul (1993) provides five major goals that should guide service system development. The first goal is to develop and provide a full array of community-based services. One failure of service systems is that they do not allow for a range of service capacities, and to be successful, available service options must go beyond traditional outpatient or inpatient treatment. The second goal for a comprehensive service system is to reduce reliance on restrictive forms of treatment and out-of-home placement. The rationale for this is simple. Restrictive settings and out-of-home placements have been overutilized, do not necessarily improve a youngster's functioning (particularly related to life skills), and represent the most expensive form of service. In addition, at some point youngsters are discharged from such settings, return to their communities, and remain in need of community-based treatment. Therefore, except in cases of dangerousness or psychotic behavior, the family and community are the preferred location for service delivery.

A third goal, as written by Stroul (1993), is to increase interagency coordination and collaboration in the planning, development, and delivery of services. The idea is again simple. When people share responsibility and decision making, their commitment is increased, and better service plans are created and implemented. This also means that more people must participate in the process. No one group has all the answers, and to develop integrated comprehensive service plans, decision makers must include families, family advocates, and professionals from the fields of mental health, substance abuse, child welfare, juvenile justice, education, and others (e.g., housing and Medicaid). This ensures that all the needs of a child and family are taken into account and that children and families are viewed holistically.

A fourth goal is to provide individualized services that are tailored to the unique needs of each child and family. This concept, often referred to as "wraparound" services, identifies the need for service systems to develop individual service plans and to create funding strategies that are flexible and noncategorical. Too often youth receive services that already exist because they meet the required category, and little thought is given to other service options. This should not be the case in an integrated service delivery system in which individualized service plans are tailored to meet the needs of each child and family.

The final goal for a system of care is to demonstrate cost-effectiveness. Most of the dollars spent on mental health service delivery are for services at the most restrictive end of the continuum. Residential and hospital-based treatment are by far the most costly—often costing between $50,000 and $200,000 per child per year. In a community-based service system the goal is to divert money from the "back end" of the system to the "front end," allowing for more dollars to be spent on services that are alternatives to more restrictive care.

Service System Components

To accomplish these goals, Stroul and Friedman (1986) and Stroul (1993) indicate that multiple service components must be available in a comprehensive and coordinated system of care. These authors divide local systems of care into seven broad service components:

- *Mental Health Services:* These include a range of activities from prevention and early identification to outpatient and home-based treatment to therapeutic out-of-home services
- *Social Services:* These include child welfare activities (i.e., protective services), financial aid, and home aid and respite care
- *Educational Services:* These range from resource room assistance to self-contained classes to home-bound and residential school instruction.

- *Health Services:* These include primary medical care, health education and prevention, and long-term care
- *Vocational Services:* These are particularly germane to adolescents, and include career education, skills training, job finding, and supported employment
- *Recreational Services:* After-school programs, camps, and special recreational projects are included in this category
- *Operational Services:* These include activities such as transportation, legal services, service coordination, and advocacy.

Katz-Leavy and Tesauro (1998) indicate that children with serious emotional disturbances require a range of services. Historically, these services have been broadly conceptualized as residential and nonresidential. However, within each of these categories an appropriate system of care provides an array of individualized services. Katz-Leavy and Tesauro (1998) and Kutash and Robbins-Rivera (1996) write that this array of services is better defined as outpatient, case management, inpatient/residential, and substance abuse.

Outpatient Services. Traditional outpatient psychotherapy (e.g., individual, group, family) continues to be a strong service component within a system of care. Kazdin (1993) indicates that psychotherapeutic approaches, such as insight-oriented, behavioral, and cognitive treatments, have positive effects when compared with no treatment, and Robbins-Rivera and Kutash (1994) state that psychotherapy does create notable improvements in functioning. However, a growing trend in outpatient care is to provide the service in the home or school rather than a clinic or private office (Armbruster, Andrews, Couenhoven, & Blau, in press; Eyberse, Maffuid, & Blau, 1996; Gullotta, Noyes, & Blau, 1996), and to offer an intensive level of outpatient care (e.g., two or three times per week). Current research reflects this trend, and a variety of studies suggest that services can be particularly effective when delivered in a nontraditional manner (Eyberse et al., 1996; Stroul, McCormack, & Zaro, 1996).

A more intensive outpatient approach can be found in day treatment. Day treatment often includes special education, counseling, vocational training, and life skill development, and typically occurs for 5 hours a day. This high level of treatment is considered a necessary component in a continuum of service delivery.

For children and youth with serious emotional disturbances, individualized outpatient approaches may be particularly important. Wraparound services, family support activities, and crisis availability are specific examples. The wraparound model, which is distinctive in that the child and family are significantly involved in all decisions, allows services to be tailored to the unique needs of the child and family. Dollars are typically set aside and can be used for mentoring, tutoring, recreation, or a host of otherwise nonreimbursable activities. Family support services may include informal groups, peer assistance, or respite care. Respite care, designed so that families can take a break from highly stressful situations, has proved to be a successful intervention strategy (Blau & Long, in press).

Case Management/Service Coordination. Service coordination, a friendlier term than case management, is perhaps the single most important component in creating an integrated service delivery system (Blau & Brumer, 1996). Having a person who can coordinate across services, monitor treatment goals, provide linkage to appropriate services, and advocate on behalf of a child and family has been proven to reduce hospitalizations, lower lengths of stays in restrictive settings, and increase consumer satisfaction measures (Katz-Leavy & Tesauro, 1998).

Inpatient/Residential Treatment. In order to provide the availability of a full array of services, there is a need to include structured 24-hour treatment settings in an integrated service delivery system. These settings can have limited levels of restrictiveness (e.g., therapeutic foster care) or maximum levels of restrictiveness (e.g., locked inpatient). The key to the successful utilization of these types of services is the inclusion of aftercare and significant linkages to the community (Kutash & Robbins-Rivera, 1996).

Substance Abuse. Although substance abuse service models are consistent with the above approaches, the increasing problem of drug and alcohol abuse warrants separate attention. For example, Petrila, Foster-Johnson, and Greenbaum (1996) indicated that upwards of 50% of adolescents with serious emotional disturbances

have a co-occurring alcohol and drug problem. Child welfare
studies reveal that nearly 70% of parents who have a child removed
due to abuse or neglect have an alcohol or drug problem (Blau,
Whewell, Bloom, & Gullotta, 1994). This alarming reality illustrates a clear need to integrate substance abuse treatment modalities
into systems of care.

Service System Examples

Many local communities across the country have implemented
the system of care model described above. Most are accomplished
through local programs and reflect a community's commitment to
this type of service philosophy (Cole & Poe, 1993). Examples
include Kentucky's Impact Program, the Ventura California Project,
the Alaska Youth Initiative, the Robert Wood Johnson Foundation's
Mental Health Services Program for Youth, the Ohio Connections
Program, the Oregon Partner's Project, the Vermont New Directions Program, the Pennsylvania Parent and Child Cooperative,
Wisconsin's Project FIND, and the Fort Bragg North Carolina
Initiative. Data from these projects demonstrate significant accomplishments from which several trends have been identified (Behar,
1992; Cole & Poe, 1993; Robbins-Rivera & Kutash, 1994). One
trend in the data is that children receiving services in an integrated
organized system of care are less likely to be placed in restrictive
environments such as a hospital or residential facility (Rosenblatt
& Attkisson, 1992; Stroul, 1993). In addition, if the youngster is
placed, the length of stay is reduced as compared to youngsters not
receiving services as part of an organized system of care. Another
finding is that children receiving services within a system of care
have fewer contacts with the juvenile justice system, and they
demonstrate improvements on dependent variables such as school
attendance and school performance (Illback, 1993). Parents of
these youth also report more satisfaction with the services and
support they receive, and initial cost data suggest that services
provided within a system of care are cost effective. For example,
Cole and Poe (1993) reported that the Kentucky Impact Program
reduced per child spending by $4,300 a year, and the New Direc-
tions Program in Vermont reduced the average yearly cost per child
from $57,218 to $43,025.

These data and initial findings reflect a growing body of evidence that systems of care, based on the guiding principles outlined in this chapter, allow for better outcomes from both the clinical and administrative viewpoints. However, such statements are not without controversy (Bickman, 1996; Bickman et al., 1995; Friedman & Burns, 1996).

In an example of this controversy, one study investigated provision of a coordinated continuum of children's mental health care as compared to traditional services. The Fort Bragg Child and Adolescent Mental Health Demonstration Project was funded in August 1989 by the Department of the Army through a contract with the North Carolina Department of Human Resources. The project sought to determine the feasibility of an alternative to the existing high-cost delivery system. This study examined whether a comprehensive and coordinated continuum of care developed for children receiving health care benefits through the Civilian Health and Medical Program of Uniformed Services (CHAMPUS) worked better than their receiving an array of services administered in a traditional manner. The project emphasized provision of single point of entry with comprehensive intake assessment; case management providing coordination and access to a full continuum of services, including extensive family involvement and support; and utilization of alternatives to institutional settings. This longitudinal research, funded over a 5-year period by the State of North Carolina and the National Institute of Mental Health, was conducted by the Center for Mental Health Policy of the Vanderbilt Institute for Public Studies at Vanderbilt University. They examined 984 children and their families in two comparative population groups. The study investigated the implementation, service quality, clinical outcomes, and the costs related to this alternative system of care and service continuum method.

Results indicated implementation took place as planned with quality services delivered. Such services included a single point of entry and a standard intake process providing comprehensive evaluations. Also provided were an array of services from traditional outpatient to acute hospitalization, as well as intermediate services including home-based, school-based, crisis management, and therapeutic homes. Coordination of services was provided through case management and interdisciplinary teams. Contracts provided full cost reimbursement with no limitations on services. According to the results obtained by Bickman et al. (1995), there were no differences in clinical outcomes between children in the demonstration project and those in the control group. Children in both groups improved with no advantage identified by one over the other. In addition, the total child service costs at the demonstration project exceeded those of the comparison participants by 50%. The higher costs were attributable to longer time spent in treatment, more extensive use of intermediate services, greater quantity of services utilized, and a lack of cost control and utilization review through the cost-reimbursement contract.

Other authors have identified that the Fort Bragg project demonstrated several positive outcomes (Friedman & Burns, 1996). First, children can be served in less restrictive settings. The project was successful in the development and implementation of an array of community-based services (Behar, 1996). Second, parental satisfaction in such a model is increased (Heflinger, Sonnichsen, & Brannan, 1996). And third, there was increased access provided to children who were in need of services (Behar, 1996; Friedman & Burns, 1996). In addition, these authors identify that the Fort Bragg research did not take into account the need for different levels of care. That is, a system of care is primarily designed to serve youth with serious disturbances. The Fort Bragg service continuum was available to all participants, regardless of their clinical severity. Thus, the research methodology did not reflect system of care program theory, and comparisons made between the experimental and control groups were not appropriate. Clearly, however, the findings that there were no differences in clinical outcomes and higher costs have spurred significant controversy. Readers interested in the details of this controversy are directed to the 1996 special issue of the *Journal of Mental Health Administration,* Volume 23, Number 1. This special issue provides a detailed point-counterpoint approach from professionals connected to the Fort Bragg study.

Despite the controversial findings at Fort Bragg, other studies have demonstrated that coordinated systems of care can be highly successful, especially for children with serious emotional disturbances. For example, research has found that children with severe disorders can be maintained in the community while appropriately providing for their multiple and often intensive needs. The Mental Health Services Program for Youth studied more than 200 seriously emotionally disturbed youth in demonstration sites located in California, Kentucky, North Carolina, Ohio, Oregon, Pennsylvania, Vermont, and Wisconsin. Evaluation information obtained in these demonstrations suggests that systems of care work to maintain children in their community when there is appropriate organizational and financial support. While systems of care in this project varied greatly and were implemented in different ways, all included case management, an array of traditional outpatient services, brief or emergency intervention services, intermediate services of moderate intensity, and access to hospitalization or residential treatment when necessary.

Building Integrated Service Delivery Systems: An Example

During the 1990s, the authors of this chapter have been involved in attempts to develop a statewide system for local service delivery systems. Their experiences, both successful and unsuccessful, serve as lessons learned to other individuals interested in building systems of care. In the early part of this decade, the Connecticut Department of Children and Families (DCF), the state agency responsible for children's services, began to serve as a catalyst for community organizing and the development of local systems of care. A local system of care in Connecticut is one or more contiguous towns or cities where a common vision regarding children's emotional and behavioral needs is shared. Service delivery includes a comprehensive, coordinated array in which the needs of each child and family dictate composition. Memoranda of Agreement (MOA) and collaborative participation from community service providers, state and local agencies, schools, families, and other organizations, articulate the shared vision and common values consistent with the department's philosophy. Importantly, these systems include parents of children with serious emotional disturbance at each level of planning and decision making.

Establishing a system requires not only collaborative efforts of the community, but, more important, the sharing and commonality of values and intent regarding children and their families. The participants must commit resources and demonstrate a willingness to make decisions within a partnership of community agencies and families. To date, 20 localities are developing, or have been participating in, such a system of care. Each system is in different evolutionary stages. Some are fully developed while others are in their infancy. When creating local systems of care it is important to allow the community to develop at its own pace. Issues such as political climate, availability of resources, and historical relationships will impact the rapidity with which a service system can develop. On several occasions communities were pushed too quickly, which caused some participants to withdraw or to lose commitment to the process. A better approach would have been to cultivate more community ownership and local decision making. By doing this, the local community would have been more empowered (Stroul & Friedman, 1988; Stroul, Goldman, Lourie, Katz-Leavy, & Zeigler-Dendy, 1992).

Establishing a System of Care Model

The initial development of local systems of care is often assisted by identifying a systems coordinator. These coordinators can organize systems of care and provide technical assistance regarding the formation and functioning of teams. It is also important to establish guidelines and parameters. A system of care structure and philosophy will provide a framework that all participants can espouse. At the same time, it is critical to allow for local differences based on creativity and needs. However, collaboration, shared decision making, and interaction among the state, families, schools, and service providers remains the ultimate goal and a primary component of the care systems.

Local communities provide coordinated comprehensive care through partnerships of families, private providers, local and state agencies, and community members. While providing services through an array, local communities maintain responsibility and provide assistance to the families and children in their service area. The Connecticut system of care model developed three levels.

Child Specific Teams (CST):
   Membership: family, state social worker, case manager, providers, family advocate

Functions: individualized planning, designation of a case manager, implementation of services. Receive consultation and assistance if necessary from a local Case Review Committee (CRC).

Case Review Committee (CRC):

Membership: families, family advocates, mid-management administrators, state supervisor, and case managers.

Functions: triage, case review administrative/clinical/financial support, and assistance to child-specific interservice teams, case-specific program planning, and development. Reports to the Interagency Management Team

Interagency Management Team (IMT):

Membership: family advocates, high ranking agency administrators

Functions: establishes interagency agreements, identifies local needs and barriers, creates of new services, assesses effectiveness of CST and CRC, and, most important, serves as a Steering Committee for the local community

Each locality participating in the development of a system of care has done so in a unique manner specific to local needs. The broad parameters of infrastructure have allowed for differences and creativity. However, the components of Memoranda of Agreement (MOA), Interagency Management Teams (IMT), Case Review Committees (CRC), and Child Specific Teams (CST) are consistent around the state. Based on the shared components, it has been useful to chart or map the status of each local system of care. This map provides an illustration of each system's evolution and serves as an overview that can be used with consumers, providers, and legislators.

Continuum Access and Availability

Systems of Care must focus on the need to ensure component capacity while ensuring a comprehensive array of services is available. In an attempt to determine priorities for resources, it is important to establish a continuum of services. This continuum can guide funding decisions and provide the basis for needs assessments. On behalf of Connecticut, the chapter authors organized a service delivery continuum that included five broad areas. Services begin from the least restrictive setting within a child's home and/or community and flow to the most restrictive, out-of-home and/or community placement. These areas include Prevention and Early Intervention, Home and Community-Based Crisis Stabilization, Treatment and Support, Residential Services, and Inpatient Psychiatric Hospitalization. For each level of care the treatment or placement setting is identified, the services available are identified, and the educational arena is identified. Figure 8.1 illustrates this continuum of care outline.

Developing the Service System

Care Management. In addition to infrastructure development and formal partnership, care management service is viewed as an integral component within any successful system of care. Care management is defined as a service involving direct client contact that provides the availability of an accountable individual to serve as an advocate, helper, service broker, and liaison on behalf of a child and his or her family for coordinating service components. Services are coordinated to ensure that the elements of treatment, domicile, and supportive services are planned and provided.

The chapter authors have identified three levels of care management dependent on the needs of the child and family. These include:

> *Level 1:* For a child involved in only one service component, the child's service provider or a member of the multidisciplinary team assigned to the child is responsible for care management in partnership with family

> *Level 2:* For a child who has a state worker, the child's worker serves as the care manager in liaison with the child's primary service provider or member of the assigned multidisciplinary team

> *Level 3:* For a child involved in multiple agencies and identified as needing care management independent of any particular service received, care management is performed by a full-time care manager. Such care managers have a small caseload and often report to a local system of care team.

Most children receive Level 1 care management or service coordination and services by a single provider through the existing network of clinics, private practitioners, and other providers who constitute the system of care. Some children with multiple needs, however, are also receiving services from the state. In these situations,

Level 1 *Placement*
         Parent's or relative's home
         Treatment Services
         Juvenile Justice Tracking Program
         Birth-To-Three Services
         Therapeutic Child Care
         Emergency Mobile Psychiatric Services
         Parent Education & Support
         Outpatient M.H./Substance Abuse
         Intensive Case Management
         Family Preservation/In-Home
         Extended Day Treatment
         Respite
         Family Advocacy
         Parent-Aide Services
         System of Care Case Management
         Education: Public/Community-Based School

Level 2 *Placement*
         Therapeutic Foster Care
         Intensive Therapeutic Foster Care
         Medically Fragile Foster Care
         Juvenile Justice Foster Care
         Exceptional Needs Foster Care
         Group Home
         Treatment Services
         Outpatient M.H./Substance Abuse
         Emergency Psychiatric Services
         Foster-Care Respite
         Independent Living Training
         Education: Public/Community-Based School

Level 3 *Placement*
         Independent Living
         Foster Care
         Permanent Foster Care
         Transitional Living
         Emergency Shelters
         Treatment Services
         Outpatient M.H./Substance Abuse
         Independent Living Training
         Emergency Mobile Psychiatric Services
         Respite
         Education: Public/Community-Based School

Figure 8.1. Continuum of Care Outline

(continued)

Level 4   *Placement*
          State Diagnostic & Res. Facilities/Residential Treatment Centers
          Treatment Services
          All inclusive treatment & support
          Education: On Grounds Schooling

Level 5   *Placement*
          Brief Community-Based Hospital
          Moderate-Term Hospital
          State-Operated Psychiatric Hospital
          Long Lane School
          Treatment Services
          All inclusive treatment & support
          Education: On Grounds Schooling

Figure 8.1. Continuum of Care Outline (continued)

care management (Level 2) is provided by a partnership among the state, the family, and the service provider. Children requiring intensive services from several agencies, and who are at risk of or have already been placed out of their home to receive mental health services, may be referred to a local case review committee. Such committees, made up of a multidisciplinary team of family representatives, other state agencies, and private providers, offer recommendations to providers or refer the child and family for intensive care management services (Level 3).

Family Advocacy. A successful and operational system of care must include significant representation from families who have children with serious disturbances. These individuals must be able to articulate a family's perspective for planning and decision-making activities. Lambert (1998) writes that the literature on family involvement in the mental health system demonstrates improved outcomes. In treatment, the inclusion of families increases medication compliance, reduces isolation, averts relapse, and increases the use of community-based services. Systemically including families in planning and decision making improves access and service delivery (Fisk, Allen, & Johnson, 1998).

Legislation. In order to institutionalize systems of care, several states have enacted legislation. In Connecticut, Public Act 97-272 represents such legislation. Public Act 97-272 was created to encourage further development of systems of care for children with behavioral and emotional difficulties and has provided a framework for system of care development in Connecticut. The following is text of that legislation:

Sec. 2. (a) The following shall be established for the purposes of developing and implementing an individual system of care plan:

(1) Within available appropriations, a child specific team may be developed by the family of a child or adolescent at placement risk, and include, but not be limited to, family members, the child or adolescent if appropriate, clergy, school personnel, representatives of local or regional agencies providing programs and services for children and youth, a family advocate, and other community or family representatives. The team shall designate one member to be the team coordinator. The team coordinator shall make decisions affecting the implementation of an individual system of care plan with the consent of the team, except as otherwise provided by law. If a case manager, other than the case manager from the Department of Children and Families, has been assigned to the child and is not designated as the team coordinator, such case manager shall not make decisions affecting the implementation of the individual system of care plan without the consent of the team, except as otherwise provided by law;

(2) Within available appropriations, case review committees may be developed by each regional office of the Department of Children and Families and shall be comprised of at least three parents of children or adolescents with serious emotional disturbance and representatives of local or regional agencies and service providers including, but not limited to, the regional administrator of the office of the Department of Children and Families or his designee, a superintendent of schools or his designee, a director of a local children's mental health agency or his designee, the district director of the district office of the Department of Social Services or his designee, representatives from the Department of Mental Retardation and Mental Health and Addiction Services who are knowledgeable of the needs of a child or adolescent at placement risk, a representative from a local housing authority and a representative from the court system. The functions of the case review committee shall include, but not be limited to:

(A) The determination of whether or not a child or adolescent meets the definition of a child or adolescent at placement risk;

(B) assisting children or families without a child specific team in the formation of such a team; and

(C) resolution of the development or implementation of an individual system of care plan not developed, implemented or agreed upon by a child specific team.

Such functions shall be completed in one hundred twenty days or less from the date of referral to the case review committee.

In the event of the need for an individual system of care plan for a child or adolescent with no identifiable community, a representative of the child or adolescent shall make a referral to the state coordinated care committee, established pursuant to subdivision (3) of this subsection, which shall designate responsibility for the development of an individual system of care plan to a case review committee. The case review committee shall also monitor the implementation of an individual system of care plan when appropriate.

The Department of Children and Families may assign a system coordinator to each case review committee. The duties of the system coordinator shall include, but not be limited to, assistance and consultation to child specific teams and assistance with the development of case review committees and child specific teams.

(3) A Coordinated Care Committee shall be developed by the Commissioner of Children and Families and shall be comprised of a parent of a child or adolescent with serious emotional disturbance who is currently serving or has served on a case review committee, a person who is now or has been a recipient of services for a child or adolescent at placement risk, representatives of the Department of Children and Families, Education, Mental Health and Addiction Services, Social Services and Mental Retardation who are knowledgeable of the needs of a child or adolescent at placement risk, and a representative of the Office of Protection and Advocacy for Persons with Disabilities who is knowledgeable of the needs of a child or adolescent at placement risk.

(b) The commissioner, in consultation with the coordinated care committee, shall submit a report on the findings and recommendations of programs for children and youth at placement risk, including recommendations for budget options or programmatic changes necessary to enhance the system of care for such children or youth and his family, to the joint standing committee and the select committee of the

General Assembly having cognizance of matters relating to children, on or before January 1, 1998, and annually thereafter.

(c) The provisions of this section shall not be construed to grant an entitlement to any child or youth at placement risk to receive particular services under this section in an individual system of care plan if such child or youth is not otherwise eligible to receive such services from any state agency or to receive such services pursuant to any other provision of law.

(d) The Commissioner of Children and Families may adopt regulations in accordance with chapter 54 of the general statues for the purpose of implementing the provisions of this section.

The above legislation has been an important catalyst in the creation of systems of care in Connecticut. In particular, Public Act 97-272 provides a framework for system of care infrastructure development and provides a requirement for parent consumer involvement in decision making. The law also mandates system of care participation from a broad constituency, including state agencies, private service providers, and schools. Unfortunately, however, the law has several shortcomings. First, the legislation is not definitive. Many sections indicate that the state "may" develop system of care teams rather than "shall." In addition, the law does not adequately address funding. Instead of identifying a budgetary appropriation, the law stipulates that system of care activities be developed "within available appropriations." These shortcomings have hampered implementation by creating confusion about responsibilities, procedures, and funding.

Opportunities and Barriers

Significant strides have been taken since Jane Knitzer's (1982) work *Unclaimed Children*. Integrated service delivery systems have been developed across the country, and despite the controversial results obtained in the Fort Bragg study, the overwhelming majority of research has indicated that a system of care approach yields positive outcomes. This is particularly true for children with serious disturbances. Fortunately, opportunities continue to exist. As this chapter is being written, many states are responding to a system of care Request for Proposal (RFP) issued by the federal Center for Mental Health Services (CMHS). CMHS plans to increase the number of these pilot projects across the country, and community collaboration, service integration, and parent involvement remain the hallmark of this approach.

At the same time integrated service delivery systems are increasing and there are growing opportunities for expansion, these same activities may be fraught with obstacles and barriers. First and foremost is the impact created by managed care. Concurrent with the activities involving local community system development, managed care is also creating networks for service delivery. These activities are often parallel, which results in fragmented funding and services. This fragmentation between systems of care and managed care must be fully addressed if true integrated service delivery systems are to be created. Developing blended and flexible funding streams, and combining socially and medically necessary service components and better linkages between funders and providers are examples of how systems of care and managed care can improve their coordination.

Another significant issue involves the need to reexamine the program theory associated with systems of care (Friedman & Burns, 1996). If system of care research and program development is to be meaningful, and based on appropriate methodology and effective interventions, a consistent program theory must be fully articulated (Weiss, 1995). This theory will serve to guide practice and evaluation decisions. Although much has already been accomplished in this regard (Stroul, 1993; Stroul & Friedman, 1986), there remains a clear need to standardize definitions, develop standards for service delivery, improve consistency in evaluation methods, and create agreed-upon outcome measurement criteria (Hernandez & Hodges, 1996). Each of these areas will warrant separate and significant attention.

Finally, the successful development and implementation of integrated service delivery systems will not occur unless attention is given to training curricula and human resources. Service delivery professionals, parents, and others have not been equipped with the skills or knowledge necessary for this work. Navigating managed care, conflict resolution, developing partnerships with parents and consumers, creating nontraditional service plan arrangements, and understanding real-world politics are not typically part of university course work. In addition, developing a culturally competent workforce and providing opportunities for paraprofessional and parent/consumer-professional involvement will be similarly important if this type of service model is to flourish.

This chapter has attempted to describe the historical development and current implementation of child and adolescent systems of care. By way of conclusion, the authors assert that integrated service delivery systems utilizing a comprehensive array of services enhance outcomes for children with serious disturbances. The authors also believe that the system of care model will guide service delivery for these youth into the next century. Based on continued support and funding, these activities will expand into the future. However, much work needs to be done to further this development. As we move into the 21st century, practitioners and researchers must continue to improve their sophistication so that the many issues facing children and families can be successfully addressed.

References

Armbruster, P., Andrews, E., Couenhoven, J., & Blau, G. M. (in press). Collision or collaboration? Not-for-profit school based health services meet for-profit managed care. *Clinical Psychology Review.*

Behar, L. (1992). *Fort Bragg Child and Adolescent Mental Health Demonstration Project.* Raleigh: North Carolina Division on Mental Health, Developmental Disabilities, and Substance Abuse Services, Child and Family Branch.

Bickman, L. (1996). The evaluation of a children's mental health managed care demonstration. *The Journal of Mental Health Administration, 23*(1), 7-15.

Bickman, L., Guthrie, P. R., Foster, E. M., Lambert, E. W., Summerfelt, W., Breda, C. S., & Heflinger, C. A. (1995). *Evaluating managed mental health services: The Fort Bragg experiment.* New York: Plenum.

Blau, G. M., & Brumer, D. (1996). Comments on adolescent behavior problems: Developing coordinated systems of care. In G. M. Blau & T. P. Gullotta (Eds.), *Adolescent dysfunctional behavior: Causes, intervention and prevention.* Thousand Oaks, CA: Sage.

Blau, G. M., & Long, D. (in press). The prediction, assessment, and treatment of family violence. In R. Hampton, T. P. Gullotta, G. R. Adams, E. Potter, & R. Weissberg (Eds.), *Family violence: Prevention and treatment* (2nd ed.). Thousand Oaks, CA: Sage.

Blau, G. M., Whewell, M., Gullotta, T. P., & Bloom, M. (1994). The prevention and treatment of child abuse in households of substance abusers: A demonstration progress report. *Child Welfare, 73,* 83-94.

Brandenburg, N., Friedman, R., & Silver, S. (1990). The epidemiology of childhood psychiatric disorders: Prevalence findings from recent studies. *Journal of the American Academy of Child and Adolescent Psychiatry, 29,* 76-83.

Center for Mental Health Services. (1997). Estimation methodology for children with serious emotional disturbance. *Federal Register, 62*(3), 5213-52145.

Cole, R. F., & Poe, S. L. (1993). *Partnerships for care: Systems of care for children with serious emotional disturbances and their families.* Washington, DC: Washington Business Group on Health.

Eyberse, W., Maffuid, J., & Blau, G. M. (1996). New directions for service delivery: Home-based services. In G. M. Blau & T. P. Gullotta (Eds.), *Adolescent dysfunctional behavior: Causes, interventions and prevention* (pp. 247-266). Thousand Oaks, CA: Sage.

Fisk, D., Allen, B., & Johnson, D. (1998). Consumers as colleagues: One more step toward an ideal mental health service system. *Breakthroughs, 2*(1), 6.

Friedman, R. M., & Burns, B. J. (1996). The evaluation of the Fort Bragg evaluation project: An alternative interpretation of the findings. *The Journal of Mental Health Administration, 23*(1), 128-136.

Friedman, R. M., Katz-Leavy, J., Manderscheid, R., & Sondheimer, D. (1996). *Prevalence of serious emotional disturbance in children and adolescents.* Baltimore, MD: Mental Health USA.

Gullotta, T. P., Noyes, L., & Blau, G. M. (1996). School-based health and social service centers. In G. M. Blau & T. P. Gullotta (Eds.), *Adolescent dysfunctional behavior: Causes, interventions and prevention.* Thousand Oaks, CA: Sage.

Hernandez, M., & Hodges, S. (1996). The System Accountability Project for Children's Mental Health: Understanding outcome information in context. *The Evaluation Exchange: Emerging Strategies in Evaluating Child and Family Services* (Harvard Family Research Project [Ed.]), 2(3), 8-9.

Heflinger, C. A., Sonnichsen, S. E., & Brannan, A. M. (1996). Parent satisfaction with children's mental health services in a children's mental health managed care demonstration. *The Journal of Mental Health Administration, 23*(1), 69-79.

Illback, R. (1993). *Evaluation of the Kentucky Impact Program for children and youth with severe emotional disabilities, year two.* Frankfort, KY: Division of Mental Health, Children and Youth Services Branch.

Joint Commission on the Mental Health of Children. (1969). *Crisis in child mental health.* New York: Harper & Row.

Katz-Leavy, J., & Tesauro, G. (1998). *Mental health components of a quality system of care for children and adolescents.* Baltimore, MD: Center for Mental Health Services.

Kazdin, A. E. (1993). Adolescent mental health: Prevention and treatment programs. *American Psychologist, 48,* 127-141.

Knitzer, J. (1982). *Unclaimed children.* Washington, DC: Children's Defense Fund.

Kutash, K., & Robbins-Rivera, V. (1996). *What works in children's mental health services.* Baltimore, MD: Brooks.

Lambert, S. (1998). What families can do. *Breakthroughs, 2*(1), 7-8

Petrila, A. T., Foster-Johnson, L., & Greenbaum, P. E. (1996). Serving youth with mental health and substance abuse. In B. Stroul (Ed.), *Children's mental health: Creating systems of care in a changing society.* Baltimore, MD: Brooks.

President's Commission on Mental Health. (1978). *Report of the Sub-task Panel on Infants, Children and Adolescents.* Washington, DC: Government Printing Office.

Robbins-Rivera, V., & Kutash, K. (1994). *Components of a system of care: What does the research say.* Tampa, FL: Research and Training Center for Children's Mental Health.

Rosenblatt, A., & Attkisson, C. (1992). Integrating systems of care in California for youth with severe emotional disturbance: III. Answers that lead to questions about out-of-home placements and the California AB377 evaluation project. *Journal of Child and Family Studies, 2*(2), 119-141.

Stroul, B. (1993). *Systems of care for children and adolescents with severe emotional disturbance: What are the results?* Washington, DC: Georgetown University Child Development Center, CASSP Technical Assistance Center.

Stroul, B., & Friedman, R. (1986). *A system of care for severely emotionally disturbed children and youth.* Washington, DC: Georgetown University Child Development Center, CASSP Technical Assistance Center.

Stroul, B., & Friedman, R. (1988). Principles for a system of care: Putting principles into practice. *Children Today, 17,* 11-15.

Stroul, B., Goldman, S. K., Lourie, I. S., Katz-Leavy, J. W., & Zeigler-Dendy, C. (1992). *Profiles of local systems of care for children and adolescents with severe emotional disturbances.* Washington, DC: Georgetown University Child Development Center, CASSP Technical Assistance Center.

Stroul, B., McCormack, M., & Zaro, S. M. (1996). Measuring outcomes in systems of care. In B. Stroul (Ed.), *Children's mental health: Creating systems of care in a changing society.* Baltimore, MD: Brooks.

Weiss, C. H. (1995). Nothing as practical as good theory: Exploring theory-based evaluation for comprehensive community initiatives for children and families. In J. P. Connell, A. C. Kubish, & L. B. Schorr (Eds.), *New approaches to evaluating community initiatives: Concepts, methods and context* (pp. 65-92). Washington, DC: Aspen Institute.

Index

About the Editors

Gerald R. Adams is Professor in the Department of Family Studies at the University of Guelph, Ontario, Canada. He is an associate editor for the series *Advances in Adolescent Development* and *Issues in Children's and Families' Lives.* He is a Fellow of the American Psychological Association, the American Psychological Society, and the American Association of Applied and Preventive Psychology. His research focuses on family psychology, adolescent development, family-school connections in predicting adjustment and academic success, and aspects of primary prevention and social interventions. He is the coauthor of five textbooks, more than a dozen books, and many research reports, chapters, and public journal articles. He is on the editorial boards of journals in sociology, psychology, human development, family science, and education.

Thomas P. Gullotta is CEO of the Child and Family Agency in Connecticut. He currently is the editor of the *Journal of Primary Prevention.* He is a book editor for the *Advances in Adolescent Development* series and is the senior book series editor for *Issues in Children's and Families' Lives.* In addition, he serves on the editorial board of the *Journal of Early Adolescence and Adolescence* and is an adjunct faculty member in the psychology and education departments of Eastern Connecticut State University. His published works focus on primary prevention and youth.

Robert L. Hampton, Ph.D., is Associate Provost for Academic Affairs, Dean for Undergraduate Studies, and Professor of Family Studies and Sociology at the University of Maryland, College Park. He has published extensively in the field of family violence and is editor of *Violence in the Black Family: Correlates and Consequences* (1987), *Black Family Violence: Current Research and Theory* (1991), *Family Violence: Prevention and Treatment* (1993), and *Preventing Violence in America* (1996). His research interests include interspousal violence, family abuse, male violence, community violence, resilience, and institutional responses to violence.

Bruce A. Ryan is Associate Professor in the Department of Family Studies at the University of Guelph, Ontario, Canada. He earned a doctorate in educational psychology from the University of Alberta and has served in numerous positions of responsibility at the University of Guelph and in child and family service associations and agencies in Ontario. His current research interests and most recent publications are focused on the relationship between family processes and school outcomes for children.

Roger R. Weissberg is Professor of Psychology at the University of Illinois at Chicago (UIC), where he is Director of Graduate Studies in Psychology and Executive Director of the Collaborative for the Advancement of Social and Emotional Learning (CASEL). He also directs the NIMH-funded Predoctoral and Postdoctoral Prevention Research Training Program in Urban Children's Mental Health and AIDS Prevention. He also holds an appointment with the Mid-Atlantic Laboratory for Student Success, funded by the Office of Educational Research and Improvement of the U.S. Department of Education. His research interests include school and community preventive interventions, urban children's mental health, and parent involvement in children's education. He has been President of the American Psychological Association's Society for Community Research and Action. He is a recipient of the William T. Grant Foundation's 5-year Faculty Scholars Award in Children's Mental Health, the Connecticut Psychological Association's 1992 Award for Distinguished Psychological Contribution in the Public Interest, and the National Mental Health Association's 1992 Lela Rowland Prevention Award.

About the Contributors

Gary M. Blau (Ph.D., Clinical Psychology) is currently the Bureau Chief for the Office of Quality Management at the Connecticut Department of Children and Families (DCF). He also holds a clinical faculty appointment at the Yale Child Study Center. In his capacity as Bureau Chief, he has the responsibility for DCF's interaction with community service providers, emergency shelters, group homes, and residential treatment centers. He is also responsible for DCF's administrative case reviews, program planning and development, policy and regulation, and the DCF Training Academy. Prior to this, as DCF's Director of Mental Health, he provided leadership and oversight to Connecticut's mental health service delivery system for children and adolescents. He is an active member of the National Association of State Mental Health Program Director's Division of Children, Youth and Families, and from July 1, 1998 through June 30, 2000 he will be the Chairperson. He has received several awards, including the Phoebe Bennet Award for outstanding contribution to children's mental health in Connecticut, the Making a Difference Award presented by Connecticut's Federation of Families for Children's Mental Health, and an outstanding contribution award for his involvement in Connecticut's Medicaid managed care initiative. Since receiving his Ph.D. from Auburn University (Auburn, Alabama) in 1988, he has worked in children's mental health with a primary emphasis on issues of victimization, child custody, permanency planning and innovative service models. He has held an appointment on the editorial board of the *Journal of Primary Prevention* and has numerous publications and presentations in the areas of child custody, primary prevention, managed care, and clinical service delivery.

317

David A. Brumer (M.A.). Prior to his untimely passing, he was the Director of Community Mental Health Services for Connecticut's Department of Children and Families. Following his undergraduate training at the University of Louisville, he attained an M.A. in Community Psychology form the University of New Haven and a 6th-year postmaster's Professional Diploma in Human Relations from the University of Bridgeport. He also held certificates in family therapy from the Graduate Center for Family Clinical Studies and in adolescent outreach from Yale University's Drug Dependency Institute. In his role as Director of Community Mental Health Services for Connecticut, he led the state in planning, development, and implementation of the state's Children's Mental Health Plan and System of Care Development initiative for children and adolescents. He was also Associate Director of the Sterling Center for Counseling and Family Relations, a community-based counseling and treatment center. He had extensive training and experience in system development, adolescent treatment, Ericsonian approaches to treatment and hypnosis, and sexual offender treatment.

John G. Day became Professor in Residence at the University of Connecticut School of Law in January 1999. Prior to joining the Law School, he was Senior Vice President and Chief Counsel of CIGNA Corporation, where he was responsible for the legal and regulatory support for CIGNA's individual life insurance division, its health and pension employee benefit businesses, and CIGNA's domestic and international investment operations. Before coming to CIGNA, he was Insurance Commissioner for the Commonwealth of Virginia, and Deputy Superintendent of the New York Insurance Department. Between 1962 and 1967, he held a number of positions in the federal government, including Assistant to the Vice Chairman of the Federal Power Commission and Special Counsel to the U.S. Secretary of Transportation. During the intervening years between his federal and state service, he was a Visiting Associate Professor at Osgoode Hall Law School in Toronto, Canada and Of Counsel with Steptoe and Johnson in Washington, D.C. Since 1991, he has been a lecturer at law at the University of Connecticut School of Law, and since 1995 he has been an adjunct professor at the University of Hartford. He is a Trustee of the Employee Benefit Research Institute in Washington, D.C., a member of the Research Advisory Committee of the Connecticut Bar Foundation, and the Health Systems Advisory Board of the University of Connecticut's Center for Health Systems Management. He received his A.B. from Oberlin College and his J.D. from Case-Western Reserve Law School.

Joy G. Dryfoos is an independent research and writer from Hastings-on-Hudson, New York, supported by the Carnegie Corporation. Her latest book is *Safe Passage: Making it Through Adolescence in a Risky Society.*

Michael M. Faenza is President and CEO of the National Mental Health Association, where he has demonstrated his ongoing leadership and commitment to community mental health advocacy. Following 13 years of direct service to children and adults with mental disorders, he has spent the past decade focusing on state and federal legislative advocacy and improving society's commitment to helping people with mental illnesses. He is social worker by training, and brings a public health perspective to issues of individual and community health. He has held clinical and management positions in public sector and juvenile justice mental health services, child protective services, and vocational rehabilitation. He holds a B.A. in Sociology from Indiana University and an MSSW from the University of Texas in Arlington where he also briefly served as an adjunct faculty member. Prior to joining NMHA, he directed the Dallas Mental Health Association for 5 years.

Nancy J. Kennedy (Dr.P.H.) has had over 25 years of professional experience in mental health and substance abuse, areas in which she is a renowned speaker and author. She is currently the Director of the Office of Managed Care, Center for Substance Abuse Prevention, Substance Abuse and Mental Health Services Administration, Department of Health and Human Services. She has traveled throughout the country speaking to purchasers, providers, and consumers about integrating preventive interventions into the health care system. Previous to this area, she worked as an epidemiologist at the federal government's National Institute on Drug Abuse. She also has academic experience, teaching at Towson State University, Baltimore. Her other job settings have included the Mental Health Association of Maryland and the Maryland State

Drug Abuse Administration. Her doctorate in Public Health is from Johns Hopkins University in Baltimore. She also has a master of public health degree from the University of North Carolina.

William D. Marelich (Ph.D.) is a Postdoctoral Scholar in the NIMH AIDS Research Training Program, Department of Sociology, University of California, Los Angeles. He received his doctorate in Social Psychology from the Claremont Graduate University, Claremont, California. His research interests include decision-making strategies in health and organizational settings, the influence of social norms on health-related behaviors, and statistical/methodological approaches in experimental and applied research. His work has been published in journals such as *Journal of Personality and Social Psychology, Journal of Personal Relationships,* and the *Journal of Studies on Alcohol.*

Christie Provost Peters is a Social Science Research Analyst at the U.S. Department of Health and Human Services. An analyst with HHS since 1990, she works on Medicaid policy within the Office of Legislation at the Health Care Financing Administration.

Robert W. Plant (Ph.D., Clinical Psychology) is currently the Director of Clinical Services at Child and Family Agency of Southeastern Connecticut and a practitioner in private practice. Child and Family is a comprehensive community-based child and family guidance facility that provides an array of clinical, health, early childhood, prevention, and education services. In his role as clinical director, he oversees the delivery of outpatient services, consults to school systems and child serving agencies, performs statewide advocacy work, and is responsible for grant writing and program development. He is an active member in the Connecticut Association of Mental Health Clinics for Children and a leader in his region's local system of care for children and youth. In his private practice, he provides direct clinical services, consultation, and education and training activities. He was educated under fellowships from the National Institute of Mental Health and the National Institute of Drug Abuse. He received his doctorate from the University of Rochester and was a clinical and research fellow at Yale University Medical School. He is the former Director of Substance Abuse Services and the Affective Disorders Program at the Sterling Institute where he oversaw outpatient and partial hospital treatment programs. He is a frequent lecturer on psychotherapy and has published numerous articles on motivation for treatment, substance abuse, family support services, and a variety of clinical and practice issues.

Mary Jane Rotheram-Borus (Ph.D.) is a Professor of Clinical Psychology and Director, Clinical Research Center, in the Division of Social and Community Psychiatry, Neuropsychiatric Institute, University of California, Los Angeles. She received her doctorate in Clinical Psychology from the University of Southern California. Her research interests include HIV/AIDS prevention with adolescents, suicide among adolescents, homeless youths, assessment and modification of children's social skills, ethnic identity, group processes, and cross-ethnic interactions. She has received grants from the National Institute of Mental Health to study HIV prevention with adolescents, the chronically mentally ill, and persons with sexually transmitted diseases; to study interventions for children whose parents have AIDS and for HIV-positive adolescents; and to examine national patterns of use, costs, outcomes, and need for children's and adolescents' mental health service programs. In 1986, her work on suicide prevention was selected as the Outstanding Child and Adolescent Mental Health Program by the New York State Department of Mental Health, and her assertiveness training with children was chosen as an exemplary model by the American Psychological Association. Her research also has been funded by the National Science Foundation, National Institute on Drug Abuse, Society for Research in Child Development, and the W. T. Grant Foundation.

Elizabeth Steel has more than 20 years of experience in the mental health and substance abuse arenas. She has developed, implemented, and analyzed mental health policies and programs that affect children and their families. Career highlights include positions with the federal Center for Mental Health Services and National Institute on Drug Abuse and, most recently, with the National Mental Health Association. She received her M.S.W. from Catholic University and has taught health and mental health policy at the graduate level.